Money Talks

Also by Alan Weiss from McGraw-Hill

Million Dollar Consulting

Money Talks

How to Make a Million as a Speaker

Alan Weiss

McGraw-Hill

New York   San Francisco   Washington, D.C.   Auckland   Bogotá
Caracas   Lisbon   London   Madrid   Mexico City   Milan
Montreal   New Delhi   San Juan   Singapore
Sydney   Tokyo   Toronto

Library of Congress Cataloging-in-Publication Data

Weiss, Alan.
　　Money talks : how to make a million as a speaker / Alan Weiss.
　　　　p.　　cm.
　　Includes index.
　　ISBN 0-07-069614-4 — ISBN (invalid) 0-07-069615-2 (pbk.)
　　1. Public speaking—Handbooks, manuals, ets.　2. Oral
communication—Handbooks, manuals, ets.　I. Title.
PN4098.W45　1997
808.5′1—dc21　　　　　　　　　　　　　　　　　　97-41226
　　　　　　　　　　　　　　　　　　　　　　　　　　CIP

McGraw-Hill

A Division of The McGraw·Hill Companies

4 5 6 7 8 9 0   DOC/DOC   0 9 8 7 6 5 4 3

ISBN 0-07-069614-4 (HC)

ISBN 0-07-069615-2 (PBK)

*The sponsoring editor for this book was Betsy Brown, the editing supervisor
was Penny Linskey, and the production supervisor was Sherri Souffrance. It
was set in Baskerville by Victoria Khavkina of McGraw-Hill's Professional
Book Group composition unit.*

Printed and bound by R. R. Donnelley & Sons Company.

McGraw-Hill books are available at special quantity discounts to use as
premiums and sales promotions, or for use in corporate training programs. For more information, please write to the Director of Special
Sales, McGraw-Hill, Two Penn Plaza, New York, NY 10121-2298. Or contact your local bookstore.

This book is printed on recycled, acid-free paper containing
a minimum of 50% recycled, de-inked fiber.

For all those who mount a lonely platform to speak their minds, irrespective of popular opinion, conventional wisdom, and political pressure. May you be rewarded for your honesty and your courage.

Contents

Part 2. Steak

Preface

At age 5, I stood in front of my kindergarten variety program audience, who regarded me with great affection, and introduced the acts. My "patter" consisted of audibly wondering when I could visit the rest room. At age 26, I faced my first professional audience, who stared back at me and waited for something I might utter to make their day, and my thoughts ran pretty much along the exact same lines as they had that day in kindergarten, albeit with somewhat greater urgency.

My first professional speaking gig was for $750 for a full day. Today, I'm paid more than 10 times that for a 45-minute keynote. The difference is not due to inflation (a lot of speakers are working for that $750—or less—today). The modern fees of the top-flight speakers are due to a combination of superb material, captivating delivery, and shrewd marketing. You need all three in this business, make no mistakes. I call the combination "steak, sizzle, and savvy."

This is not a book for individuals who want to control their nerves in front of colleagues at a business meeting. Toastmasters, a fine amateur organization, does that superbly well. Nor is it a book for those who look at "the fear of speaking" in the hackneyed, cliché manner of the general public, this being the first and last time you'll read about public speaking as the greatest fear of the person on the street.

I'm tackling herein *professional* speaking, not *public* speaking. You can make a million bucks if you do the former well. I know, because I have. You can be the latter speaker without being the former, but you have to be the latter if you are the former. The hallmark of the *profes-*

sional speaker is the ability to create value for a client through the transfer of skills, learning, and/or enjoyment, and to be paid commensurate with that value. That's why large fees can be the norm, because they're based upon the value delivered *and not the length of the presentation nor number of members of the audience.*

So this book embraces those *whose business is that of* keynoters, trainers, workshop leaders, facilitators, seminar instructors, emcees, after-dinner speakers, humorists, panel moderators, and all variations thereof. If you make your living (or seek to) by standing up in front of audiences and delivering value through speaking in these or other fashions, this book is intended to help you maximize your fees, attract new clients, enhance repeat business, and generally, enjoy life a whole lot more. The operative word is *business.*

Professional speaking is, first and foremost, a *business.* That is, it's intended to show a profit for the practitioner after the checks have cleared the bank and the expenses have been paid. For those who claim they "have a message to deliver," well, they're only storytellers if they're not putting money in the bank or under the mattress. I'm not against good works, but I am opposed to starvation. After all, even missionaries are paid a salary, and martyrs are in it for a longer-term payback.

In the chapters that follow, we'll discuss the steak, the sizzle, and the savvy—the content of your message, the aspects of your delivery, and the requirements of your business. Buckle your seat belt. It ain't what you think.

Alan Weiss

Acknowledgments

Although I didn't always realize it at the time, my deep appreciation goes to all of those who helped launch and refine my career as a professional speaker. I'd particularly like to thank those bureau principals who were the first to take the risk of booking a nonconventional, contrarian speaker: Susie DeWeese of Speakers Corner, Kiela Hine of Convention Connection, Michelle Lemmons of International Speakers Bureau, and Mark French of Leading Authorities. A tip of the hat to Lou Heckler, a superb and unselfish speaker, who introduced me to the bureau relationships.

With a frenetic consulting, speaking, and writing schedule, I could not have completed this work without my crack research team, Claire McCarthy, Laurie Marble, Phoebe Weiss, and Paul Dunion, and my technological experts, Terry Brock, Rebecca Morgan, Marlene Brown, and Darek Mislewski. I'm indebted to the finest editor I've worked with, Betsy Brown of McGraw-Hill, whose total support and insightful guidance have been the key part of our collaboration through two books.

My heartfelt thanks to the clients of Summit Consulting Group, Inc. who have placed me on their conference agendas and, consequently, food on my table. I'm especially indebted to those who have invited me back repeatedly, including GE, Coldwell Banker, GTE, Mercedes-Benz, the Institute of Management Studies, and Merck.

Profound thanks to the denizens of the New England Speakers Association, who elected me their president and then made me their king, proving that unending assaults of undiluted affection can cause even a hardened cynic to begin hugging vague acquaintances.

I'm greatly influenced by my daughter, Danielle, working at MTV, and my son, Jason, working as an actor, who are both, in their ways, carrying on the speaking tradition. And I'm greatly comforted by the love of my first wife, Maria, who also happens to be my current and only wife, through these past 29 years.

Finally, to my close collaborator and fellow bon vivant, L.T. Weiss, whose unerring editorial assistance has been an integral part of my work through seven books.

PART 1
Savvy

1
What Is a Professional Speaker?

"Is it like a professional breather?"

Some Common Ground

What on earth is a professional speaker? We all speak every day, and a lot of people do it in the course of paying jobs. A flight attendant has to give those captivating safety descriptions before takeoff. Tour guides speak incessantly about art, history, and the homes of Hollywood stars. Is a TV game-show host a professional speaker? What about the public address announcer at the ballpark? Surely, politicians are professional speakers . . .

The answer is: Who cares? This book is not for those seeking to focus on definitions and categorization. It's for those who want to create a significant, wealth-developing enterprise based upon their ability to communicate with, and improve the well-being of, audiences. It's not a profession for the faint of heart, but no profession that deals with ideas, behavior change, and public reaction ever is.

There are chapters in this book which will appeal situationally to some speakers. For example, the politician who must communicate well to get elected might find the chapters on "sizzle" of significant help. A salesperson who has to make presentations to prospects or trade associations might find the chapters on content and organization of assistance. (And a lot of people, regardless of their calling and station, will have raced immediately to Chapter 4. Welcome back.)

The entire work, however, has been created for the true speaking professional: someone who makes his or her livelihood from presentations made in front of audiences. As in some conventional books on the topic, I've included the mechanics in Parts 2 and 3, covering content and delivery. But unlike those other books, we're beginning here with the business side of the enterprise.

If you don't agree with the fact that this is a business first and foremost, aren't able to master basic business requirements, and/or don't wish to organize yourself in that fashion, then all the sophisticated techniques of topic development and all the dazzle of platform subtleties won't buy you tomorrow's newspaper. There are, approximately, a kibillion people who consider themselves professional speakers, but only a few thousand are making serious enough money to live a good life without a day job.[1] There is far more *need* for good speakers than there are good speakers. In fact, *there are more people giving advice about how to be a good speaker than there are good speakers*. What's wrong with this picture?

A few years ago, I was working on a project for the American Institute of Architects and had the opportunity to interview Art Gensler, a well-known, highly regarded architect who is CEO of a huge firm bearing his name. I asked him why he was so successful in an age when architects were being pushed around by general contractors, designers, and engineers, and when professional income was declining.

> "I'm running a business," he said, "which happens to revolve around architecture and design. But it's a business first and foremost, and the aesthetic decisions do not take precedence over business decisions."
>
> "What does that mean in the pragmatics of daily operations?" I asked.
>
> "It means that we won't take projects that we'd love to build at a loss, and attempt to make it up on volume."

As a speaker, if it costs you $2500 to acquire a client and if you charge that client a fee of $1000, and that is your only assignment for that client, there is a term for your approach to the market. It's called bankruptcy.

In General, About Whom Are We Speaking?

Professional speakers include, but are not limited to, the following major delivery profiles:

---

[1]And if you remove the celebrity speakers—those who are sought because of their fame in other pursuits, such as Colin Powell, Tom Brokaw, or Gloria Steinem—that number plummets still further.

- *Keynoter.* Literally, the person who sounds the "key note" for a conference or meeting by opening it with a relatively brief (30–90 minutes) speech intended to establish a theme and motivate people to become engaged. Keynote has been transmogrified by the speaking profession to mean anyone doing a general session (as opposed to a concurrent session), but how many keynotes can you have?

- *General session speaker.* The person addressing the entire audience of a convention or meeting, usually in a 1- to 2-hour time frame.

- *Concurrent speaker.* The person presenting to smaller groups during a convention or meeting. Those groups are either selected by the organizers or by the participants themselves. Concurrent presentations can range from 45 minutes to a full day, but they're usually no more than a half day.

- *Trainer.* The person who conducts workshops or seminars of varying durations (not infrequently on multiple days) expressly intended to create skills transfer. Trainers typically incorporate exercises, case studies, group activities, and generally, more interaction and involvement with the participants. Although size can vary, workshops and seminars tend to accommodate about two-dozen participants.

- *After-dinner speaker.* This is a general session of a dozen or a thousand people being addressed to conclude an evening. It is one of the most difficult types of speaking in that the audience has usually experienced an open bar, a heavy dinner, wine with the meal, often an awards ceremony, some boisterous banter, and some droning talks by the top executives. It is not for the unconfident, inexperienced, or thin-skinned.

- *Humorists.* These folks may appear anywhere on an agenda to lighten things up (if they're good) or poison things for everyone who follows (if they're not good). They often incorporate information about the organization and personalities sponsoring the event into their humor. (Once again, we're not talking about celebrities such as Jay Leno or Jerry Seinfeld, although they'll do this kind of work if you pay them enough.)

- *Character portrayers.* There are people who dress like Ben Franklin, Albert Einstein, Marilyn Monroe, Abraham Lincoln, and presumably, Zorro, who use the persona of their subject both to entertain the audience and to convey some pertinent points about personal and professional development. They frequently provide an exegesis of their subject's famous speeches or roles. These are novelty acts, tightly choreographed, that are often quite successful in schools as well as businesses.

- *Facilitator.* Facilitators facilitate—that is, they are supposed to enable groups to communicate better, to resolve issues more expeditiously, and to deal with difficult issues in a collaborative, constructive manner. The best facilitators allow the groups to do most of the speaking, but they are often required to present summaries, demonstrate what's occurring, describe obstacles, and provoke debate.

- *Moderator.* This is typically the panel emcee who provides brief explanations of subjects and procedures, introduces the panelists, handles questions from the floor, and keeps the proceedings on time.

The best speakers fill a variety of these roles according to their own skills and the needs of the client. The more client needs you can meet, the more valuable you become. A humorist can be a general session or concurrent session speaker, for example, just as a keynoter can later serve to facilitate a senior group.

Let's take one more slice of the speaking demographic based upon income and some descriptors I've arbitrarily created:

Stratospheric. These are celebrities whose name recognition alone is an audience draw. They include politicians, performers, book authors, and media personalities. Fees in this rarefied atmosphere are generally in the $20,000–$75,000 range. We won't consider them further because they do not represent the normal evolution of this food chain.

Circuit stars. These are people well known for the speaking abilities per se and their repute with past audiences. They are generally represented by a variety of speakers bureaus. Fees are in the $10,000–$20,000 range.[2]

Well-networked. These are people who are of the same quality as the circuit stars but who haven't reached that level of marketing heft. However, they have efficient networks of buyers and referrals, are often represented by bureaus, and work steadily. Their fees are in the $2,000–$10,000 range.

Climbers. These aspirants are sometimes making a living from speaking, but usually not. Some are quite good, but in need of marketing savvy. Some are adept marketers, but they don't have much in the way of content (one-trick pony) and/or delivery. Their fees may range from $500–$2000.

---

[2]These are the ranges they could charge if they so desired. Some superb speakers deliberately price themselves at lower levels to make themselves more appealing to a wider range of potential buyers. It's a smart strategy if volume of work isn't an issue. In other words, three speeches at $4000 create more income than one speech at $10,000, and the profit is unaffected if someone else is marketing you.

Gazers.   These are the folks thinking about entering the profession or dabbling in it. They may get an engagement by fluke or because of a fortunate connection. They generally don't have marketing materials, haven't created a coherent plan, and simply see what the next day brings. They may work for free, for a small honorarium, or for a modest fee. (Further comparisons appear in Figure 1-1.)

I realize that you can cite some exceptions to these lists. So can I. And sometimes it snows in May. But most of the time, most of the conditions will prevail for most of the people in each category.

Nowhere on my lists do I include the phrases "full-time" or "part-time." That's because those delineations make no sense in professional speaking, despite the fact that so many people seem preoccupied with them. I spoke 50 times last year. Am I a part-time speaker? Would you have to speak every day to be full-time? And seldom is speaking all that

Category	Fee Range	Repute	Marketing	Image
Circuit Stars	$10,000–$20,000	Well known among bureaus, corporate buyers, and the media. Name can serve as a "draw."	Primarily through bureaus or agents. Often has a book in print. Featured in brochures.	Professional demo videos, testimonials, accolades at high level. General session speakers.
Networked	$2000–$10,000	Well known by bureaus and some corporate buyers. Appear in the media if they have a specialty.	By personal contacts, client referrals, hired staff, and bureaus. Some will "cold call."	Sometimes a demo video, demo audio. Usually have articles in print, testimonials.
Climbers	$500–$2000	Unknown outside of immediate locale, if there.	Shoestring. Appear in some listings. Network extensively.	Usually constrained by budget. Generic look.
Gazers	$0–$500	None.	None.	Unknown.

Figure 1-1. Comparisons of speaker success.

you do, especially when successful. You're probably doing a little consulting, perhaps serving as a coach, maybe creating and selling products, and generally, seeking ancillary sources of income. Full-time and part-time are irrelevant. Paying the mortgage is relevant.

> *The client does not know or care whether you are full-time or part-time, work out of your home or in a skyscraper, have 25 suits or only the one you're wearing. The client only cares that you provide value for the audience. Perceived value ahead of time results in high fees. Perceived value after-the-fact results in repeat bookings. Does anyone need written instructions?*

Most of the people making most of the money in professional speaking today are trainers. That's right, they are networked people, working regularly conducting seminars and workshops of anywhere from one-half day to a full-week's duration. Most of them are doing this for themselves, but some work on behalf of large seminar firms.[3]

I suspect that you're thinking, "Wait a minute! The big money is in keynoting. Those people near the top of the chart aren't doing training sessions." No, they're not. But I said, "Most of the people making most of the money." The highest paid speakers are, indeed, the "draws" who can anchor a major conference. *But most of the overall money being made by most successful speakers is in the training business.* That business alone represented an investment of about $40 billion from U.S. organizations in 1995.[4]

I'm not advocating that you focus on the training business. In fact, I advocate that you master as many of the speaking formats as you can, although the skill sets needed are considerably different for keynoting and training, for example. Nonetheless, a lot of us can do a lot of things.

---

[3]These are firms such as Fred Pryor Seminars and CareerTrack. This is an excellent way for people in the climber category to acquire regular work and build a following.
[4]According to statistics gathered by the American Society for Training and Development in Alexandria, Virginia.

Improving the Client Condition

We've briefly examined the what and how, but the question still remains as to why. Why do we need professional speakers? Isn't it something naturally done, like listening, breathing, or sleeping? Does it rate a separate profession and separate discipline?

People who address audiences have the potential to create tremendous value or create tremendous harm. The only reason to hire a speaker—no matter what his or her specialty—is to improve the condition of the audience and, frequently, the organizations which they represent. That improvement may come from the transfer of skills, the awareness of a condition, the appreciation of their potential, the provocation of their emotions, the interactions among them, the motivation to pursue additional help, or the initiation of immediate action. No matter what the improvement or how you define it, it must be perceived and valued by the client.

A few years ago, a speaker in the climber category told me that it was her belief that all of us were on the platform to validate ourselves and to receive the affection of the audience. She is still in the climber category, and I doubt that she'll ever emerge from it if she continues to believe that we are on stage basically as a public indulgence in narcissism and therapy. (The last time I checked, the patient pays the therapist, and if we're up there for validation, commiseration, and assurances that we're "all right," then we should be paying members of the audience. If they charged by the normal 50-minute hour, that would reduce the duration of most speeches substantially.)

We are paid to deliver value, not to soak it up. We are paid to meet and exceed client objectives, not our own. And we are paid to understand the current state of the participants and move them from it, not ignore it. The status quo is not the desire, or people wouldn't assemble in the first place.

As you can see in Figure 1-2, there are three primary ways to approach an audience. If you are speaker-centered—if you are, indeed, in it for the personal feedback and gratification—then your best effect will be one of having provided an interesting persona, and your worst will be one of an egomaniac. Speaker-centered speakers feel they've failed if they don't get an immediate indication of how much they're loved and how good they are. In this business, that's the standing ovation.

Audience-centered speakers are far more effective and are often considered the avatars of the profession. They are highly effective with groups in rapidly establishing rapport and in providing a variety of devices to create early involvement, no matter what the size of the audience (see Part 3 for these techniques). And all of us have to

Speaker-Centered	Audience-Centered	Buyer-Centered
focus		
▪ what's comfortable	▪ pleases the listeners	▪ meets buyer goals
risk-taking		
▪ none—always look good	▪ mild, but play to majority	▪ always—stir emotions
humor		
▪ get a laugh	▪ get them on your side	▪ to make a point
stories/anecdotes		
▪ personal and ego-driven	▪ create commonality	▪ to make a point
delivery style		
▪ insincere sincerity	▪ choreographed	▪ natural and flexible
reaction to disruption		
▪ personal affront	▪ minimize the effect	▪ admit and resolve
response to questions		
▪ personal examples	▪ asks for examples	▪ combines examples
*self-disclosure**		
▪ excessive and irrelevant	▪ as it relates to listeners	▪ as it relates to goals
measures of success		
▪ standing ovation	▪ "smile" sheet ratings	▪ buyer rehires
overall demeanor		
▪ controlling, in the spotlight	▪ false "involvement"	▪ targets actions
lingering, most positive effects		
▪ "interesting person"	▪ "great presenter"	▪ "let's do it"

*Self-disclosure is a much-abused term which generally means revealing personal aspects of yourself on the stage. It's sometimes used with the equally mysterious "authenticity," or the redundant "self-authenticity." I'm using it here in the sense of how much of your personal feelings and life you volunteer during a speech.

Figure 1-2. Three approaches from the platform.

be audience-oriented to the extent that we have to create a willingness to listen. But it can't end there. Whenever I interview audience-centered speakers, they hand me their evaluation sheets and point to their "numbers." I actually know one such speaker—who is quite good on the platform—who keeps these things for life. He can go back 20 years or more and tell you what his cumulative average is over thousands of groups. My reaction is simple. "That's nice, but what did the buyer say? How was the organization helped? What were the results 6 months later?"

The trouble is that audiences know what they want, but they seldom know what they *need*. The buyer, presumably, knows what they need, and if he or she doesn't, then it's your job to provide still more value and help discover what those needs are.[5] Audience-centered speakers are often quite popular, and sometimes that's good enough.

Buyer-centered speakers include enough audience orientation to create a willingness to listen, but their main thrust is in meeting and exceeding the buyer's objectives. This is where the fun begins. Sometimes meeting a buyer's objectives means deliberately *provoking* an audience, making them think "out of the box," creating dissatisfaction with the current state, forcing them into a new action. You don't often get standing ovations or universally high ratings on evaluation forms if you do this consistently and well. But you do get rehired.

---

*Be speaker-centered in your profit motive, audience-centered in your delivery, but buyer-centered in your results focus. Confuse these at your own peril. There are a **lot** of speakers who work 200 days a year and barely make a living. If you're going to starve, you can probably do that working only 20 days a year.*

---

[5]See my book *Million Dollar Consulting: The Professional's Guide to Growing a Practice,* McGraw-Hill, 1992, revised 1998, for lengthy descriptions of how to find the real buyer of professional services. For the moment, let me make it clear that it is seldom a meeting planner, which is another conventional myth in this industry. Meeting planners are feasibility people. They seldom know what the economic buyer's real objectives are, and they're seldom in a position to pay for value. The meeting-planning industry has been clobbered by corporate downsizing.

A Performing Speaker, or a Speaking Performer?

There is a raging and mostly irrelevant debate in speaking circles about such esoterica as:

- Should you use notes or memorize your talk?
- Do you use a lectern or move among the audience?
- Are audiovisuals mandatory these days?
- Should you take questions or remain in the expert role?
- Should you sell products from the platform?
- Do you require acting and movement coaches?

Most buyers I've spoken to regard speakers as a viable alternative for some combination of providing knowledge, transferring skills, creating awareness, and provoking action. Many of the speakers I've seen and heard, however, seem to consider themselves as viable alternatives to a traveling road show, Disney World, narcissism, and self-therapy. Let me explain.

From a business perspective, you have not succeeded unless the buyer believes that his or her objectives were met and therefore would consider both hiring you again and recommending you to others. Nothing else matters. Your applause doesn't matter, the rating sheets don't matter, the meeting planner's thank-you notes don't matter, and your feeling of enhanced self-esteem doesn't matter. Whether it's a salesperson selling a Buick, American Express offering their card, or United Airlines providing a trip to San Francisco, nothing else matters unless the customer is satisfied with the product or service, agrees to come back, and tells others to try you out.

The bullet-point debate that opens this section is irrelevant because everything depends on what the buyer needs to meet the organization's objectives. That's why every presentation needs to be tailored and tweaked to the client's specific needs.[6] I've heard speaking gurus pontificate that you can't deliver speeches anymore without sophisticated visual aids that have moved from overheads to slides to computer-generated graphics. Yet one third of the time I use no visual aids at all, and some superb speakers never use them. In fact, there are occasions when they

---

[6]Every speaker you can find says that he or she customizes speeches for client needs. That customization generally means they change the title of the talk and nothing else. So "10 Steps to Quality Service" becomes "10 Steps to Quality Selling" and "10 Steps to Quality Inventory Management" and so on.

should never be used, such as after dinner, when low lights and the requirement of focused attention are guaranteed to induce narcolepsy. One association in Idaho asked if I was going to be using "a lot of computer stuff." I told the organizer that I never used computer aids in the presentation. He sighed in relief, telling me that their prior year's speaker had turned everyone into Luddites by inadvertently focusing on all of his technological whiz-bang at the expense of his message.

In later chapters on steak and sizzle, we'll talk about the best way to use whatever techniques you've decided on, but here are the *savvy* reasons for determining what you'll do, prior to deciding how you'll do them.

1. With regard to speaking versus performing, there is a spectrum in speaking that ranges from totally choreographed and orchestrated to totally ad hoc and responsive (see Figure 1-3). Both extremes are occasionally appropriate, but I submit that you'll more often find yourself in the middle. For example, all of your stories and anecdotes—no matter how natural and spur-of-the-moment you want them to sound (and, in fact, the *more* spontaneous you want them to sound)—need to be carefully rehearsed and practiced for timing, inflection, and movement. Yet your talk should also be flexible enough to allow you to play on some recent development in the organization, a uniqueness about the audience or setting, a question that arises, and so forth.

Impersonators are often on the left side of my continuum and humorists on the right. Most excellent speakers move around a broad range in the middle.

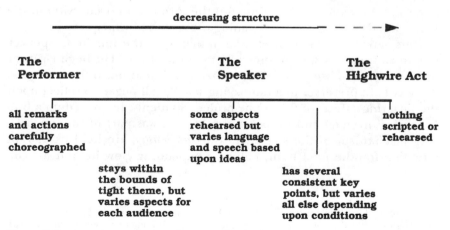

Figure 1-3. A continuum from performer to daredevil.

2. Visual aids are of use only if they enhance the message and help to improve the client condition. They are plain silly if they do neither. I once saw a speaker use a videotape to show someone drawing on a flip chart! Another speaker used slides to show still pictures of some of the people he was referring to. When I asked him why he went through the trouble (of dimming lights, working with remote controls, orchestrating his movements), he told me, "I always use slides, no matter what, because they show the audience a certain level of sophistication." Yes, they do. A low level, in this case.

Some of the worst abuses occur with computer-generated graphics because they have a relatively high degree of technological glitch.[7] When they work perfectly, they can overwhelm the audience to an extent that the medium becomes the message and actual content is ignored. McLuhan is rolling in his grave.

3. There is, today, a legion of coaches who have emerged from the shadows to provide speakers with techniques about gestures, movement, and interaction with the audience. Let's place things in perspective. No buyer has ever been recorded as having declared that a speaker will be rehired because of the superb, exaggerated hand gestures that were used, nor has one ever made a referral to a colleague because a speaker paused and moved with such dramatic flair. Do these jots and tittles of speech and manner make a difference in the impact of the delivery? Yes, but a very minor one.

The audience will walk away influenced or not influenced by the content of your message, be it humor, motivation, direction, anger, or provocation. To the degree that a message is enhanced by the use of stage and dramatic touches, fine. But the former can occur without the latter, and the latter have no meaning without the former.

Years ago, I attended an ethics seminar, and the luncheon speaker was introduced as an engineer from somewhere. He began rather uncertainly, established little eye contact, and held on to the lectern as if it was a life preserver in a rampaging sea. We all began to reflect upon the lingering effects of the crème brûlée. Suddenly, he picked up a broken piece of metal and rubber and told us it was part of the failed O-ring mechanism of the space shuttle *Challenger*. He held us in rapt attention for the next hour, haltingly explaining how he and his col-

---

[7]One of my favorite parodies was the old Apple commercial, in which a speaker using Windows can't get the computer to project an image, and audience members in the dark begin yelling out arcane instructions, such as "Try doc.ff/file.launch."

leagues in engineering were overruled by corporate executives and politicians, right up to the launch. His former employer was Morton Thiokol.

Believe me, the message is everything. Keep the coaches on the sidelines and confer as needed, but don't let them get onto the field.

4. The type of presentation you use will rely heavily on the degree to which you are able to subordinate ego. Like baseball or sex, it's an easy concept to grasp but extraordinarily difficult to do well.

I and three other speakers were appearing at one point on a "fast-track" seminar for Meeting Planners International. Each of us was given 45 minutes. I had delivered the keynote to the convention earlier; now I was to address an elite group of two-dozen executives and board members, followed by the other speakers. Prior to my opening, two facilitators had been chosen to "break the ice" and prepare people for the learning.

The facilitators manufactured a 90-minute "show" of their wares. That's right—the content sessions were 45 minutes, and the icebreaker was twice as long! Very thick ice, one would suppose. On top of the artificial opportunity to remain on stage, one of the facilitators managed to work into her summary of a response to a participant's question that she had won a prestigious award recently and then milked the place for applause. It was so egregiously egomaniacal that I had to laugh. Yet this nonsense is going on every day.

You should never sell your books and tapes (if you have them) or other services from the platform, despite the fact that there are "experts" who do nothing other than teach you how. If you're good at what you do, people will flock to buy them based upon your ability to have helped them during your talk, not because you mercilessly flog them from the platform. This is simply an abuse and an unethical intrusion on the audience's time.

You should involve or not involve the audience to the extent that such interaction furthers or impedes your progress toward the buyer's objectives. You should use notes or not use notes based upon your comfort level and the help or hindrance that results in terms of delivering your message. (No one measures speakers on their ability to memorize, except other speakers.) I once had a stunned participant confront me after a session in which I obviously shuffled my notes around—and kidded about it—during my talk.

"You were a smash today," she proclaimed, "and yet you used notes. I was told only amateurs use notes, and that the audience would never accept it."

"Only amateurs accept uncritically every piece of loony advice that comes down the pike," I replied. "Audiences want the speaker to succeed, and they're very forgiving. Give them what's obviously your best effort, provide a new idea that can improve their lives tomorrow, and they won't care if you use crayons and finger paints on the walls."

The Vagaries of the Trade

The odds are that most of your college professors were deadly dull. That's because they were (and are) compensated to perform a task, which is to hold a class session and deliver information. If teaching is defined as imparting knowledge, few of them actually teach, since precious little knowledge is transferred and only a scintilla is retained, let alone utilized, postexamination.

Most speakers approach our profession in the same manner. They believe that they are paid to deliver a speech. Nothing is farther from the truth. Yet that is what most convey in their interactions with the buyer, and that is what most cite in their fee schedules. It has become a commodity business, with bureaus (and speakers themselves) representing hourly or daily rates for the presence of a body on stage. That's roughly the equivalent of a doctor who performs open-heart surgery charging by the hour or an architect charging by the size of the building. Plumbers, who do charge by the hour, do noble work; but it's much more difficult for me to ensure that my speaking pipes will hold water.

Speaking is a business that provides for the enhancement of the buyer's objectives in return for remuneration to the provider. So let's establish some definitions and parameters prior to delving into the rest of the book and its specific techniques.

The **buyer** is the person who signs the check or causes it to be signed. The buyer is rarely the meeting planner, although that is the person with whom some bureaus are most comfortable working, which is one of the weaknesses of that system. A buyer is not necessarily the CEO, although he or she may well be in smaller companies or in larger ones organizing a top-level meeting. When I speak at GE, Jack Welch doesn't hire me. People 12 levels down hire me, but they are able to make the decision and cut the check. The buyer is inevitably that person whose objectives are to be enhanced. He or she "owns" the *outcome of the event.*

Whether you are pursuing an organization or responding to a contact they have initiated, try to find the buyer. In so doing, you can connect your involvement to his or her desired business outcomes, thereby increasing not only your chances of obtaining the assignment, but also your ability to obtain higher fees.

> *The more you focus on objectives and end results, the more valuable you are. The more you focus on events and tasks, the more vulnerable you are. A client can easily replace a 1-hour talk with another 1-hour talk. A client can rarely replace "the ability to close sales at a faster rate" or "the improvement of customer service to decrease failure work" quite so easily.*

Objectives are the results that are to be achieved through your participation. Delivering a keynote, speaking after dinner, facilitating a breakout group, and conducting two concurrent sessions are not results. They are tasks, and therefore they are commodities, subject to tough comparative shopping. This is why you'll hear a meeting planner so often say, "We've got $5000 for this slot. Who can you get for us?" It's the height of absurdity. The real question is, "Here's what we want to achieve. What value do various alternatives provide so that we can make an intelligent ROI (return on investment) decision?"

Listen carefully: The mere act of helping to explore, understand, and clarify the buyer's objectives will add tremendous value to your contribution. That's why you should relentlessly pursue discussions with the buyer and submit your proposal directly to that person. Only they have the volition and capacity to arrange for investments based upon return (meeting planners merely have budgets which they're incented to stay within, and they sacrifice quality for economy every day). A key aspect of what the consultants call "process consultation" is that a collaborative, diagnostic approach is, itself, intrinsically valuable. Many buyers tell me that they aren't sure that the objectives have been formally articulated. "Well," I respond, "wouldn't that be useful to do now so that you have a standard by which to measure success?" It's hard not to get the business after that.

The **process** you engage in is more valuable than your actual time on stage. The reason that the heart surgeon is so valuable is not the hours it takes to remove diseased arteries. The value is in the 20 years, the continuing study, the experiential base, and the superb judgment that enable the surgeon to perform such a delicate operation in those few hours. Doctors don't get paid by the blood vessel, and you shouldn't get paid by the adverb.

The process behind virtually any speech includes the following:

- initial talks with the client to determine outcomes and your contribution to those outcomes

- often, additional conversations with intended audience members to determine their points of view, their challenges, and to develop some client-specific examples
- a study of the industry in general, the competition, and the client's role within that scenario
- design of the actual speech, which may include 50 percent of standard points you would make, 25 percent of specific client-centered material, and 25 percent of audience exercises, interactions, new material, etc.
- discussion of your speech with the client and coordination with what precedes and follows you, as well as with any other speakers on the agenda[8]
- preparation of visuals, handouts, and/or performance aids
- practice
- actual delivery of the talk
- postsession follow-up with the client to determine what else may be necessary (e.g., another copy of some of the visuals), what the reactions were, how well the objectives were met, etc.

If you accentuate the process—and you may well have additional components—then the buyer can understand the comprehensive contribution to his or her objectives. If you emphasize the 60 or 90 minutes, or even the full day you're on stage, then the buyer perceives that payment is only due for that relatively brief duration. You have the ability to educate the buyer, but you can't do that if you're not talking to the buyer and/or if you don't understand your own value in terms of that process.

Summary

Professional speaking is a craft that revolves around words used to meet buyers' objectives. The outcome of a successful speech should be an overjoyed buyer, whose resultant testimonial is a paean to your skills. You manage and guide this process by focusing on the outcomes,

---

[8]When I offer to call both participants and other speakers to coordinate and customize my message, the client is always highly impressed. This enables me to cite higher fees because additional value is already established in the buyer's mind. There's another pragmatic reason: I once opened my talk only to find from the audience that a speaker 2 days prior at the conference had covered the first third of my 90-minute session. I improvised quickly and resolved never to appear "blind" again.

understanding the overall value of the process that culminates in your time on stage, and dealing with people who make investment decisions based upon value delivered, not minutes spent.

Professional actors aren't speakers. While it's important to be thoroughly prepared, it's sterile to be so tightly orchestrated that the audience perceives an off-the-shelf performance rather than an engaging interaction. People choose the plays and professional performances they attend, but they usually have their speakers chosen for them. If you do a thorough job at the front end, understanding the audience and basing your value upon the difference you can make in their personal and professional lives, then you'll be positioned to reap huge rewards. Ego-needs fulfillment, product sales, and adulation will follow as by-products. They should never be pursued as primary goals. When speakers appear primarily to meet their own needs, they are as obvious as a ham sandwich (emphasis on the *ham*).

Now that we have some common understanding of what professional speakers do and why, let's take a look at how to choose a market and why most speakers inexplicably foreclose options rather than expand them.

2
How to Choose Your Market

"But those people all know more than I do."

Get the Dummy Off the Cover

I was speaking at a "marketing laboratory" sponsored by the National Speakers Association in Tempe, Arizona. The audience was composed of professional speakers who wanted to broaden their appeal and, commensurately, increase their business. I had addressed the need to allow a wide variety of buyers to contact you, a concept I call "enabling the buyer to buy." For example, on the practical side, a buyer can't buy from you if he or she doesn't know how to reach you. On the conceptual side, the buyer can't buy if you don't appear to cover the appropriate topic areas, know the industry, have the experience, and so forth. It's ironic that so many speakers break their backs providing for the pragmatic reachability (even to the extent of plastering their photos on their business cards), yet manage to discourage potential buyers with an incorrect perception of their abilities.[1]

At the conclusion of my presentation, one of the participants asked if I would critique his promotional materials. He told me that he wanted to appeal less as an entertainer who appeared after dinner and more as

---

[1]Someone should do a sociological study of the "tchochkes" and ancillary doodads that speakers either give away or sell. There is an array of laminated cards with fortune-cookie wisdom, bumper stickers, bookmarks, self-published vanity books, can openers, paperweights, wall hangings, and peculiar club memberships (e.g., The International Association of Bubbas). If that energy went into increased fees rather than tangential dust-collectors, the entire industry might improve its revenues.

a change agent who appeared as a general session speaker or keynoter amidst the conferences. His proposition, which was quite logical, was that his entertainment was merely a vehicle to convey his techniques about managing change, and he was not a humorist per se.

He handed me his brochure, which was an expensive 9×12 piece. On the cover was a picture of him seated in a chair with a large dummy on his lap. It turned out that his entertainment was ventriloquism.

Here was a talented guy energetically engaged in turning off buyers.

"Lose the dummy," I suggested.

"You mean move that aspect of my act to the inside?" he wondered.

"No, lose it altogether. As long as it's here, you're a ventriloquist, and you'll have to work mightily to convince any buyer that you also can deliver a powerful message about change that will be the focus of your value. And stop talking about your 'act' unless your buyer is the manager of the lounge at the Golden Nugget."

He made the changes and thanked me profusely for the advice. Whether we're new to the business or veterans of the platform, we all get too close to our "act." We see ourselves from the inside out, yet buyers can only see us from the outside in. Perceptions are reality. The bad news is that our perceptions of ourselves are almost always different from the potential buyer's. Longfellow pointed out that "we judge ourselves by what we feel capable of doing while others judge us by what we have already done." The good news is that we can manage that process if we care to take an objective look.

Here are the logical, simple steps for choosing the scope of your markets. Notice that I didn't say "your market." I advise that you be as broad in casting your net as possible. Experience and circumstances will intelligently narrow it as needed, but that winnowing process is often a gentle erosion around the edges, not a sharp knife slicing a pie into eighths.[2] These steps are equally applicable for the neophyte or the veteran. (In fact, those with a few years' success in the business might find they've been arbitrarily and unconsciously limited in their growth.)

---

[2]If you want the opposite view, there's an otherwise charming and wonderful woman named Juanell Teague who makes a living coaching speakers in her concept of "Specialize or Die," which I think is the motto on New Hampshire's license plates. You can reach Juanell at People Plus, Inc., in Dallas (972/231-2831), presumably to learn how to specialize and how not to die, but be advised that a great many successful speakers have chosen to do neither.

Five Steps to Choosing Your Market Scope

1. Determine what value-added you bring to a potential client.
2. Determine what types of clients most need that value.
3. Determine where those clients live.
4. Determine how you will reach the buyers within them.
5. Reach them.

1. Determine What Value-Added You Bring to a Potential Client

If you don't leave the client in a better position than the client was in before you got there, then there is no point in having you there at all. You must be able to clearly define and articulate *how you will improve the client's condition*. This is never answered by the response, "I'll make a speech" or "I'll conduct a training session" ("Hey, let's put on a show!").

Clients are entitled to a return on their investment. If you can't suggest what that return is using the prospect's language, then who can? Never talk to a buyer unless you can describe that return in terms that the prospect can relate to.

Value-added must be described in terms of some output, some result, some bettered client condition. These don't have to be on the order of world peace (and in fact, too many of us kid ourselves into believing that what we offer has cosmic significance). Figure 2-1 provides some examples of the value-added that you might bring. Buyer terms and typical speaker terms appear in the figure.

The key element is to stop thinking about what we *do* and to begin thinking about what we *leave behind*. Your value should never be encapsulated in your speaking appearance, but rather be extended through the ongoing results of your appearance. (We'll get to this in later chapters, but that's why your marketing material and testimonials should focus on those lingering effects, not the brief time you actually spent on the client's property.)

Speaker Terms	Buyer Terms
■ conduct sales training	■ improve sales closing rates
■ deliver the keynote	■ create a need to listen and learn
■ entertain after dinner	■ alleviate day's stress, emphasize camaraderie
■ talk about stress reduction	■ improve productivity
■ deliver my message of hope	■ enable people to resolve their own problems
■ provide a motivational talk	■ challenge participants to exceed higher goals
■ convey time-management skills	■ improve productivity
■ introduce quality techniques	■ reduce failure work that erodes profitability
■ instill customer service attitude	■ improve customer retention rates, cut attrition
■ describe my battle with illness	■ broaden solution options for personal tragedy
■ provide investment advice	■ maximize financial security
■ teach interpersonal skills	■ reduce conflict on the job

Figure 2-1. Translating speaker terms into buyer terms.

List on the left everything that you think you do, deliver, speak about, convey, provide, etc. This can include your personal life experiences, concepts you've developed, humor, anecdotes, techniques, exercises—anything that you believe you are (or could be) adept at providing from the platform. Complete that column first, and take a day or two or ask friends to help if you're not confident the list is accurate and/or complete.

Then attack the second column. Translate everything into an outcome for a potential buyer. If you can't translate it, cross it out (get the dummy out of the act). Keep at it until you're absolutely comfortable describing that outcome orally and in writing. *Then try it on a real, live person.* Ask a friend—or better still, someone in a potential client organization—if your statements ring true in terms of benefits for his or her enterprise, be it private, government, nonprofit, education, whatever. Use the feedback to adjust your value statements.

The first step is always to analyze what value you are capable of providing. Only then can you determine who needs it.

> *Listen carefully because few in speaking heed the
> following, and I'm as sure of this advice as any I've
> offered in seven books: Always define yourself in terms
> of your lasting value to the client. When someone asks
> you, "What do you speak about?" it's an amateurish
> question. But when you dignify it and satisfy it with,
> "I speak about x, y, and z," that's a career-limiting
> response.*

2. Determine What Types of Clients Most Need That Value

This is the step that can dramatically narrow or expand your field. Most of the conventional wisdom recommends that you engage in a narrowing process to enable you to "focus" and "target" and not to fritter away your resources. Funny, but I'm under the impression that this is a business, and businesses thrive on profit, and profit is a derivative of growth.

Note that I've said clients who "need" the value, not those who "want" the value. Every prospect I've ever met knows precisely what he or she wants. But very few of them know what they *need*. That difference—the intelligence you can provide in assisting the prospect to discover needs that were heretofore unknown and that you can uniquely address—is a key component of your value-added proposition. Marketing is nothing more than creating need, which we can describe as results that are attractive to the buyer. Selling is the ability to convince the buyer that you have the best alternative to provide those results. Now, I ask you: Would you rather be selling an alternative that is vying against everyone else's for a generic result (the want), or would you rather be uniquely positioned to provide the best answer to a very specific result (the previously unknown need) that you and the buyer collaboratively have identified? Do you really need to think that one over?

I know a fine speaker named Roberta. She has meticulously created a speaking business that supports her, and she is a voracious learner. Periodically, she has come to me for advice, which is a mutual-learning experience. One of the most striking aspects of Roberta's business, however, is what she's neglected to do. Roberta is expert in helping people who are in tough situations find the talents, resources, strengths, and assets that they innately possess and build upon them to create a brighter future. She deals with people who have been downsized, outplacement clients, the chronically unemployed, and others who have lost jobs and/or have trouble finding meaningful work. Her reviews and results are excellent.

I asked her why she didn't apply the exact same skills and processes to those who are doing well, but therefore may be blind to what they could additionally accomplish. Current success blinds a lot of people to their true potential (especially in the speaking business). She told me that her specialty was dealing with troubled people and that her comfort level was in that arena. Yet Roberta is constantly seeking ways to grow her business to the point where it does more than cover the bills.

Roberta defines herself in terms of past success, current audiences, and a tiny playing field. There are people who seek and want her help. Yet there's a much larger playing field of people who need that same boost and introspective examination, but don't realize it. I'm convinced that Roberta would be equally comfortable there, but she doesn't want to risk leaving her current comfort zone. Longfellow was right: At least for ourselves, it's useful to define what we're capable of doing, not just what we've done.

A consultant named Gary, who left GTE to try to make it on his own, showed me his unique technique of "killer gap analysis," which he used to help organizations overcome gaps caused by better-performing competitors. It was a disciplined, systematic approach which was exactly what senior managers wanted to help reduce the distance between front-runners and themselves. Gary thought he was in good shape because the methodology applied across industrial lines. He was far from a narrow specialist, right?

Not so fast. I asked Gary why he didn't market to the front-running firms by establishing the need for them to *create* "killer gaps" to continually outperform and outdistance the competition. Why did he have to appeal to a remedial audience who wanted to catch up? Why couldn't he create the need to use his approaches to forever stay ahead, especially since firms in the latter category have more money to spend and tend to be more innovative? In other words, if he could create the need, they were perfect clients for his value-added.

Gary looked at me as if I hadn't heard a thing he had said. It took another hour to pound the point home. Then he told me, almost morosely, that he would have to totally rethink his approach to the market. Congratulations. That's what we should all be doing on a regular basis.[3]

---

[3]Roberta continues to grow her business, branching out and gaining visibility by serving as one of the star presenters for a major seminar company. This provides her with a solid economic base and the free time to invest in building her own practice. Gary has gone back to corporate life in a highly insecure job as the director of training of a troubled utility.

> *Define your value in the broadest conceptual terms,*
> *studiously avoiding industry, niche, and segment*
> *alignment. Enable any buyer to buy. Every word you*
> *use to narrow your impact eliminates thousands of*
> *potential buyers. So don't use too many words.*

Make a broad list of industries and markets that could profit from the value-added you've defined for yourself. Don't engage in destructive testing, which means arbitrarily eliminating those you feel don't have money (education and nonprofits), are logistically impossible (too far away), are saturated (too many well-known people doing sales skills training), are uncomfortable (senior executives are too tough), or are too sophisticated (high-tech is beyond my comprehension). All of those rubrics are untrue. For example, there is a lot of money in the education market if you know how to access it, and I recently spoke at one of the leading high-tech firms in the country, where they had to use an ashtray and a phone book to balance their ancient slide projector. Was that because they normally use only state-of-the-art computer graphics? No, it was because most of us are cobbler's children, running around with holes in our shoes.

Don't define yourself by presumed audience; define yourself by value delivered. Who can profit from that value? Your answers will tend to be very broad. *Keep them that way.* You can always narrow things later, if you're obsessed with limiting your income. But for now, describe those who benefit from your value. As an example, let's assume that in speaker terms you provide delegation skills, but in buyer results we'll translate that as "enabling people to improve teamwork, push decision making downward, and leverage work through others." Here is just a partial list of some potential clients:

- managers remaining in downsized organizations of any type
- firms emphasizing multidisciplinary and cross-functional teams
- volunteer organizations (Salvation Army, Red Cross, PTA, Scouting)
- boards of directors and trustees
- municipal government
- complex sales (e.g., technical support, product maintenance, etc.)
- trade association staffs interacting with members
- high-potential, fast-track people slated to become managers

■ Newly appointed supervisors and managers

■ high-pressure occupations, such as emergency response teams

Note that I'm not delimiting my choices by the kinds of materials I have, the past groups I've worked with, my personal experiential base, or any other circumscribing factors. I simply want to determine who might have need of my value, whether they know it yet or not!

3. Determine Where Those Clients Live

Once you've defined your value, you can determine where your prospects "live." In the examples just listed, the local volunteer, emergency response teams, and downsized businesses might be an immediate target. But notice that my list includes not only types of organizations (e.g., municipal government and trade associations) but also demographic slices within virtually any organization (e.g., newly appointed supervisors and fast-track people) as well as functions found in most organizations (e.g., boards of directors and trustees).

I was once asked while appearing as an expert witness, "Who constitute your potential clients?" My reply was, "Everyone. I just have to determine where they are on the priority list." For once, an attorney was rendered momentarily speechless.

Speakers too often engage in a sheltered journey that takes them to insulated, safe havens, within which they build safe nests. And so I encounter people who speak only to mortgage bankers, solely to food service workers, and exclusively to telemarketers. The best of them are whales in carp ponds, and the worst of them can't put food on the table. To give you an example of how quickly a market can be penetrated, a couple of years ago, through sheer happenstance and some bureau placements, I wound up speaking to 90 percent of the senior executives of every retail and independent bank in New York State. Don't forget, I'm a generalist, not a banking expert, and yet I was able, with no strategy to do so, to almost totally penetrate that market. If that were my only market and that were my strategy, what to do for an encore? Move to Pennsylvania, then Maryland, and through all 50 states? Perhaps, but unlikely. Return to New York again with a different topic? I don't think so—most trade associations prefer new faces every year or the membership doesn't believe they're doing their jobs securing outside resources.

In terms of the value you provide, and the likely candidates you can provide it to, you should have a list that's widely encompassing. The idea now is to pare it down into priorities. As you grow and succeed, ensuing priorities will rise to the positions of attention, but that will depend on your level of growth.

At the outset, your priorities might be guided by:

- resources for marketing (travel, advertising, listings, etc.)
- existing visibility (articles written, interviews, media exposure possible)
- existing contacts among the target prospects
- referrals from others among the target prospects
- most long-term potential (large organizations over local nonprofits)
- easiest case to establish need (downsized organization)
- individual experience/knowledge (you've worked in the hotel industry)
- current trends (news media hitting poor board performance)

These criteria are based not upon specific industries or specialties, but rather upon your ability to gain a rapid, positive response to your value proposition. It's silly to pursue the aerospace industry, for example, just to establish a specialty and focus. It makes more sense to focus on demographic slices, functions, or types of organizations most conducive to your ability to produce results. The newer you are to the field, the more important speed and the efficient use of scant resources become. The more experienced you are, the more important long-term penetration, repeat business, and ability to pay large fees become.

So, the more experienced speaker's priority list might have grown to also include:

- ability to sustain high fees within my value proposition
- multiple booking potential (corporations with numerous sites)
- high-level audiences composed of potential buyers (trade associations)
- international potential for expansion (global organizations)
- exposure in parts of country I haven't worked (travel is welcome)
- ability to purchase added products/services (books, consulting)
- potential for additional value propositions beyond original
- bureaus that market to my priority list

The items on my "experienced" list might not be feasible for the beginner, but they should be consciously added as success permits. We'll talk more about bureaus later on, but they serve a very useful purpose in marketing for you. In particular, they should be providing marketing *further down your priority list,* in areas you might not otherwise reach. The mistake that veteran speakers make is that they utilize bureaus to help them reach customers they would have reached anyway, except they've paid 25 percent of their fee (the usual bureau commission) to obtain the same sale. Bureaus have to provide their own value proposition in marketing, or they're not worth the fee. That's how I wound up speaking to all those bankers I otherwise wouldn't have reached. The bureaus involved earned their commissions, and it was money well-spent on my part.[4]

You'll find sources in the appendix to help with locating potential client organizations once you've reached this point. But here are three major search alternatives you can engage in daily. There's absolutely no reason why you can't turn up a dozen high-potential leads a day if you've completed these three steps with vigor.

1. For local leads, network. Attend civic functions. Serve on committees and fund-raisers. Have lunch with successful entrepreneurs.

2. Read those major publications which run stories on organizations that may fit your priority list and note the details for follow-up. Typically, these include *The Wall Street Journal, The New York Times, Fortune, Forbes, Business Week, Industry Week, The Nation's Business,* etc. In addition, there are specialty publications that may help in certain areas, such as *Chemistry Week, Mortgage Originator, Culinary Trends, CIO Magazine,*[5] etc.

3. There are "passive" listings of trade associations and organizations, such as *Business Phone Book USA,* which contain every major organization's phone number, address, e-mail listing, web sites, etc. *National Trade and Professional Associations of the United States* provides the name, location, chief executive, conference sites and themes, membership, and budget of every major trade association in the country.[6]

There is no acceptable reason why you can't establish a dozen prospects a day at the local and/or national level for your top priority list criteria. That's 60 a week, 3,000 a year, not counting those that will come to you by other means (e.g., referrals). If you close 10 percent of your leads for an average of $2500, that's a $750,000 base business without repeat engagements, ancillary product sales, referrals, or any other

---

[4]In late 1996, I spoke at a cattle feed lot convention and was the hit of the show. This is not a place I would normally even know about, much less appear as the featured speaker. As a result, the goat- and sheepherders association is now interested in me. Go figure.
[5]CIO is Chief Information Officer.
[6]See the appendix for sources.

sources of income. Of course, there's nothing stopping you from generating two-dozen prospects a day, closing 15 percent of them, and charging $3500, is there? To find out how to raise those numbers, read on.

4. Determine How You Will Reach the Buyers Within Them

There is only one way to reach a potential buyer: Determine how that buyer makes decisions, *not how you would make the decision*. Very few buyers respond positively to "cold calls" in this business (those who do respond are seldom the real buyers). Remember, you want the person who can sign a check, not a gatekeeper or intermediary.

Buyers usually make buying decisions about speakers in this order of priority:

1. personally having heard the speaker and been impressed
2. heard from a trusted peer that the speaker is excellent
3. heard from a trusted subordinate that the speaker is excellent
4. heard from a trusted third party that the speaker is excellent
5. heard from a bureau or agent with whom there is a relationship
6. seen or heard something about the speaker (e.g., media interview)
7. received promotional material from the speaker

Note that this is a relationship business. Whether it's a colleague, a subordinate, or a bureau with which the buyer has previously worked, the trusting nature of a continuing personal relationship is the key unless the buyer has personally seen you.

How do you enable the buyer to buy?

Buyer's buy. That's why they're called buyers. But they can also decide not to buy. Your job is to enable them to buy through an appeal to their most comfortable buying channels. Your hardest work should be done prior to contacting the buyer.

The first rule is to speak. Speakers are supposed to speak, and they should do so often. The more visibility you achieve, the more likely you are to have impressed buyers in your audiences. Regularly approach those organizations which are likely to have audiences composed of potential buyers, trusted recommenders to those buyers, bureau representatives, and/or media people. Obviously, this requires several different kinds of disparate groups, but you don't have to eat all the chicken dinners if you don't choose to. This technique, however, takes care of every important item on the buying priority list.

Seek out chambers of commerce, all of the service clubs,[7] the Better Business Bureau, charitable events, business roundtables, nonprofit groups, and anyone else seeking a speaker at lunch, dinner, to kick off an event, or to close it. The larger and higher-quality the audience the better, but you never know who will hear you. Always have a press kit and handout materials available and always provide a "leave-behind" for every participant to keep.

You'd just be sitting at home anyway, so don't view a freebie as some harsh penalty. *You're better off speaking for free in front of potential customers than you are not speaking at all in front of no one.* The fast way to fees is to do a lot of stuff for free. Successful veteran speakers follow this rule as well. While pro bono work is usually intended as a legitimate investment in an organization that values a speaker's talents, it seldom fails to rebound to a speaker's advantage. That's because those nonprofit and charitable board members sitting there captivated by your speech are, in their day jobs, vice presidents, general managers, and head honchos of organizations on your priority lists.

Bureaus are much more comfortable taking on new speakers if they have seen them first. Newspaper reporters and local radio talk-show hosts are much more likely to write about or interview someone they've seen have an impact in the community. These groups are always worth the investment. Prepare as carefully as you would with a paying client because they are the route to that client.

The second rule is to publish. Get your name in print. It doesn't have to be *War and Peace* and it needn't be in *The New York Review of Books.* Get an article about one of your topics in the local supermarket shopper, weekly newspaper, state business publication, or association newsletter. If you write a two-page article twice a month, that's two dozen a year. If a quarter are accepted, you'll have six articles published yearly—one every other month—not counting those that others ask you to write or repeats on the initial acceptances. Of course, you can always write three articles a month and have one third accepted for publication. Use both the published articles and the unpublished articles in your media kit. The latter should be printed nicely on your computer

[7]To name a few, the Elks, Lions, Rotary, Moose, Shriners, etc.

with a title such as, "Rogers & Associates: A White Paper on Retaining Good People."

Listen carefully: If you write, use the results whether or not they are published. Never waste any effort. Prospects will be impressed by well-written, well-presented articles on topics of importance to their business. Focus each article. Don't create 20-page treatises attempting to cover all the ills of modern humanity. You're better served with three to six pages on a specific, relevant topic, such as fostering teamwork, how to terminate problem employees, faster responses to customer complaints, and so forth.

The third rule is to network. There are sources in the appendix to help with networking skills and alternatives, but the commonsense formula is to follow the buyers. How will you appeal to the items on the buying priority sequence listed earlier? How will you make it comfortable for them to purchase your services? Attend the trade association meetings they attend. Read the publications they read. Publish in the newsletters that speak to their industry. Become involved in clubs, events, and associations that include people who work in that industry. Volunteer to work on projects in the community with which they are involved.

Speakers, by nature, are voluble. They needn't be persuaded to introduce themselves to strangers. You should be a natural at social events and business meetings. Attend and make yourself known. Build relationships. It's free and relatively painless marketing.

5. Reach Them

If you've traveled the road successfully to this point, you've met buyers who are potential clients. Build upon the relationship, not with a quickly proffered business card or an impersonal bundle of promotional materials, but with inquiries about the prospect's business. Listening is much better than telling.

Find out what the key issues are, the major problems, the desired innovations, the competitive challenges. Keep probing until you can begin to make connections—privately and internally—between the value proposition you can provide and tangible results for the prospect in his or her greatest perceived areas of need. Offer other insights and thoughts—help to create additional need—as you learn what the prospect truly values (i.e., higher profitability, greater teamwork, decreased attrition, improved communications, heightened public image, etc.).

Build a relationship, not a sales pitch. Build trust as a colleague, not a proposal as a vendor.

When you believe that you've explored what the prospect wants, offered insights into additional needs, developed a tight connection between your value and relevant results, and built a trusting relationship, present your case. Do it in writing so the buyer has the luxury of reviewing at leisure what your contribution is and what the ROI looks like.

You might be rejected. All of us are. When it happens, do two things that few of us do:

1. Ask why, so you know what you missed and can correct it next time.
2. Continue to build that relationship.

People who say "no" today often say "yes" in the future, and people who say "no" for good reason may have equally good reason to refer you to others.

You might be accepted. All of us are. When it happens, do two things that few of us do:

1. Ask why you were given the business.
2. Continue to build that relationship.

The relationship building can now continue on a more intimate basis. Also, we focus too much on reasons for our failures and not nearly enough on the causes of our successes. Only by finding out why we were chosen can we replicate the steps and attributes that resulted in our success.

Maintaining the Radar Array

I came across a particularly agitated colleague at a management conference that featured a half-dozen major speakers on the agenda. He was pacing and moving his lips soundlessly.

"What's up, Mark? You've done this a hundred times, right?"

"Yeah, but this time it's a very sophisticated management team. They've just had a hell of a year. I don't think my usual stuff is going to do it."

His usual stuff did just fine. All speakers suffer through periods when we're convinced that the client knows far more than they do. What can we possibly offer that the client hasn't already heard and doesn't already know? Some of my most successful presentations followed the momentary belief that I would be thrown out not long after I said "good morning."

People at Mercedes-Benz know a whole lot more about making automobiles than I do. But they don't know nearly as much about building an innovative culture. People at *The New York Times* know infinitely

Content Knowledge	X	Process Skills	=	Results
• autos		• decision making		• profit
• chemicals		• problem solving		• productivity
• insurance		• negotiating		• morale
• banking		• interviewing		• safety
• electronics		• coaching		• image

Figure 2-2. Process skills leverage content knowledge.

more about the newspaper business, but they aren't as adept at conflict resolution. People at Hewlett-Packard understand computers far better, but need some help with consultative selling skills.

The route to success is in providing *process* skills that people can use to leverage their already existing *content* knowledge (Figure 2-2). Processes are constant and can be applied cross-industrially, which is why specialization is anathema to me. But if you position yourself as a content expert (how to build cars, how to telemarket), then you not only narrow your field to those content areas, but you'd better be superior in your knowledge to those engaged in those businesses. The value-added of content experts is better content knowledge. The value-added of process experts is their tools, which the content people don't know how to employ.

There are speakers whose value is in their content knowledge. They are expert in financial operations, the fine points of the law, chemical analysis, and so on. But most speakers are *leveragers,* catalysts who can provide a turbocharge for the fuel that already exists in all organizations. Many people will tell you, "You don't know our industry." There are two responses to this.

The first is that you do know that the industry suffers from poor retention of good employees or a weak public image or chronic lack of innovation or whatever other process needs you've discovered. That will immediately create relevance and a focus on issues, not your experience.

The second is for you to be conversant, not expert, in the industry. If you read the sources referred to earlier and if you concentrate on your priority targets, your target vocabulary will improve daily. For example, if banks are on your list, learn what a loan defalcation is. If the health industry is a target, learn to discuss capitation. If you plan to do business with insurance providers, understand the meaning of churn, and why it's not a good sign.

The combination of focus on process issues of relevance and a vocabulary that embraces the buyer's frame of reference will offset any notions about your lack of extensive work in aerospace, foods, dog kennels, or funiculars.

> *If you insist on stacking the deck, at least do it in your*
> *favor. Learn to speak the client's language; don't try to*
> *be better versed in the client's business. Learn to focus*
> *on process needs, not content details. Show me an*
> *organization that doesn't need better communication*
> *skills, better teamwork, and improved profits, and I'll*
> *show you that it's merely a CIA cover.*

Your "radar array" has to be as encompassing as possible. You have to be continually vigilant for prospects, buyers, and opportunities to reach them. That means that the devices you use to identify them can't be unnecessarily narrow in their scope, shouldn't misidentify targets, and can't have any blind spots.

If you only receive an occasional "blip," then the chances are high that your equipment is either too restrictive or broken. Rigorously apply the five-step approach to setting priorities, finding buyers, and reaching them. Use discipline in networking, writing, and speaking at high-potential events. I've suggested very modest goals for your output in terms of articles, leads, and speeches. I've also suggested that there's nothing stopping you from establishing and surpassing a more aggressive standard.

By my estimate, close to 98 percent of all speakers, no matter what their proficiency or success levels, are sole practitioners. That is, we work alone, without marketing staffs, publicity people, or sales representatives. "Feet on the street" is not a wise alternative to increasing our business. In fact, mass approaches to the market are a genuinely bad idea, and million-dollar speakers don't engage in such wastes of time and effort. We all need to focus on the highest potential buyers and *enable them to buy our services.*

Choose your markets based upon your value proposition and connection with buyer needs, many of which you can create in the buyer's consciousness once you've established a trusting relationship. Does it take time? Sure, but no more time and a lot less money than spinning your wheels with cold calls, impersonal mailings, and uninterested third parties. The good news is that you manage the process, not the buyer and not the competition. Speakers' greatest marketing enemy is their own sloth and lack of creativity.

In the old *Cheers* television comedy, the bartender named Coach once told one of the leads, Diane, that he had been working on a book for 6 months. Diane was amazed and said, "I didn't know you were a writer."

"A writer?" asked coach. "I've been trying to read it."

It doesn't take 6 months to read a book (or to write one). Even veterans procrastinate about that book they wanted to write, that tape series they wanted to record, and that radio show they wanted to host. This afternoon or this evening, start it. There's no one stopping you.

3
Positioning Yourself in the Field

"You're a fish. Whaddya mean you can't swim?"

Only Life Itself Is a Full-Time Occupation

There is a tremendous debate among professional speakers as to how one should progress from part-time to full-time status. In fact, there are two deeply revered beliefs among veterans of the business, and like many deeply revered beliefs, they are egregiously false. As Oscar Wilde observed, a thing is not necessarily true just because someone dies for it.

Deeply Revered Belief 1. You are not a professional, indeed you haven't "made it" in the business, unless you are engaged in it full-time.

Deeply Revered Belief 2. The longer you are at it, the better you are.

I recall attending my first speakers' conference in the late 1980s. All of the "wheels" were there,[1] and as I tended to my drink during the cocktail reception, a legend in his own mind walked over to introduce himself. Seeing my "newcomer" nametag, he graciously informed me that if I watched the veterans carefully, accessed them as mentors, and

---

[1]An interesting phenomenon: With the possible exceptions of Zig Ziglar, Nido Qubein, and the late Og Mandino, none of these people is a common name among American business, but they create a "star" status for themselves within the industry's trade associations.

generally, paid the proper homage, I just might be as successful as they were someday, fates willing. At the time, I was making about a half-million dollars a year, wasn't spilling my food on myself, and could utter comprehensible sentences. But his criterion for success was longevity and membership in the "in crowd."

My criterion for success is pleasing people who can write checks that clear the bank. Peer recognition—if based on merit and not slobbering adulation—is wonderful, but it doesn't pay the mortgage and seldom impresses the buyer. Don't tell me about the industry awards you've garnered and the strange initials after your name. Tell me about how you'll improve my business.[2]

It doesn't matter how often you speak because we're all part-timers. No one is speaking 5 days a week, 50 weeks a year, at least not for money. If your fee were $10,000 per speech and you spoke once a week, that would earn you a cool half million for getting out of bed just 20 percent of the time. Sound ridiculous? Well, $5000 twice a week does the same thing, and even $1000 twice a week will earn you $100,000 and leave you with 3 days plus the weekend. (Yeah, I know about marketing, preparation, networking, practice, and all that time investment. We'll get to that. It's not as bad as most would like to make it.)

Last year, I spoke about 50 times, which has been my average over the past 5 years. I did not pursue any of the engagements. Bureaus booked me for about half, and half came from people calling me. Over the next year, it appears that I'll be speaking slightly more, with bureaus representing about 65 percent. If one's average fee for these engagements is $7000, that's $350,000. Over the past decade, speaking revenues have moved from a quarter to a third of my total income (with consulting work representing about 60 percent and publishing about 10 percent).

I'm a part-time speaker. A lot of people could live nicely on those 50 days of income.

> *It's not how much you speak or how long you've spoken that's important. It's how well you speak and how effectively you meet the buyer's objectives. Oh, and it's also a matter of charging for it.*

---

[2]The speaking business is the only one I've ever observed with people so desperate for image credibility and recognition that many place their masters degree after their names in print, as in Jane Jones, MA. I used to think a disproportionate number of them were from Massachusetts until I caught on.

We'll discuss fees in the next chapter, but while we're on the subject of the "full-time fallacy," let's debunk one more piece of horrid advice. There's an industry rubric that states you should raise fees when demand exceeds supply. That's roughly akin to saying you should swim away from the beach until you can see land again. There's an awful lot of water out there.

And there's an awful lot of time in a year. In this case, is supply 5 days a week? Actually, you might be able to speak twice a day, and even on weekends. Maybe supply is 700 speeches a year? Supply and demand are commodity measures. They are not measures of value. Raise your fees— no matter how many times a year you speak—when your value to the buyer increases.

If full-time/part-time isn't the indicator of speaking success, does that mean one can (*shudder*) work at another job and also be a speaker? Of course it does. Let's take the most extreme case. Suppose you're holding down a 40-hour conventional nine-to-five career. However, you've managed to secure local speaking opportunities in the evenings and on weekends (or during vacations). If you're paid for them, you're a professional speaker, and you might be quite happy with the arrangement.

The point isn't your lifestyle or how you choose to spend your time. The point is whether you earn money for working on the platform. I know a dental hygienist named Denise who is married with children. She works full-time in her field. She also addresses dental groups, medical offices, conventions, and trade associations as her schedule permits. She's funny, effective, and highly regarded. She chooses her assignments based upon the demands of her professional schedule and her family's needs. Denise is an excellent professional speaker, a fine dental hygienist, a wonderful mother and wife . . . well, you get my drift?

Too many speakers waste too much time trying to determine how to leave their present occupations and/or reduce their other time commitments to spend more time on professional speaking *as if that were an end in itself.* If speaking is to be your total calling, you'll naturally gravitate there because the gratification, job offers, and involvement will result in that evolution. But you can't force it.

People who pursue other interests or have additional careers (which I do, as a consultant, or Denise does, as a hygienist) are speakers. They are not poor stepcousins of professional speakers; they *are* professional speakers, no less than someone who tries to speak every day and travels 95 percent of the time.

Fish swim. Speakers speak. No one challenges a fish at rest with, "I see you're not swimming, so for the moment we're not going to accept you as a fish."

Being Around a Long Time
Makes You Older,
Not Necessarily Better

Don't be awed by the size and scope of this industry. There are people
who have been embraced by the bureaus, who have the connections,
and who are most visible at industry conventions. But many of the newcomers I've seen are a lot better than the veterans who seem to rely on
name recognition and a hackneyed "act" rather than trying to meet the
business challenges of their contemporary customers.

There are approximately 7500 trade associations, labor unions, professional societies, and technical groups that hold conferences each
year, many of which hold dozens of them annually.[3] If we add over
120,000 businesses[4] in the nation and their conferences and meetings,
even eliminating those which have no need for external resources, we
can realistically assume there are in excess of 100,000 meetings a year
utilizing professional speakers. (After all, 2000 per week is only 40 per
state, or eight per state a day; there are probably hundreds in New York
City alone, every day.)

The meeting industry is in need of new talent. No meeting planner
wants to present the "same old, same old," and every bureau wants to be
able to propose fresh faces and new topics to its clientele. Don't make
the mistake of assuming that you have to earn your merit badges
through long apprenticeships and careful climbs to the top. If you want
to climb the mountain, fine, but there are helicopters available.

One of the worst fates of an actor is to be typecast, which means that
people can only credibly accept the actor in a role with which he or she
has been identified before. That's a career-limiting dynamic. Some can
escape the fate—Tom Hanks went on to diverse, award-winning roles
after starring in a vacuous television sitcom. But Ted Danson and Shelly
Long have had a much tougher time post-*Cheers*. Similarly, veterans in
the profession have often stumbled into a success trap, in which they
were able to establish a niche but then fell victim to it. Speakers should-
n't be typecast either. If you're relatively new to the business, you have
the advantage of being lighter on your feet and more versatile.

So disregard both deeply revered beliefs. It doesn't matter how many
speeches you make a year, and it doesn't matter how long you've been

[3]All of these groups are covered in an extremely useful publication called *National Trade
and Professional Associations of the United States,* Columbia Books, New York. See the
resources guide in the appendix for more information.
[4]Another useful reference work, *Business Phone Book USA: The National Directory of
Addresses and Telephone Numbers,* Omnigraphics, Inc., Detroit.

in the business. All that matters is that buyers hire you, you meet their objectives, and you're paid for doing so. The degree and amount are up to you. But I know of no full-time speakers.

10 Best Practices to Increase Your Business

Here, then, is a brief practicum of 10 best practices for the novice or the established speaker who wants to increase business dramatically and take an easier way to the top of the mountain.

1. Never Respond to the Question, "What Do You Speak About?"

Your orientation should always be on what's *accomplished* for the client. Don't focus on what you do, but on how the customer benefits. Don't talk about why you're good; talk about what the buyer needs. Above all, don't prematurely and arbitrarily narrow your appeal, which a "topic list" will invariably do.

2. Prepare Well, but Not Fanatically

It's as important *not to be perfect* as it is to be well-prepared. No speech you or I ever make will mark the turning point of modern civilization. With luck, they might mean a bit of improvement in a person's professional and/or personal life. The difference—to the customer—between being 95 percent prepared and 100 percent prepared (whatever that is) is infinitesimal. It is not perceived. But the energy expended in moving from 95 percent to 100 percent is immense, much more than that required to move from 75 percent to 95 percent.

Heresy? I know. But it's time we took apart the fantasy of perfection in this business, along with its attendant fanatical preparation. We are not building the space shuttle. We're not even trying to build a Toyota. There's just no need for frenzied anticipation. At 95 percent, your slides are rehearsed and placed correctly, you have a backup bulb for the projector, your examples have been adjusted for the audience, and you can alter your timing given the progress of those before you. Enough.

I once heard a very well-known speaker tell a crowd that he gave the same speech about 100 times a year and that he never failed to practice it *every time* prior to delivering it. The speech was 3 hours long, and he spent 3 hours practicing *the same speech* every time. He claimed that this was the path to success.

My immediate reaction was that he was either deliberately lying to create false barriers of preparation for others or that he was the slowest learner I had ever encountered. The Gettysburg Address was written on the back of an envelope.

One of the best ways to prepare is to record your speech a week or so earlier and then listen to it a few times. Practice some ad libs to throw in each time, think about how you'll manage the visual aids during each segment, and work on making smooth transitions. When you're tired of listening to it, you're done practicing.

3.   Adhere to Basic Adult Learning Needs

There are those who will tell you there is a formula to a speech: You open with a humorous story, make a point, tell an anecdote, repeat your point, and close with a deeply personal revelation. That might help you deliver a speech in a choreographed manner, but I think you can see it coming a mile away.

Adult learning generally occurs in the sequence depicted in Figure 3-1. This sequence shouldn't be a lock-step formula, but it does reflect what we know about human learning. We are presented with information of potential usefulness, practice with it to explore its utility, receive feedback on our use or performance, and then apply it in real life. Without the final step, all else is academic.

The discussion aspect can include humor, audience participation, and a host of other devices. It needn't be simply a "talking head" (although that's what it usually was in school). The practice element can include exercises, role plays, games, and simulations, or it can be as simple as focusing someone on how a concept might be applied. The feedback constitutes the need to provide insights for the practice, and it can be self-feedback, from colleagues, or from the speaker. Application means that the audience has done something more than merely sit through your presentation.

Discussion ➤	Practice ➤	Feedback ➤	Application
• lecture	• alone	• oneself	• immediate
• interaction	• in teams	• partner	• delayed
• demonstration	• mentally	• speaker	• independent
• example	• in writing	• delayed	• with others

Figure 3-1. An adult learning sequence.

These steps apply more to a workshop than to a keynote, but they have applicability for all adult learning. Even in a brief keynote, you want to present ideas and instill action in the participants. (Which is why keynotes require different skills and can be harder than much longer presentations.)

4. Understand Your Role as a "Motivational Speaker"

There is a difference between motivation and inspiration. To be inspired is to be spiritually moved, emotionally involved, uplifted, and to take solace in words themselves. Its derivation is from theology. There's nothing wrong with being inspired, but it's usually a temporary, euphoric feeling, not a long-term focus on action.

Motivation is intrinsic. It comes from within. It is a willingness to act based upon a belief that the actions are important and will be gratifying. I cannot motivate you; you can only motivate yourself. However, I might be able to help establish an environment and atmosphere that is conducive to your motivation. (Which is why motivation in the workplace is most directly a function of the immediate leadership and environment. It's plain silly to have a speaker try to motivate an audience which then returns to a gulag.)

Every good speaker is a motivational speaker because he or she helps people to take action. Motivation and self-esteem are intertwined, and self-esteem is heightened when someone receives tangible skills which, when used, add to their success, encouraging them to apply those skills repeatedly (see the adult learning sequence in the previous section). In essence, the more successful I am, the better I feel about myself, and the better I feel about myself, the more successful I am. But that's a tautology. The key to influencing that circle is to provide discrete skills that I can rely on for success (Figure 3-2).

To the extent that we impart those skills in others, we are all motivational speakers. I've never known how to reply when someone asks, "Well, are you one of those 'motivational' speakers?" I guess I'd better be.

Motivational speaking has developed a bad name because it's sometimes delivered as an empty, quasi-inspirational talk filled with platitudes, bromides, and the bathos of personal struggles. "You can't take away my best friend, myself," and "You can knock me but you can't reach me" are cute phrases, but hard to apply in the workplace the next day. On the other hand, learning a technique to resolve conflict with a coworker or learning how to influence the boss's delegation style are techniques that can help me tangibly and immediately.

What's more motivational: Being told I'm my own best friend or being able to eliminate some of the stress in my life?

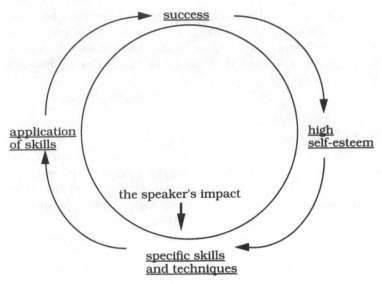

Figure 3-2. The motivation circle.

5. Self-disclose Only If You Have a Point

Among professional speakers, the personal revelations known as self-disclosure have moved from minor technique to the main attraction. When involving ourselves and our experiences on the platform, we've too often moved from modest litotes to egocentric hyperbole. Here's a satire I use with my mentorees to make the point:

> "The astronaut had traveled to the moon with only a tenth of an inch of metal between him and the void. He had landed a quarter of a million miles away and walked tentatively but triumphantly on the cratered surface. Now, he was to return home in the final, tiny stage of his rocket that awaited him.
>
> "But something went terribly wrong. Instead of heading for Earth, he tumbled out of control in the direction of deep space. All attempts to correct his errant capsule failed, and he sailed, helplessly, into the abyss.
>
> "Ladies and gentlemen, I am that astronaut…"

Believe me, it's not so farfetched. I've seen speakers break down into tears on stage (always in the same spot, night after night, as sincerely as you can imagine, trying to regain control for exactly 46 seconds), speakers invite parents they hadn't spoken to in 10 years to join them on stage, and speakers reveal more about their personal lives, struggles with disease and loss, and intimate problems than I'd ever want to know. I've heard more from speakers 60 feet away on a stage than I've heard in the privacy of my own living room. It's not a pretty sight.

Self-disclosure works if there's a point the audience can use to improve their condition. Telling me you were born poor and now you're not (presumably because you're making money telling me this story) does not help me unless I can relate to the *techniques* you used to make that transition. Sharing with me your heartbreak, disease, loss, or vicissitudes may help you unburden yourself weekly, but it doesn't help me unless I can translate it to my condition and my life.

I always face an audience with the belief that they *are not* damaged. All of us, of course, have experienced the vagaries of fate. We all have had tragic times as well as wonderful times. But that's simply a condition of human existence. There's no need to turn yourself inside out or violate my privacy by violating your privacy unless there's a pragmatic set of skills that results.

There usually isn't. While I'm happy with your reunion or conquest of adversity or recovery, I'm a lot better off longer-term with something I can use tomorrow to close more sales, better manage my time, communicate better with others, or more adroitly lead teams.

Some approaches to speaking actually claim that the speaker's relationship with the audience is a function of the audience's need for help and the speaker's need for approval.[5] That sounds like a bad case of codependency to me. I believe that the speaker-audience relationship is based upon shared values (we'd like to improve), trust (the speaker is factual), pragmatism (these are useful techniques), and relevance (this applies to us). If, as a speaker, you need approval, see a therapist.

If you're lonely, get a dog. If you want to practice, get a volunteer audience. Only if you think you can improve an individual's and/or organization's well-being, however, should you try to get a client.

---

[5]See, for example, *I Can See You Naked,* by Ron Hoff, Andrews & McMeel, Kansas City, MO, 1992.

6. Cultivate Two Speakers Bureaus As Though They Were Potential Clients

Speakers bureaus are not like money in the bank, meaning the more the merrier. They *are* the bank. You don't want casual relationships with a dozen, unless you first have an intimate relationship with a couple.

We'll discuss the most sophisticated ways to acquire and work with bureaus in Chapter 7, but for now, here are some guidelines if you haven't done much bureau business in the past or if you've been unhappy with either the quantity or quality of your placements:

- Always establish a relationship with the principal first. You might work with subordinates later, but you need the owner's personal belief in you.

- Although you may work out of your bedroom or den, don't be so lenient with a bureau. You want a multiperson operation (all the more to market with) that has access to sophisticated equipment (for copying, duplication, messages, etc.). If you call during working hours and rarely talk to a live person, it's too small an operation—picture all those potential clients having to leave voice-mail messages. I returned one bureau's call and spoke to the "principal" herself, while a baby screamed and two dogs barked in the background. Is that the image you want your representative to convey?

- Provide a fee schedule with options so the bureau can have some flexibility in negotiating for you (e.g., you take a percentage off your fee if the client is within 100 miles of your base).

- Find intermediaries who are represented by the bureau or are known to the principal to act in your behalf. References and referrals work with bureaus just as they do with buyers.

- Make your case to the bureau in terms of their outcomes, not your benefits. "I've noted that you're very active in the financial community, and I spent 5 years in mortgage lending. I have some contacts who plan meetings, and I'd be happy to put you in touch with them." Send a potential client to them. Such largesse gets a lot more attention than the continuing pleas for placement.

7. Have Something to Say Before You Write; Then Write Often

I once heard a speaker advise others that "If you have a speech, you have a book." Well, you might have a very, very brief book.

Don't use secondary sources because they're often actually farther removed than that and can be highly misleading. Find your own sources. More important, form your own opinions. Look around in awareness and digest what you see. Are people more stressed when they work at home? Do decisions actually have poorer quality when made participatively? Does most training accomplish next to nothing 6 months later?

Don't be afraid to be contrarian, but be scared out of your mind to be trite. It's better to stand out in a crowd through controversy than to blend into the wallpaper through blandness. Your favorite color shouldn't be plaid.

Writing will enable you to express your thoughts, examine your cognitive processes, and anneal your concepts. It doesn't matter whether you get published, although your odds are strikingly higher if you have written something as compared to having written nothing. Writing and speaking are synergistic and symbiotic. John Updike once explained that to understand how people speak—to be able to write dialogue— you had to understand how they think. I believe that to speak to people you have to understand how you think.

8.   Develop and Use Only Personal Anecdotes and Stories

Everyone is sick to death about the boy who throws the sand dollar back into the ocean.[6] The naval ship that keeps requesting the lighthouse keeper to move to avoid a collision is about as old. They were poignant and funny once. So were silent films.

All around our personal lives revolve stories, incidents, circumstances, and travails of family, friends, and strangers. Jot them down, record them on tape, create reminders for yourself (I keep an "anecdote file"). Periodically go through them to select those with the potential to prove a point or highlight a concept. Feel free to embellish— after all, it's your story, and the key is the audience's improved condition, not personal historical veracity.

Never discard the anecdotes. Even those that seem to hold no promise may emerge as brilliant departure points as you mature, your speeches evolve, your clients change, and society diversifies. In the worst case, the anecdote takes up some space, but if you discard it, you lose it forever.

---

[6]A passerby says that the effort can't make a difference because there are thousands washed up on the beach. "But it made a difference to that one," says the now-stereotyped, philosophical child.

Personal stories immunize you from being copied and keep you unique no matter who else in on an agenda. No one can tell your stories as well as you can, and no one has your personal history and experiences. Collect and nurture the stories of your life. They are your continually renewing resource.

9. Subordinate Your Ego

Stop trying to be the center of attention every time. I was invited to speak in Atlanta once, and the group's officers hosted a dinner for me the night prior, presumably to meet me on more intimate terms and to learn what they might. However, the association's president waltzed in, and she promptly dominated the discussion. When one of the group raised a basketball question, she even had some irrelevancies to insert about a game she had never played and didn't care to watch.

That woman was incapable of sitting quietly and listening because she judged her success by how often she opened her mouth. Our success is actually a function of communication which, the last time I checked, was a dialogue. If you're not on the platform, don't feel that you have to be the center of attention (and even then, you're only a conduit and shouldn't be a hero).

You might have a better story than the one that was just told. Save it for another time, rather than practicing one-upmanship. You might have visited more places, earned higher fees, worked with tougher audiences, and had a more harrowing travel experience. So what? Allow others their moments in the light of their friends' attention.

The best speakers I've ever seen are terrific listeners. They don't need to be on center stage when they're not on the stage. They don't have to tell you continually what they've done because their accomplishments speak for themselves.

I love the airline pilot who, with superb talent and comprehensive experience, has just landed a $160-million 747 filled with 500 people after a transoceanic flight and comes on the public address system to say, "Thank you for flying with us. We really appreciate your business and hope you'll choose us again." That's humility. It's a rare trait.

10. Understand That Sometimes It's the Audience, and Get on with Your Life

I've had a few speeches that I wish I'd never accepted. Both the client and I had acted in good faith, but conditions (or client judgment) deteriorated. For example, I've faced audiences who have just arrived from a 2-hour open bar; who have been awarded prizes and trophies after

grueling competition and pressure; who have had terrible news presented to them (deaths, layoffs, divestitures—I kid you not); who have been
exposed to too many speakers or activities, some of which were dreadful
and dull; and who were just plain ornery for no good reason at all.

I don't hold it against the client, and I certainly don't hold it against
myself. I do the best I can and I leave. That's all that I can do, and I'd
propose there's little more that you can do.

If you haven't prepared, blow your lines, are hungover, or become
insulting, you're at fault and should return the client's money. But if
you've done everything you can to your best ability, go home to work
another day. The money has been earned much more than when you're
hot and having a great time for yourself. Some audience can't be
pleased, no matter what you do. All you can do is your best.

No speaker that I know of who has been successful turning around a
very difficult crowd ever went to the buyer and said, "That was much
tougher than expected, but I turned them around, so I want you to pay
twice my fee." Conversely, no buyer should say to you, "You did your
best, but they were tough and you didn't make any headway, so I want
my money back."

Occasionally, it doesn't work. The only real downside is if you allow it
to affect you in the future. The longer you're in this profession, the
more of these immovable obstacles you'll hit. I hit one every year or
two, bounce off, spend the money, and move on. This business is not
about somebody else's idea of perfection or arbitrary credential. It's
about preparing well and doing your best. Just think about what a world
this would be if everyone, in every client, prepared well and did their
best every time.

Wind in the Sails

This section of the chapter is for those of you who are relatively new to
the profession or who seem stalled at a low level of activity. Once you're
moving, with some headway, it's relatively easy to change direction. But
as long as you're becalmed, you're helpless to set a course.

There are many options available to create your own power. They
include:

- working for a seminar training firm
- obtaining sponsorship
- securing another speaker's castoffs
- volunteering services in return for exposure

- broadening your scope
- serving as a backup

Working for a Seminar Training Firm. These firms include organizations such as CareerTrack and Fred Pryor Seminars. Quite a few very successful speakers began with these companies. They offer very inexpensive seminars (typically $39–$99) for a day's duration, around the country, drawing from a cadre of speakers and trainers who comprise the "faculty."

The seminar companies either create or purchase their course content independently; the instructor doesn't need to bring his or her own material (in fact, they prefer that you don't). You learn the content, practice teaching with a veteran, and you're off and running. You'll be asked to commit to a basic number of days—say, 10 per month—in return for that guarantee from the company. The pay is low, generally about $400 per program at this writing, although there are some exceptions for high performers and commissions on book and tape sales.

The advantages include exposure all over the country, accolades for your press kit ("Lou was the highest rated CareerTrack trainer for 2 years in a row!"), experience dealing with diverse audiences, a guaranteed cash flow, learning new concepts (you can teach several different programs), and at least half of your time free to market yourself as a professional speaker.

The disadvantages include a demand on half your time (reducing flexibility), considerable travel (which is part of our business anyway, however), very low pay, constraints on what you can and can't do in the seminars, and continual monitoring—these firms are paranoid about instructors developing their own prospects during the courses, and with good reason.

All things considered, these arrangements are quite helpful *if* they are seen as temporary bridges to the next step in your career growth. As a permanent job, they're roughly equivalent to the rowers in the Roman galleys.

Obtaining Sponsorship. Some organizations will pay a speaker to appear on their behalf. For example, Apple Computer might hire someone to address school groups on the best uses of technology in the classroom, a communications company might hire someone to address police and fire departments about crisis management, or a health maintenance organization might employ someone to address community groups on the benefits of early screenings for certain illnesses.

These are not sales pitches. They are informative presentations whose sponsors want to increase their profile, goodwill, and long-term business through their support of such efforts. Utilizing a professional speaker, and not a company spokesperson, creates much less of a sales environment and much more of a professional presentation.

A friend of mine is an expert on public safety and has written a book on the subject.[7] He is trying to align himself with manufacturers of safety paraphernalia, such as mace, whistles, and alarms. Someone with experience as a professional nurse might be perfect for the HMO alluded to earlier. A former volunteer firefighter might have an advantage with the public safety agencies cited.

The advantages include guaranteed work, exposure, the ability to use your own concepts and techniques in support of your sponsor's needs (they might ask you to help design the session), and a firm client to cite. Depending on the nature of the organization, the pay could be menial or meaningful. The disadvantages include a probable lack of buyers for your future speaking in your audiences and the potential of being cast in a narrow niche (she's a healthcare specialist).

Sponsorships virtually never seek you out. Your best bet is to find a firm that is practicing such tactics (or could benefit if they did) and present your case to the buyer. Relatively few people do this aggressively, and you could have their undivided attention if you make a strong case, again, *toward their objectives.*

Securing Another Speaker's Castoff Business. All of us who have arrived at certain levels of success receive inquiries about business we don't want to pursue. It is usually because the client can't afford the fee, it's in an area in which we're not sufficiently relevant, it calls for travel that isn't attractive, and/or it conflicts with other professional or personal activities. It happens to me at least once a month, so it's happening out there every day as you read this.

Reach out to speakers in this situation. I don't mean that you should call them once a week and ask for a handout because that's what it would be if there's no quid pro quo. Develop a relationship as you would with a client, bureau, or banker. Can you do some research for the speaker in return for first call on appropriate business he or she can't handle? Do they need some office help, some temporary staffing, some computer work? Can you walk the dog and wash the car? (All right, I'm kidding, but not by much.)

---

[7] *The Safety Minute: How to Be Safe in the Streets, at Home, and Abroad So You Can Save Your Life!* by Robert L. Siciliano, Safety Zone Press, Boston, 1996.

Establish that kind of relationship with three or four busy speakers, and you might get their castoffs on a regular basis. If you're good, you'll be able to address the topic and earn credibility with the audience (which won't always be the case in these situations). Your fee will be no problem, since you'll be a bargain compared to the original, and you'll probably receive a higher fee than if you had been contacted directly.

The advantages are in the association with proven pros, the ability to work with firms that never would have called, and the opportunity to "test the envelope" in terms of your versatility and appeal. There are few disadvantages if you are able to establish a truly trusting relationship, and you're not simply around for legwork and as a "hanger on." One person who took on castoffs from me was able to work at a fee twice what she otherwise would have demanded, put days into preparation, and blew the client's socks off. He told me that, no offense, he really didn't see how anyone (meaning me) could have been better for them.[8]

He was probably right.

Volunteering Services in Return for Exposure.   Every service organization, community group, social club, youth group, and local professional society can use speakers, especially if they're for free. The key in volunteering for these roles is that you want to do it for groups that will have potential customers in the audience. The ironclad rule for addressing these groups is simple: Always bring a lot of business cards.

The Rotary, for example, typically has both small-business owners and managers from larger organizations, as well as community leaders. Civic organizations will have, by design, top people from large businesses on their boards and committees (e.g., The Greater Peoria Business Improvement Coalition). Occasionally, these entities will pay, at least an honorarium. But it's more important to achieve the exposure to the people in the group than it is to make small change.

Recently, I spoke pro bono for the board of a shelter for battered women, helping them to define their strategy and goals. One of the board members was the chief of police of the second largest force in the state, and he immediately hired me to do the same session for all of his senior officers. These things happen all the time. But they can't happen if you're not in front of these groups.

---

[8]Not long ago, I recommended another colleague, who is a humorist, to a client who couldn't afford my fee. He received a second, larger booking after the engagement because the wife of a major business owner was present and insisted her husband hire him for his next staff meeting. You never know.

Broadening Your Scope. Try to look at your skills on a much wider basis. As a speaker, you can be a panel moderator, an emcee, a visiting college lecturer, a spokesperson, a mediator, a facilitator—just about anyone of whom communication skills and stage presence might be required.

One day, flying home from San Francisco, I returned a message from my wife from the airplane.

"What are you wearing?" she asked.

"Maria, not here," I whispered.

"Knock it off. Are you wearing a suit?"

"Well, no. You know I travel casually."

"Okay, listen. As soon as you land, rush home, put on a suit, and meet me at the public television station outside of Providence."

"Why? Is there a benefit or a fund-raiser?"

"No. You're hosting tonight's debate for the League of Women Voters."

It seems the local television anchor who emceed the event was sick, and the backup was on vacation. My wife, a committee member, confidently volunteered me. When I arrived 30 minutes prior to airtime, the director was nearing meltdown. But when he realized I could walk, talk, and follow stage signals, he recuperated.

The show went flawlessly, and I was subsequently hired to do a local awards banquet as the after-dinner speaker at full fee. I never considered that I couldn't host that show. You can do a variety of things if you let people know. They might not all be perfectly consistent with your speaker's image, but they will provide opportunities for you to shine in front of people who will require that image later.

Serving As a Backup. Here's a technique that most new speakers miss. Provide your name, credentials, and abilities (it's always about relationships) to organizations that can be seriously hurt if they have a no-show. (In areas hit with hard winters, this is particularly relevant.) Provide your name to local speakers bureaus, hotel banquet managers, company meeting planners, service organizations, newspaper columnists, talk-show hosts, and anyone else who might hire, or influence the hiring of, outside speakers.

You will be competing with no one else, in my experience. Tell people that you're not expecting them to hire you for the gig, but that having a backup is always prudent, and you work for 75 percent of the original speaker's fee when called upon at the last moment. (Use your own percentage or rate. Don't worry—you're not going to be called if Colin Powell can't show up, so the rates will be reasonable.)

I appear on radio all the time. Locally, I'm interviewed in the studio. One day, the host of a talk show I had appeared on twice told me she was going on vacation. "You're really good on the air," she said, "so how about pinch-hitting for one day?"

Thus, I became a talk-show host for 3 hours. The producer kept whispering through the earpiece, "Don't forget to promote your latest book."

Yeah, I think I can do that.

Fish Swim, but Different Strokes for Different Folks

There is no single way to make it in this business. Bertrand Russell once said, "Don't ever be absolutely sure of anything—not even if I tell you."

Professional speakers help people and organizations improve their condition. They do it in a wide variety of ways, employing a vast array of talents. You have to decide what your "playing field" is and what kinds of plays make sense once you're on it. Ignore the stentorian, dire pronouncements of those who, with fingers pointed skyward, proclaim that you must specialize, you must speak only for a fee, you must speak full-time, you must work with bureaus, you must have a demo video, you must eat bran every day.

The only "must" is to be flexible and not to rule out options that may be of utility as you advance your career. And we are all trying to advance our careers, every day, newcomer and veteran, high profile or low. Some of us are simply less part-time than others.

Nothing succeeds like success. Don't listen to vacuous directives. Instead, watch what a variety of successful people have done. Then do that.

Observe what people whom you respect have done. (Don't just listen to advice because it's too easy to give it.) And watch a wide variety of people. Adapt those techniques that seem most relevant to you, and perhaps a few that will help you to stretch. Through this exploration, you can determine your true value to the client, and that will help you establish your fees, commensurate with that value.

Someone once asked me why I didn't farm out all of my administrative work, such as sending out invoices.

"Are you mad!" I raved. "That's one of the truly great pleasures of the profession, setting up that invoice and sending it to the client. That's the apotheosis of the work, the tangible evidence that you're providing such value that the client deems it a worthwhile return on the investment."

You can't help others until you effectively help yourself. So let's turn now to the chapter that most of you may have already begun with: How do you establish fees?

4

Establishing Fees

"How much do you cost?"
"How much you got?"

No One Is Worth Very Much
by the Hour

Many of you have turned immediately to this chapter. Welcome. I hope you'll go back and glance at some of the others when we're done here.

Nobody is worth all that much by the hour. My auto mechanic makes about $75 per hour for his shop, some speakers command $7500 for a keynote, and Colin Powell, the former Chairman of the Joint Chiefs of Staff, commands about $75,000 for an hour appearance at a convention. That's 10 times the high-end keynoter fee and 1000 times the mechanic's rate. How can this be so? Does Colin Powell have 10 times or 1000 times their life experiences, skills, preparation, intelligence, and abilities?

The fact, of course, is that the hour (or half day or day) on the platform is not the value of what any of us bring to the client, *yet we insist on charging fees for that time commodity, rather than our true value.* In reality, the mechanic is able to charge $75 an hour because of his or her experience, training, expertise, and talents to fix your car, provide the proper preventive maintenance, and ensure that the proper performance endures long after you're out of the shop. That same *process* applies to you, me, and Colin Powell, as well.

People in the audience come to hear an hour keynote,[1] but the buyer

---

[1] This logic applies equally well to speeches of any duration, including multiday training sessions. I'm simply using the hour keynote as the most dramatic example.

is paying you to deliver it because of some combination of the following factors. I call it "the value list" because it represents those aspects of what you do which the buyer finds of worth.

The Value List

- your repute in the field
- the talents you bring to bear to deliver it
- your singular knowledge or approaches
- your particular platform skills
- the visual aids or demonstrations you provide
- your ability to speak to that particular industry
- the skills you'll impart to the audience
- your experiences, stories, anecdotes, and/or humor
- the behavior change that will ensue
- the improvement in the business that will result
- the reference point you create, which will be an ongoing focus
- the provocation to reconsider positions
- your perspective from other companies
- motivation that people will generate from your message
- a sense of unity, direction, and purpose that you can provide
- your credibility
- your personal accomplishments and results
- your ability to serve as an exemplar
- the client's intrinsic trust in you

The more of these factors that apply, the more valuable you are. If you think about it, Colin Powell delivers virtually all of them. That $7500 keynoter delivers most of them. How many do you deliver?

Note that my list of valuable attributes focuses mainly on the past and the future. While there are some items that are strictly in the present, such as platform skills and delivery, even these are the result of your past training, experiences, and practice. In other words, there are two major aspects underlying your value to the buyer:

1. Your combination of past experiences and development that has produced the qualities you convey today.

2. The long-term results the client will realize as a result of your time on the platform.

Your real worth is in the unique combination of factors that have resulted in your current value to the client and in the skills, behaviors, beliefs, and approaches that the audience will apply after your presentation which will benefit the business permanently. *The hour itself is incidental, being nothing more than the delivery vehicle which enables your own past to benefit the audience's future.*

The platform is simply a vehicle which enables the speaker to transfer his or her own value—gleaned from past experiences—to the audience's future.

A taxi ride from the airport is not worth $35. However, being conveyed from the airport, where you don't need to be, to the office, where you do need to be, is worth $35. A bus can take you for only $5, but it's slower, less reliable, makes more stops, and is far less comfortable. A private limo can take you for $65, with more comfort, a private phone, better climate control, and door-to-door service. We all invest in the kind of ride that makes the most sense.

On a per hour basis, a keynote is far more expensive than a full-day seminar. Someone charging $5000 for a keynote isn't going to charge $40,000 for a full day ($5000 times 8 hours), if they do both types of sessions. They'll probably charge around $7500 for the full day. A keynote is much more expensive on a commodity basis because it's the limo ride—in far less time, in far more comfort, people are arriving at the destination that the buyer has chosen.

The basic process involved in speaking, from the buyer's perspective, has to be the one in Figure 4-1. It is your responsibility to educate the buyer that his or her value list is being achieved not through an hour or half day, but through the substantial body of work that has taken place in the past and through the results that will accrue on an ongoing basis well into the future. Few name-brand drugs that we buy cost very much to manufacture—certainly, nothing near their purchase price. However, Merck and Upjohn and Bristol-Myers have spent billions on the research and development that finally brought the drug to the consumer in a safe, reliable, convenient form. And the drug's effect will have a long-term impact on your condition, either curing it or ameliorating it.

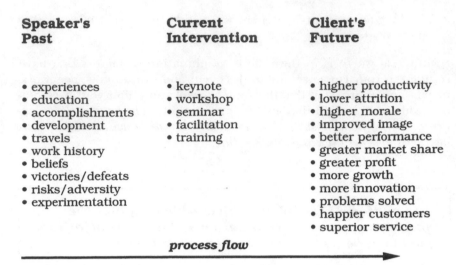

Speaker's Past	Current Intervention	Client's Future
• experiences	• keynote	• higher productivity
• education	• workshop	• lower attrition
• accomplishments	• seminar	• higher morale
• development	• facilitation	• improved image
• travels	• training	• better performance
• work history		• greater market share
• beliefs		• greater profit
• victories/defeats		• more growth
• risks/adversity		• more innovation
• experimentation		• problems solved
		• happier customers
		• superior service

process flow

Figure 4-1. The value process.

The speaking process is no different from that of pharmaceutical research and manufacturing. We're not paying for the aspirin capsule, but for the work that brought it to us and the salutary effect it will have on our health. Buyers shouldn't be paying for the hour's speech, but for the long-term processes that created its value and the longer-term salutary effects on the organization.

The key to establishing high fees is to establish high value in the eyes of the buyer. Let me make this absolutely clear because most speakers focus on the wrong results. Value has very little to do with standing ovations and "smile sheets" that rate the speaker a 9.9 on a 10-point scale. The only thing that matters to the buyer is how well his or her objectives are met, and that seldom involves audience ratings *unless the speaker is the one who emphasizes them.* There is far more value in improved sales, lower attrition, and greater innovation in the business than there is in a speaker's rating by the audience. The rating applies to a relatively brief moment in time. The results apply to the company forever.[2]

---

[2]Let me make it clear that I'm talking about legitimate corporate buyers who are usually line managers or executives. I'm not talking about meeting planners, who often are solely concerned with saving money and audience ratings because that's how they, themselves, are evaluated by their company. Line managers are paid to get results, and money is seldom an object if the results are significant enough. For an in-depth discussion of buyers and approaches, see my book *Million Dollar Consulting: The Professional's Guide to Growing a Practice,* McGraw-Hill, 1992, 1998.

No company or corporate buyer has ever said, "Remember Mary Speaker? She received a 9.9 rating. What a great contribution to our business." But they do tend to say, "Remember the sales improvement that resulted from Mary Speaker's work? Maybe it's time to get her back in here again." Focus on your own ego, and you might get stroked. Focus on the buyer results, and you will get repeat business.

So, it's vital to do the following to this point:

1. Understand your own value package.

2. Translate your value into long-term results for any given client.

3. Educate the buyer so that he or she reaches the same conclusions.

4. Only then suggest your value options.

Now for the key question. Who is the buyer?

Listen Carefully: Buyers Sign Checks

Note that I seldom use the words "customer" or "client" when I allude to obtaining business. That's because the buyer is the key, and speakers often don't have a clue about the true buyer. A buyer is someone who can authorize a check (or in primitive cultures, actually sign one). The buyer is usually near the top of the hierarchy in smaller organizations, but can be anywhere in larger ones. Titles are highly deceiving.

In the speaking industry, there has been great focus on the role of the meeting planner. In most cases, a meeting planner is actually a feasibility or implementation buyer, not an economic buyer. By that I mean that the meeting planner is given a strict budget (by the real buyer) and is paid and rewarded to conserve it. Meeting planners tend to be low-level people, rarely involved in corporate strategy or departmental missions, and invariably evaluate speakers as commodities to fit time frames and budgets.[3] Meeting planners love to evaluate potential speakers by viewing demo tapes for a few minutes, making visceral decisions on such ephemera as a funny story, stage movement, and appearance. I have had meeting planners tell me, without blinking an eye, that they didn't want a woman to address their group (this from a woman plan-

---

[3] Please send your cards and letters elsewhere. I know there are fine meeting planners and some who are actually closely tied to key business goals. But that is the overwhelming rarity. Speakers who focus on meeting planners as their primary buyers will never be able to escalate their fees dramatically because the value/results dynamic is simply not important to that buyer.

ner), they thought someone was too old, they felt someone was "too New York," and they felt someone had too much content.

Speakers bureaus tend to deal through meeting planners. If you work with bureaus, you won't miss that potential buyer because the bureau will do it for you.[4] But for your own approaches, eschew the meeting planner and focus on the economic buyers who themselves are focused on results. They are the ones to whom you can make your value/results appeal. Since they are paid to achieve results themselves, they will find the money to pay for anyone who can help engender them. The equation for them is simple: ROI (return on investment).

Whenever possible, market and sell to economic buyers. If you find that you've been introduced to a feasibility or implementation buyer, use that entry point to gain access to the economic buyer. Bureaus will otherwise attend to the meeting planner market, although the good ones will pursue economic buyers as well. Your strategy should look something like that depicted in Figure 4-2.

The primary thrust of the speaker (and any marketing or staff personnel who are employed toward these pursuits) should be to establish a

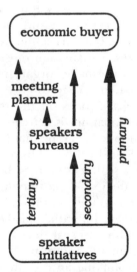

Figure 4-2. Speaker marketing priorities.

[4]The meeting-planning industry has taken a vicious hit over the past decade from the corporate downsizing movement, which tells you immediately how valuable executives consider this function. When I was the keynoter for Meeting Planners International a couple of years ago, I found many of the attendees out of work, including a couple of the members of MPI's board of directors. This is a dying profession, and speakers bureaus are going to have to establish credibility with line buyers if they are to survive.

relationship with the economic buyer. A secondary thrust should be toward those bureaus that can place you with economic buyers, although they will invariably also work with meeting planners. Only the tertiary thrust—meaning if there is time or in the case of serendipity—should be geared toward the meeting planner in the event this path may lead to the economic buyer. In my experience, most speakers reverse this sequence, thereby securing a poor return on their scarce resources.

So, our steps might really look like this:

1. Understand your own value package.

2. Translate your value into long-term results for any given client.

3. Find the economic buyer in your target customer.

4. Educate the buyer so that he or she reaches the same conclusions.

5. Only then suggest your value options.

The Trek to the Economic Buyer

How do you know one when you see one? Is it like the Yeti, rarely seen with just enough tracks in the snow to suggest a sentient being? Or is it Waldo, hidden in some crowd awaiting your scrutiny?

My economic buyers have had titles like director, manager, business process consultant, vice president, and of course, CEO. At higher levels, it's fairly easy to tell. You might be talking to the vice president of sales who is interested in a speaker for his or her sales conference. There's not much detective work required. But what if you're talking to a sales director who tells you that he has been given the task of securing the speakers for the meeting? How do you tell if this is the economic buyer, or merely a feasibility buyer, without offending that person?

Here are the questions I've found useful to ferret out the real economic buyer. You don't need to ask all of them, and you should choose

> *The reason it's imperative to find the economic buyer is that he or she is the only person who can appreciate your value in terms of the results generated and will make an investment decision on that basis. Otherwise, you'll be purchased like produce.*

those that best fit your style, since I'm prone to simply ask, "Are you the one investing the money?"

Questions to Find the Economic Buyer

- Whose budget is supporting this investment?
- Who will evaluate the final results?
- To whom do the participants all commonly report?
- Whose objectives are at stake?
- Which executive will open and/or close (be featured at) the meeting?
- Who approves the final agenda?
- Will you make a decision or a recommendation to someone else?
- If there are conflicts over the agenda, who makes the final call?
- Who is most affected by the success or failure of the participants?

Committees are seldom economic buyers. By definition, they are evaluators and recommenders. You can ask these questions in as blatant or subtle a fashion as you wish, just as long as you do ask them. Too often, we're so delighted merely to have been considered for a speaking engagement that we fall all over ourselves trying to impress whomever will see us. That's fine if we want to secure jobs, but it doesn't contribute anything if we want to create million-dollar businesses.

(Incidentally, sometimes we find ourselves magically with the economic buyer at the outset. Here's some complex advice: Don't leave. It's not uncommon for the speaker to react to the initial contact by accepting delegation down to a feasibility buyer. If you actively participate in the intent to delegate you downward, you'll experience a vertiginous drop through the organization, landing dazed and bruised in the office of someone who will ask you, as soon as you've revived, "So, how much can you reduce your fee if we cut the slot from 2 hours to 45 minutes?")

And what happens when we meticulously apply the questions and discover that we are, indeed, dealing only with a gatekeeper who resists allowing us to talk to the economic buyer? We've all encountered the palace guards, bloviating about how busy the management is, but whose actual sworn duty is to protect the decision makers from actually receiving information which might lead to a high-quality decision. Do we resign ourselves to the ignominy, or do we scale the ramparts?

Get your ladders and climbing gear. Here's how you convince the gatekeeper to either open the gates or get out of the way while you open them.

Leverage Points to Get to the Economic Buyer

- I have to ensure that his/her objectives are met.
- I have to be sure there are no unreachable expectations.
- I have to ensure that the full value of what I can deliver is understood.
- I must tailor my approach to his/her style/theme/philosophy/agenda.
- Ethically, I must see the person investing the money.
- It's unfair for you to do my marketing for me.
- There are technical details which only I can explain.
- It's imperative that I hear his/her strategy and tactics.
- You and I can collaborate once we've both received his/her advice.
- I do this with every client. It's why I've been recommended to him/her.
- This is what outstanding professionals do in this business.
- It's for his/her protection. Objectives sometimes change.
- It's a strict quality policy, and I can't work with him/her unless we meet.

In the event all of these fail, you may want to simply contact the economic buyer and advise that person of the same types of issues. You do risk irritating the gatekeeper and, perhaps, losing the potential business. However, no risk, no reward. It's simply that important to find the economic buyer and secure your agreement with him or her because only that person can appreciate your value package and the long-term results for the organization in terms of an appropriate investment.

Providing the Choice of "Yeses"

I've spent the entire first half of this chapter leading up to fee structure, and we're not quite there yet. That's because your fee strategy is irrelevant if you're dealing with the wrong people or if you're not in a position to establish value and results. On the assumption you've accomplished that, however, we're at the final step:

1. Understand your own value package.
2. Translate your value into long-term results for any given client.
3. Find the economic buyer in your target customer.

4. Educate the buyer so that he or she reaches the same conclusions.

5. *Only then suggest your value options.*

You never want the buyer to be making the decision as to whether or not to use your services. You want the buyer to be making the decision *as to how to use your services.* To accomplish that, you must provide the buyer with options. You control this dynamic. If you provide options, the buyer will consider them. If you don't, it's unlikely that the buyer will say, "Why don't we develop some options that provide me with a range of ways in which to use you?"

This is not abstruse reasoning. The buyer will do what's in his or her best interest. You must manage the relationship so that what's in your self-interest is in the buyer's self-interest: getting hired.

If the buyer's decision is how to use you rather than whether to use you, your chances of being hired are multiplied by a factor of 10 or more. You are the only one who controls that dynamic.

Two Examples

Let's suppose that the buyer is considering you for a 2-hour concurrent session at an annual conference. The buyer has budgeted for six speakers at $3500 each in the three concurrent sessions and $6500 each for keynoters to open and close. Here are some options you might propose:

- Conduct one concurrent session as planned for $3500.
- Conduct two of the concurrent sessions on different topics for $6000, saving the client $1000.
- Present one of the keynotes and a concurrent session for $8000, saving the client $2000.
- Present the concurrent session and facilitate breakout groups when the participants are later divided into working teams for $5000.
- Present the concurrent session and moderate a customer panel the client had planned for later in the program for $5000.
- Use any permutations of the foregoing options.

Now let's suppose you're being considered for a single keynote (or motivational or humorous talk, etc.) speech within an organization, so that there are no other speakers or variables. There has been no budget established. Here's how to provide options when you are the sole consideration:

- Deliver the speech as suggested for a $5000 fee.
- Call potential audience members in advance and build your comments around their immediate concerns and priorities for a $6000 fee.
- Provide the client with the rights to reproduce materials you provide for internal distribution for $5500.
- Allow the client to audiotape and/or videotape your comments for internal distribution for $6500–$7500.
- Provide a 30-day follow-up mailing to participants to reinforce your points and provide job aids for application of your techniques for $6500.
- Interview management to incorporate their comments and concerns and orient the audience toward the corporate strategy in your approaches for $6000.
- Incorporate a survey instrument that the audience completes and which you will then compare for the buyer to other groups you've addressed for $7500.

If you included all of the "add-ons," the total fee for the 1 hour would be $14,000, so I'd recommend that you'll provide all of the options to the client for $12,000. You may have more options than I've listed and at different fee levels. That's not the point. The key question is, *are you providing such options in every single buyer encounter, in every proposal, and in all of your literature?*

Many people ask me how to respond when the potential buyer asks, "What's your fee?" The correct answer is, "I don't know, what are your needs?" If you respond to the question with a number, then you admit that you only charge by the time unit. If you respond with a question, you're telling the customer that fees depend on his or her objectives, and there are probably options to meet those objectives. The difference between $5000 and $12,000 in the second example is minor compared with the vastly greater value that the buyer receives. Many speakers provide some of those services anyway, yet they don't segment them and end up delivering more value than they charge for. The old bromide "underpromise and overdeliver" is fine if you're in missionary work, but how about "deliver great value and charge for it" as a more equitable arrangement?

In the worst case in the two examples, the buyer may not use you. But in the next-worse case, the buyer will hire you at a base fee that is consistent with your value delivery. In the best case, you are earning a greatly increased fee (in the second example, about 140 percent) with only a marginal increase in your actual work, but a substantial increase in the buyer's perception of your value.

> **Remember: The discussion should never be about fee, only about value.**

---

29 Ways to Increase Your Value and Your Fees

1. Value is in the eyes of the client. Provide what is valuable to the buyer, not to you. Consequently, hold your features and benefits in abeyance. They may not fit the client's desired goals.

2. Value is based upon perceived worth. Build your credibility through your accomplishments (what you've done), not what you think you can do. Testimonials and client lists outweigh promises and plans.

3. Base fees on the fulfillment of objectives (e.g., sales increase, higher morale), not on fulfilling tasks (e.g., delivery of a training program).

4. Time-unit billing will always be less than your true value. Never bill by the hour, day, or program.

5. Don't worry about gaining a sale. Worry about building a long-term customer.

6. Be willing to walk away from the business. Nothing adds to your value as much as the buyer's perception that you're making judgments based upon equity and collaborative relationships, and not immediate financial gain at any cost.

7. Charge as much as you are comfortable charging for your value. Buyers expect what they pay for. A $750 speaker will be considered a minor expense and a "throw-in," whereas a $7500 speaker will be considered a major investment and an asset. (The client won't care if not many people go to hear the $750 speaker, but will personally be in the halls shepherding people into the $7500 investment.)

8. Don't propose your services based upon what the client obviously wants. Explore why the client is holding the meeting and establish the real *needs*. Every buyer knows what he or she wants, but few know what they need. The difference may be your value-added.

9. Enter into a collaborative search with the client to examine objectives, measures of success, and desired outcomes. There is great value in a collaborator, very little in a vendor.

10. Never negotiate fees. Negotiate value. If the client wants your fee reduced, ask which value should be eliminated (e.g., don't do the audience interviews, don't provide a master copy of the handouts, don't allow the audiotaping, etc.). Buyers may love to reduce fees, but they hate to reduce value. If you reduce a fee without reducing the value delivered, you come across as a hustler who has padded the price, and the question emerges, "How low will this person go?"

11. Provide options, each representing a different value package. Use combinations of those options. You won't confuse the buyer; you'll intrigue the buyer with valuable possibilities.

12. Never allow a simple "yes or no" decision to be made about you. Find ways to elevate "whether" to "how."

13. Make your least expensive option your own baseline for an engagement and make at least one option very large and comprehensive at several times that baseline. You never know.

14. Always *begin* with buyer objectives. This focuses the discussion on the buyer's needs and allows you to seamlessly build your deliverables onto existing need and desired outcomes.

15. Suggest additional objectives for the buyer to consider. If the meeting is to build time-management skills, is there also an opportunity to provide some cross-functional knowledge of others' accountabilities through small-group teamwork?

16. Make sure that prospects and clients are fully aware of all of your services. Make it clear in your leave-behinds, literature, and proposals, for example, that you have a range of products, provide consulting services, or do outplacement work.

17. Send proposals as confirmations, not explorations. Reach conceptual agreement when you're with the buyer so that the proposal is merely a formality to be signed. You don't want the buyer (or worse, a subordinate) using the proposal as a negotiating instrument, compared to other proposals.

18. Don't feel obligated to cite fees early. Wait until you know what the buyer needs and you have an idea of which options you want to

offer. It's quite acceptable to reach conceptual agreement on the range of options and include the fees only in the written proposal.

19. Let overly troublesome business go out the door. When buyers drive you crazy with demands for lower fees, additional free services, and onerous payment arrangements, take a hike. These people will cost you money every time and significantly add to your stress level. Why are so many speakers surprised when clients who gave them problems at the front end of the discussions don't pay on time or refuse to pay when it's over?

20. Do not accept lower fees to "get in the door." Once a client sees a fee, the overwhelming momentum is to lower it still more. Virtually no clients say, "You were terrific, so let's raise your fee in the future." They say, "That was good, and if we can keep the fee where it is or reduce it, I can promise you more exposure." *Start as high as you can.*[5]

21. Don't worry about market ranges, competitive fees, and the awful "supply and demand" nonsense. Base your fees on the value you deliver to the buyer, period. Other considerations will simply bog you down. I've been hired at several times the fee that others were turned down over because my perceived value was so much greater than theirs.

22. Higher fees influence buyers as higher value. Practice providing a quote with a straight face and confidence. I'm serious. Look in the mirror and say, "The options will probably be from $5000 to $9000 based on what we've discussed thus far. Would you like me to explain the difference in value?"

23. Assess your own unique background and talents in the fee equation. If you have the rare combination of an MBA and JD, for example, if you were a manager in the customer's industry for many years, or if you're about to appear in the media in the client's area, you have ample value-added right there. Make this apparent to the buyer.

24. If you work with bureaus, recognize that 25 percent of your fee will be lost to their commission. Don't pad fees, because the client gains no value from that. But keep your fee levels legitimately high enough to justify that 25 percent if the bureau is indeed creating

[5]The same holds true for bureaus. Don't accept the malarkey that they want you to lower your fee (or they want to increase their commission) because of the exposure and spin-off business that will result from your appearance. If you're good, you're good, and you don't need charity. If you're not good, you shouldn't be doing the gig.

new opportunities for you. Educate the bureau in your options and ranges.

25. Add to your fee for legitimate inconvenience or special favor. For example, I increase my fees for any booking made within 30 days of the presentation date because such short notice invariably generates scheduling headaches and unexpected time away from my family. Clients in need of such short-term, high-quality help never dispute fees. I instruct bureaus to make the same adjustment.

26. Negotiate your bureau commission structure. If you have to interact with the client to make the sale and the bureau merely introduces you, less than a 25 percent commission might be appropriate. On spin-off business,[6] less than the full 25 percent commission is easy to negotiate, and some bureaus automatically reduce their share on such business.

27. Raise fees substantially for business you dislike and don't necessarily want. I hate to do full-day programs, and I've stopped doing most of them. But I have a very high full-day fee, and if a customer wants to pay it, it's amazing how the inconvenience can disappear. I've raised my fees three times for such programs, and I still do several each year.

28. Stop doing cheap tricks. Many speakers continue to deliver business which got them to where they are. They can generally do it in their sleep and charge far too little for it (because, primarily, it isn't worth much anymore). Stop doing that. Refer the business to people who can use it, will do a more inspired job, and will reciprocate the gesture when possible. Such low-paying work drags on your energy and creates an image of you that you no longer need. As a rule, eliminate the bottom 15 percent of your business at least every 2 years. How? Either raise the fee or get rid of the work, that's how. It's no longer profitable.

29. Even if you don't choose to use options, segment your speaking into keynotes (up to, say, 90 minutes), workshops (up to a half day), and seminars (up to a full day) to provide alternative fees. Use whatever categories suit you (facilitation, training, after dinner, etc.), but provide price differentiation. That way a client can decide to use you in various ways. And you don't want a buyer to say, "Well, your fee is $4000 no matter how long we use you, so why not stay the

---

[6]Business generated from a speaking appearance provided by a bureau. Any such business, ethically and contractually, should go through that same bureau. Unprofessional speakers merely take the business and hide it from the bureau.

entire day?" or "If your fee is $3000 for a half day, and we only need a 30-minute talk after lunch, I guess that will be about $500, right?"

Increasing Fee Velocity

There's one more aspect to improving fees that most speakers neglect: the *velocity* of the fee. It means that you want to get your fee into your bank as rapidly as possible, but the default position of speakers is often "pay me whenever you feel like it." The terms and conditions of your engagement should be stipulated after conceptual agreement on outcomes and value so that it's merely an afterthought for the buyer. But if you don't establish payment terms, some purchasing agent in the bowels of the client organization is ready—and paid—to do so.

Always try to get paid in full in advance. You won't always be able to, *but you'll never be paid this way if you don't ask.* Simply state that your policy is full fee in advance to secure the date and begin any preparatory activities, such as presentation design, materials customization, participant interviews, etc.[7]

If you can't get full fee in advance, you may want to try a soft incentive, such as a 5 or 10 percent discount if the fee is paid in advance. (Don't offer this if the presentation date is imminent.) Such a discount is important for two reasons:

1. You will be holding the money and using it for a long period, sometimes as much as a year in advance.
2. The client cannot cancel your engagement if you are holding the money.

I have a myriad of letters from speakers and consultants testifying to the wisdom of this advice, providing examples of contracts that would have been canceled or delayed because of internal client changes if the fee had not already been paid.

Demand, as a minimum, a 50 percent deposit, with the balance to be paid *at the time of the presentation.* That's right, you get an envelope when you show up. Some bureaus will demand a 50 percent deposit *and keep all of it until your presentation as a "guarantee."* Tell them to take a walk. If a bureau collects a 50 percent deposit, they should keep their 25 percent full commission and forward the balance to you immediately. They'll say they need to have security in case you don't appear. But who's guaranteeing that the bureau will be around in 6 months?

---

[7]Expenses should be billed at the conclusion of an engagement, or monthly if for an ongoing engagement, and should be payable upon receipt of your invoice.

> *Payment terms are often subject to your policy. If you don't have one, the client's policy will prevail, and it certainly won't be one of paying you as quickly as possible.*

If a bureau places you and collects the deposit, the balance should be payable to you at the presentation, not to the bureau, which will further delay payment, sometimes for months.

I don't advise ever accepting less than a 50 percent deposit, or a bureau collecting its 25 percent commission, and receiving the remainder on the presentation date. (You can also try stipulating that the balance is due the week *prior* to the presentation.) Anything less is not a collaboration and leaves you vulnerable to cancellation, delay, late payments, disputed costs, client internal turmoil, and so forth.

Guarantee your work in writing, but make your contract noncancelable in writing as the quid pro quo. This is a business. Businesses turn a profit.

To summarize: Base your fees on the value you bring to the client's objectives, provide for options (value packages) so the client can decide how best to use you and not whether to use you, and increase the velocity of the ensuing payment in every way possible. If you do that, you'll have the processes in place to make a million dollars. Let's turn now to how you attract the business.

5

Advanced Marketing

"I want to be a big fish."
"Then get into the big pond."

How to Work with Bureaus:
Slavery Is Not a Highly
Leveraged Position

The key to riches in the speaking business is working smart, not working hard. That means you need to examine your own basic beliefs, understandings, assumptions, and implicit approaches to the business, since there's a distinct possibility that some of them are inaccurate and a couple may be plain wrong. That's because there are more people giving advice (and charging for it) in the speaking business than there are good speakers.

The last time anyone looked, coaching was a *leveraging* position, meaning that there are a multitude of excellent players created by a superb coach. When there is mediocre coaching, there is usually a myriad of very average players. But in no circumstances is there a rational reason to have legions of good coaches and a resultant swarm of undistinguished players. There are relatively few excellent speakers in the land (otherwise, fee competition would keep prices low, and my advice in the previous chapter about charging for value would be commonplace), which leads me to believe that the hordes of coaches aren't that hot, either.

One of the worst of the assumptions that even veteran speakers labor under is that a speakers bureau relationship is mandatory and that such a relationship's parameters are dictated by the bureau, which can be very choosy about whom it represents. Here are some facts about the bureau relationship that apply to all of us, whether we've never been asked, never chosen to work with them, work with them occasionally, or get virtually all of our engagements through them.

Five Facts to Challenge Your Assumptions About Bureaus

1. Bureaus Cannot Live Without Speakers, but the Reverse Is Not True

Last year, I worked with an insurance company whose executives warned me that the independent agents were their customers.

"What about the people buying insurance?" I asked.

"Oh, they're our customers, too," they quickly conceded.

"Well, if there were no agents, only potential customers, could you still sell insurance?" I pressed.

"Of course, and we sell directly about 30 percent of the time right now."

"If there were no potential customers, only agents, could you still sell insurance??"

"Of course not."

"Well, I think you're confused about who your customers are, and what your sales and distribution methods are," said I, as I proceeded to create a long-term relationship with my customer.

I understand who pays me for value, and it's not the bureau. We could speak if there were no such thing as bureaus, but bureaus could not exist if there were no such thing as speakers. Consequently, this has to be a collaborative relationship, wherein the bureau *earns its commission from your client's payment by providing value to you.*

I've spoken to scores of bureau principals and owners. About a quarter of them don't bother to hide their belief that speakers are the biggest pain in their lives and that their jobs would just be dandy without them. They treat the speakers they do represent as hired hands, whereas they regard speakers who seek to be represented as door-to-door con artists whose phone calls aren't returned and submission of materials isn't acknowledged.

Even if you are a neophyte struggling for business—much less if you are a veteran to whom buyers come directly—walk away from any bureau that does not treat you as a valuable, talented partner. You shouldn't take rude treatment and lack of respect from a paying client. Why on earth would you accept it from someone you are paying to market you?

2. There's No Magic in a 25 Percent Commission

The standard rate for business is 25 percent from the speaker's fee. Although some speakers increase their fees to accommodate the commission and try to net the same amount as they otherwise would have received, it's a bad practice.[1] Some bureaus try to collect 30 percent or more. For a third of your fee, they'd better be coming to your home and washing the windows.

Commissions can be negotiable. For example, if a bureau introduces your name to a prospect, works with you to develop a presentation around the client's unique needs, and closes the sale on your behalf, that's worth a lot of money because the business is probably not a relationship you otherwise would have secured. Conversely, if the bureau merely gives you a contact's name and suggests you call them and sell a deal directly, the bureau has provided a service, but at much less value because you had to do the work, and the purpose of bureaus is that *they* do most of the marketing work.

Especially if you're asked to reduce your fee for any reason (e.g., for a nonprofit organization, for a good client in a budget squeeze, for a speech that requires only local travel), ask the bureau how much it will reduce its commission level.

If a bureau isn't providing value, why should you pay them 25 percent of your income? If you continue to do this, it's not the bureau's fault. You are not managing that relationship.

Last year, I gave a speech at a reduced fee for a local insurance general agent who employed 20 people. It was an hour's presentation only 10 minutes from my home, and he promised to forward my materials and a testimonial to his corporate office, where he served on the committee for the large regional convention. Sure enough, I was later hired at full

---

[1]That's because you should never penalize the client for your marketing costs, and the client (or others who hear of it) will become mistrusting if they find you have essentially two different fees for delivering the same approximate value depending on how the sale is consummated.

fee on the basis of his recommendation. His company then asked their exclusive bureau in Washington to send me the paperwork. *The bureau actually wanted 25 percent of my fee for having done nothing but send me the paperwork!*

3. The Bureau's Customer Is the Person Who Pays Them: You

I'm sick to death of the malarkey that the bureau's customer is the organization seeking the speaker. The buyer isn't paying the bureau (although the deposit check is going in that direction); *you* are paying the bureau out of *your* fee. The commission comes from the speaker.

Consequently, a bureau's insistence that you conduct no direct conversations with the buyer doesn't serve the buyer well, since you have to explore needs and establish relationships with the person responsible for the outcome of the session. That is not done efficiently through an intermediary. The relationship with the bureaus must be collaborative, not onerous. Your material needn't be entirely "bureau-friendly."[2] But if the bureau believes that your contact with the buyer will result in an unethical deal excluding the bureau, then the level of trust isn't present to build a productive collaboration.

Most bureaus will ask for a 25 percent deposit to hold a date, which becomes their commission. The balance is then due at the presentation and payable to you. However, some bureaus ask for a 50 percent deposit (which is a good idea) but keep the entire amount until your speech (which is a ridiculous idea). In that case, the balance should be forwarded to you immediately. I know of a few bureaus that receive full payment and attempt to hold it until the speech. While addressing a bureau group one day on the subject of professional ethics, I asked how anyone could tolerate someone else holding their money.

"You don't understand," pontificated one bureau owner. "How do we know the speaker will actually appear? We have to hold some sort of guarantee."

As some of his colleagues murmured approval, I asked, "How do I know your bureau will be here in 6 months? What's my guarantee?"

There was no response to that question.

---

[2]This is the practice of providing literature, tapes, workbooks, etc. to the bureau without your address, phone, or contacts so the bureau can ensure that all client contacts are exclusively with the bureau. In other words, they don't trust you or the client.

4. If You Allow Them to, Bureaus
Will Manage Perception

There is the reality of what buyers really want to see and evaluate, and there is the perception of what bureaus want them to see and evaluate. Remember from our prior discussions that you should try to build relationships with economic buyers and that bureaus tend to build their relationships with meeting planners.

Consequently, there is a developed mythology stating, for example, that speakers must have demo videos to be considered for work. I worked with bureaus for years without such a video, as have many other successful speakers. Videos are useful, however, to meeting planners for *deselection*. It's easy to watch barely 3 minutes of tape and decide if the speaker's "look" or "style" is acceptable to the meeting planner. As the videos become more vanilla and common—because there are a relatively few "coaches," producing the same look for everyone—the meeting planners are in a position to compare like commodities and make their selections devoid of real substance and content.[3]

Bureaus also love "showcases," in which they ask speakers to pay for the privilege of auditioning their wares in front of dozens (or even scores) of meeting planners. I find these repugnant because I'd be subsidizing the bureau's marketing expenses, appearing before the wrong kind of buyer, and presenting in juxtaposition to a dozen or more competitors, which creates a commodity—hell, a meat-market—atmosphere.

If you don't make enough to pay the bills one month, the bureaus aren't going to send you something to tide you over. Listen to their advice about the market, but then make your own decisions about how you want to be perceived, what your unique value-added is, and how the customer relationship should be established.

5. There Are Terrific Bureaus and
Terrible Bureaus

To find the best bureaus to work with (and I've included some in the appendix), ask speakers who work with them regularly. There are those I direct people to, and others I divert people from. Don't believe that a bureau's mere interest is synonymous with quality. Even some of the better-known bureaus are run by people who think speakers should fall on their knees in order to do business with them. One woman said to

---

[3]Which is why the video I use today is imperfect and of a live 2-hour keynote complete with audience reaction. I want people to see me in action, and I don't want to be seen as another slick marketing piece.

me that I should change my business card, which has represented me through a practice that creates a seven-figure income, to be more consistent with what she likes to see on them.

"I'd never do that," I said.

"Then you'd never work with me," she loftily intoned.

"So what?" I asked.

There are, unfortunately, many people calling themselves bureaus who are actually lone wolves working out of a bedroom or off a kitchen table. While there are many speakers who do the same, the difference is that the bureau wants 25 percent of your fee in return for marketing you, which means, unless I've missed something, that the bureau must have marketing resources in addition to a phone and post-office box. A bureau should have staff to canvass prospects and research organizations, equipment to duplicate tapes and written materials, sophisticated communications media and computers, established business contacts, a stable of successful and happy speakers, and an identifiable and a content client base.

There is nothing wrong with asking a bureau for references! Ask them for names of speakers and those speakers' clients gained through the bureau. Don't you provide references when someone is interested in hiring you?

In some years, my bureau-placed business has been 80 percent of my work; in other years, it's been 10 percent of my work. Lately, bureaus represent about 40 percent of my speaking engagements. They can be a strong market-leverage device or a drain on your time and income. Whatever they are, you can control the dynamic.

To provide both sides of the issue, in the following lists you'll find what you must do to ensure a good relationship and, in all fairness, what the bureau needs if it's to represent you professionally.

10 Musts for a Successful Bureau Relationship: Speaker Requirements

Here are my personal guidelines for a successful bureau relationship, which can be highly rewarding for all parties concerned. However, if you don't manage the relationship for your best interests, the "default" position will not be very desirable.

1. Establish a relationship with the owner. Others may place you and market you, but you can only tell if the bureau's values are compatible with yours by working with the principal.

2. Request and receive references and examples of the bureau's marketing materials. Don't accept claims at face value. Ask if this quality represents you well.

3. Retain your identity on your materials and literature that you provide for marketing. If the bureau doesn't trust you, then don't get involved.

4. Avoid mandatory comarketing investments. Options to take out listings, showcase, exhibit, etc., are fine and valuable, provided you can pick and choose.

5. Clarify that you will speak to prospects directly and early when needed to determine how to help close the business (and if it's right for your skills).

6. Expect a callback on the same business day (or the next morning) when you leave a message with the bureau. You're entitled to professional responsiveness.

7. Require that "holds" (tentative bookings) be managed carefully and removed from your calendar as soon as the bureau determines the business will not close.

8. Ensure that all fees in excess of the bureau's commission be paid directly to you at the time of receipt and that the client directly reimburse expenses to you.

9. Request flexibility in commissions for spin-off business, multiple bookings, ancillary consulting work, and related situations which merit reduced commissions.

10. Avoid exclusive arrangements. Only by allowing numerous bureaus to represent you will you ensure your own flexibility and find your own best deals.

10 Musts for a Successful Bureau Relationship: Bureau Requirements

The excellent bureaus have legitimate needs that speakers must adhere to, especially if a trusting relationship is to be built. A great deal of this relies on ethical and professional behavior which, unfortunately, isn't always in great supply.

1. Be honest about your capabilities. Don't accept assignments unless you can serve the client well. Exceed expectations. The bureau's reputation is its main asset.

2. Be original. Don't use others' materials and don't use shopworn generic stories. Clients who hire speakers can usually spot these instantly.

3. Arrive early and stay late. Let the local coordinator know you've arrived, and don't rush off during the applause. Avoid tight connections and last-minute arrivals.

4. Be honest about outcomes. If there were problems, tell the bureau immediately, whether technical, interpersonal, or logistical.

5. Keep your materials up-to-date and professional. Provide contemporary testimonials, quality brochures, and effective handouts.

6. Join in win/win comarketing. It can make sense to appear in a special mailing or create a voice-mail sample of your speaking. You're in this together.

7. Speak to prospects quickly whenever requested. Good bureaus know when a few words from the speaker can close the deal. Don't keep the buyer waiting.

8. Recommend other fine speakers to the bureau. This is not a zero-sum game. The more the bureau succeeds, the more it can invest in your success.

9. Scrupulously forward spin-off business (business leads or closed deals gained during a bureau placement). This is a contractual *and ethical* requirement.

10. Maintain consistency in fee structure (although it may be highly diverse) and provide lengthy advance notice if scheduled fees are to be raised.

Third-Party Sponsorships

Working smart instead of working hard requires the leverage that third parties can provide. Bureaus are one type of third party. But there are others which are infrequently exploited.

For example, colleges and universities all across the country sponsor executive extension courses, community learning programs, and all kinds of management and small-business seminars. While the sponsors are often taught by the faculty (they emerged as an intelligent device to apply undercapacity manufacturing resources—the faculty), they usually employ external instructors, trainers, and speakers. This phenomenon has spread to private entrepreneurs as well, as represented by such organizations as The Learning Connection, The Learning Annex, and other private educational groups catering to the public at large.

For over 10 years, I was on the faculty at the Weatherhead School of Management at Case Western Reserve University. It meant that two or three times a year I'd travel to Cleveland to instruct two or three programs on diverse topics such as effective presentation skills, innovation, leadership, interviewing, and so on. The school and I agreed on the programs, matching their clients' needs with my talents. The customers were from a variety of medium and large organizations, public and private, that subscribed to Case's management programs. On average, I'd work with 100 people for a day at a time.

Any business gained from the organizations whose people attended these sessions was my business. In addition, I could sell books and tapes to anyone interested. So, the picture looked like this:

- Case paid me to appear and listed me in their catalogue.
- Case was an excellent testimonial and reference for me.
- Participants were free to buy my books and tapes.
- Speaking and consulting business derived was entirely mine.
- All expenses were paid.

In effect, I was being paid to audition and market my skills, while participants experienced a rich, fulfilling day of learning, and Case added to its credibility and business in the organizational community. Not a bad win/win/win is it?

The Institute of Management Studies (IMS) is based in San Francisco and Reno, and they have an international system of local chairpeople who organize seminars in their cities. About 75 faculty members deliver a curriculum that ranges from light motivational techniques to difficult issues of organization alignment. The audiences are segmented and range from frontline management to executives, depending on topic. The speakers may deliver anywhere from a single program to two dozen, and the IMS pays a decent fee for the session. Any business resulting from the 50–150 attendees for the faculty member is totally private. One of my colleagues on the faculty delivered 14 of these sessions last year and told me that he generated 40 percent of his total revenues from the ensuing contacts among participants.

The additional leverage point of organizations such as the IMS is that your colleagues on the faculty are often recognizable names and sometimes more successful in the profession than you. Consequently, the brochures and literature become useful marketing tools, and the addition of the experience in your press kit or biographical sketch can provide added credentials.

I know of speakers who have convinced healthcare organizations to sponsor their speeches at retirement homes; athletic equipment manufacturers to sponsor their talks at youth groups; and high-tech companies to sponsor presentations at technology conferences on nontechnological issues. Merck & Co., the pharmaceutical manufacturer, once sponsored my keynote at a pharmacists' convention. I spoke about managing change, a nontechnical topic, and Merck wanted the credit for bringing in such a speaker.

There are local third-party sponsors with names such as The Executive Conference, The Executives Roundtable, The Management Institute, and so forth which probably pay a moderate fee but will expose you to key decision makers in the community. I've met presidents of operations with 10,000 and more employees at such events and have closed both speaking and consulting business as a result.

Finally, there is a plethora of institutes and private "universities" which cater to a wide variety of organizational segments. For example, the American Press Institute in Reston, Virginia, provides educational programming for virtually anyone involved in the print media, from publishers to classified advertising salespeople. It pays a modest per diem for outside faculty, but places you in front of a roomful of people with the potential to hire you, recommend you to a buyer, provide publicity for you, etc. Inevitably, such programs are in fine facilities with publicity and brochure mention. The American Management Association in New York offers a host of seminars, usually led by outside speakers, and even sponsors breakfast meetings around the country for local management to receive an infusion of learning before starting their day.

Trade Association Marketing, or Being Paid to Market

My idea of the hierarchy of highly leveraged marketing through sponsors and third parties appears in Figure 5-1. The characteristics of the most potentially rewarding third-party sponsors are:

- Full and normal fees are paid to the speaker.
- The audience includes significant buyers for your services.
- The audience is large.
- The event is prestigious and the sponsor is highly regarded.
- There are other "draws" on the agenda.
- You have a general session, not a concurrent session.
- You can sell books and tapes at the event.

As you can see, a local nonprofit group is probably looking for some sage advice and professional platform skills, but the audience usually will contain, at best, recommenders. But at a national trade association meeting, all of my conditions can be met.

Increasing Impact with Significant Buyers ↑

National trade associations
- Health Industries Distributors Association
- International Association for Financial Planning
- American Bankers Association

Local and regional trade associations (or chapters)
- Minneapolis Personnel Assocation
- Houston Chapter, American Institute of Architects
- Tennessee recreational vehicle association

Management extention programs
- Universities, colleges, junior colleges
- Private programs (The Learning Connection)
- Government support (Small Business Administration)

Local non-profit business groups
- Rotary
- Chamber of Commerce
- Better Business Bureau

Local non-profit community groups
- Service clubs (Elks)
- Youth groups
- Parent-teacher leagues

Figure 5-1. The hierarchy of third-party sponsorship.

My hierarchy is not a single, linear climb. I continue to speak at local nonprofits and at every other level in the hierarchy. But I've already been to the top and continue to speak there on a monthly basis. What are you doing to get there?

Trade associations have a lot of money. They will often have a meeting planner *who is much more powerful than the private sector counterpart* because the trade association's raison d'être is education of its members, so conferences and conventions are the place to demonstrate to membership that their dues and obligations are quite worthwhile. You will either be dealing with the executive director of the association or a meeting planner who is also an officer of the organization. Don't let anyone kid you; trade associations pay as much *if not better* than private sector meetings.[4]

---

[4]I refer you again to the invaluable resource, the *NTPA: National Trade and Professional Associations of the United States,* Columbia Books, Inc., New York. See the appendix for specific contact information. This annual publication contains every trade association, its president, budget, convention sites, conference themes, membership, and other pertinent information, and no speaker's reference library should be without it.

Here are 10 tips for successfully marketing to trade associations and successfully delivering a speech to the membership that will result in leveraged business from the attendees.

10 Tips to Leverage the Trade Association Marketplace

1. Talk to members first.   Learn about their concerns and issues. If you are targeting the National Association of Music Merchants, visit some local members' retail stores and talk to the owners.

2. Demonstrate a unique nonindustry perspective.   The conferences are blanketed by speakers with content knowledge, and they're usually deadly dull. Establish conversancy with the field, but introduce your fresh, nonindustry perspective.

3. Create an intelligence file.   Using your regular business reading, the Internet, and reference resources, generate a "dossier" on the industry's strengths and weaknesses, its past, present, and likely future.

4. Orient your approach to the future.   Trade association members are thirsty for help in making sense out of changing times, particularly in volatile industries (e.g., healthcare, telecommunications, travel). Don't tell them what they already know.

5. Be provocative.   Don't be afraid to be contrarian. Give people something to talk about. You want your name mentioned in the halls.[5]

6. Create visual aids and handouts that mention the industry.   You don't have to create an entirely new speech, but you should insert examples, stories, anecdotes, visuals, and aspects of your handouts (if you use them) that embrace the industry. This helps the learning and greatly increases the likelihood of spin-off business.

7. Let the audience know you've done your homework.   I almost always include some segments in which I say, "I polled some of the members at this convention and asked them what advice they'd give someone new to your business. Over 80 percent said, 'Save your money!'"

---

[5]One association executive rushed up to me to tell me, "You were a hit in the ladies room!" You never know about all the private measurement devices that buyers use in this business.

8. Create a meeting-specific handout.   This could be a single sheet, a copy of your slides, or detailed support for your presentation. Make it something that participants want to keep. Put the conference date and the title of your speech on the cover. In addition, put your name and every piece of contact information on every page (in case individual pages are photocopied and circulated back home).

9. Offer to deliver multiple sessions.   Even highly paid veteran speakers will gladly do this. The association likes to provide the keynoter, for example, in the more intimate setting of a concurrent session. The association can save money—and you can earn more—by using you three times instead of three people one time.

10. Parlay your trade association appearances.   Prominently include in your media kit trade association publicity, testimonials, appearance dates, interviews, and so forth. Trade association speaking, as you've seen, is a somewhat specialized skill. If you've mastered it, the accolades can provide ready access to more and more associations.

Publishing and the Great Debate

If you want to make it big in the speaking profession, you have to publish. Articles in major media will do the following:

- enhance your visibility and credibility
- provide solid content for your media kit
- force you to continually generate new ideas and validate old ones
- gain entry into more and more publications through repute
- provide access to other media (radio, TV, Internet)
- generate leads
- provide handouts for your sessions
- form the basis for future books
- form the basis for future products

If you've never published, use a "staircase" technique shown in Figure 5-2. It begins with a local column for the weekly community newspaper and leads to the local daily (*The Podunk Pendulum*), the regional daily (*The Hartford Courant*), the state magazine (*Rhode Island Monthly*), the

"STAIRCASE" APPROACH TO PUBLISHING

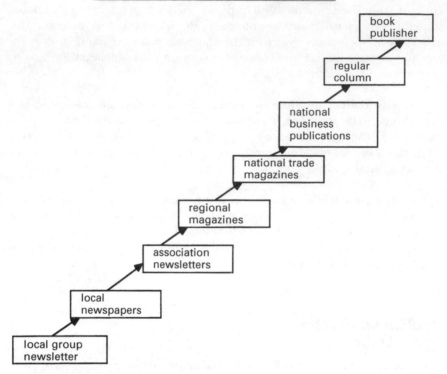

Figure 5-2. The staircase method to publishing.[7]

national magazine (*Training*), and the "media of record" (*The New York Times, The Wall Street Journal*). In other words, parlay what you do, using tear sheets and columns from the first publications to progressively sell editors of larger publications.[6]

Here are some guidelines for publishing an article in major media:

---

[6]See the appendix for catalysts, such as *Radio and TV Interview Reporter* and *The Yearbook of Leading Authorities and Experts.*

[7]The staircase method and the guidelines for getting an article and a book into print which follow are taken from my book *Million Dollar Consulting*, McGraw-Hill, New York, 1992, 1998.

How to Get an Article Published

I. Determine What Subject You Want to Write About

   A. Why are you the person to comment on the topic?
   B. How will this subject enhance your business, repute, or standing?
   C. Why is the subject relevant at this time (and for the next several months)?

Don't be afraid to be contrarian. The world doesn't need another piece on "left-brain vs. right-brain thinking."

II. Determine Where You Want to Publish the Article

   A. Who is your audience and what do they read?
   B. Don't be afraid to *ask* your audience!
   C. Where is it most reasonable for you to be successful?
   D. Research publications and study their style.

I was never published in the Times *until I sent them an article that I realized was just what they needed!*

III. Prepare a Professional Inquiry

   A. Send it to a specific editor's attention.
   B. Specify what, why, examples, uniqueness, length, and delivery date.
   C. Request specifications.
   D. *Always* enclose a SASE.[8]
   E. Cite credentials—yours and the article's.

This step must be more carefully executed than the actual article!

IV. Write It Like a Pro

   A. Use specific examples, names, and places.
   B. Write it yourself, but solicit critique.
   C. Write it to the specifications.
   D. Make sure you include autobiographical data at the end.
   E. Request free reprints or reprint permission or discounted reprints.
   F. Don't self-promote; let the substance do it for you.
   G. If rejected: resubmit, resubmit, resubmit, resubmit, resubmit.

Use prior articles as credentials to write newer ones.

---

[8]Common acronym in the trade, standing for "self-addressed, stamped envelope."

Some Other Comments.   Don't overwrite. Write what's on your mind without worrying about the great American novel. When you edit, you'll find the piece is amazingly good. Attribute things you borrow, but don't try to dazzle with superfluous references. Be critical and analytical. Readers respond best to provocation and the opportunity to look at things in a new way. When in doubt, start a new paragraph. Use graphics when appropriate, and try to load in the metaphors and similes.

There's a simple rule for publishing: First, have something to say.

The great debate is about whether or not to self-publish books. My criteria are simple. Self-publish books when:

- you want a product to sell with maximum profit
- you want a handout for your training sessions

But publish only through a known, commercial publisher when:

- you want credibility with buyers
- you want to improve your credibility as an authority

Sometimes a commercially published book will earn considerable royalties, and sometimes a self-published book with gain you credibility. But not usually. Notice that "ego stroking" is not on either list. There are a lot of bad books published commercially, and most self-published books are awful. If you need your ego stroked, buy a dog. If you need to tell people you're an author, yet have nothing to say that will sell a publisher, use the money you would have invested in the vanity publishing to secure the services of a therapist. You're not a driver unless you can drive a car, and you're not an author unless someone else pays to publish your stuff.

Harsh? Yes. Reality? Also yes.

Here's my route for getting a book published commercially once you've ascended the staircase. Book publishing is slightly easier when there is a long track record of articles and columns to support it, but these are not prerequisites. The most important aspect is convincing the publisher (or your agent) that your book will sell, and the way to achieve that is to do your own homework, because the editor hasn't the time or inclination to do it for you. It is difficult to get the first book published, but with a targeted, systematic approach, it's much easier than most people think.[9] Follow these guidelines.

How to Get a Book Published

I. Determine What It Is You Have to Say

   A. Your particular expertise from education, experience, training, circumstances.
   B. Your ability to "pull together" disparate things that others haven't.
   C. Your ideas, concepts, theories, and innovations.

If you have nothing constructive to contribute, don't write a word.

II. Determine Which Publishers Are Most Likely to Agree with You

   A. Examine their current books in print.
   B. Request their specifications.
   C. Ask people in the business.

Do not vanity or self-publish—it's a waste of time and no one's impressed.

III. Prepare a Treatment for the Publisher's (or Agent's) Review

   A. Why you?
   B. Why this topic?
   C. Why this topic handled in this manner?
   D. What competitive works are extant, and why is yours needed?
   E. Who is the audience?
   F. When would it be ready?
   G. What are the special features (e.g., endorsements, self-tests, etc.)?
   H. Provide *at least* the introduction and one chapter, a table of contents, and summaries of the other chapters.

If you can't sell it to the publisher, you'll never sell it to the reader.

IV. Write It Like a Pro

---

[9]Contrary to popular opinion, literary agents can be quite effective for first-time authors. There are some who actual specialize in the speaking field. You can find some good ones through the National Speakers Association. See reference in the appendix.

A. Invite clients and/or respected authorities to contribute.
B. Use a sophisticated computer and software.
C. Don't use a "ghost." If someone else writes your book, why does anyone need you?
D. Always take the reader's viewpoint.
E. Schedule your writing sessions just as you would your other responsibilities.
F. Use trusted others to review, critique, and suggest.
G. *Always* attribute anything that's not yours.
H. Keep it "future-current"—remember, it will be published a year from your submission.

What is published represents your values. Are you proud of what you've written?

Some Other Comments.   Don't become discouraged—keep submitting, and find out why you've been rejected. And remember, a successful business book sells about 7500 copies! Don't expect to be on *Oprah* the next Monday. Finally, read contracts carefully because they will specify author's discount, planned promotion, expenses you may incur, and so on. For example, you can almost always negotiate the indexing costs to be transferred from you to the publisher. Run the whole thing by your attorney.

Publishing will, at first, require a substantial investment of time. However, that time can usually be found on airplanes and in distant hotel rooms. Once you've broken into the field, you'll find it easier and easier to publish, both because your skills are developing and because your credibility is growing. The staircase method is useful to ensure that you also grow as an author and avoid the success trap of publishing repeatedly for a limited audience.

The Zeitgeist of Marketing

I've found that truly brilliant marketers in this business don't—that is, *do not*—take the proverbial "rifle shot" approach. I don't believe that you should target a specific promotional opportunity and focus solely on it. My experience has been to create a broad-scale visibility that gradually rises, so that after several years you are fairly constantly in the public eye.

Don't fall victim to the "numbers" approach. People ask me how many "hits" I get on my web site. I tell them that I don't care, and I mean it. I only need one—the one that's going to lead to my next $10,000 speaking engagement. I don't care how many media interviews my various listings generate because I only need the one that's going to trigger a buyer's call inquiring about a series of regional keynotes.

Perhaps you can't be all things to all people, but I've found that I'm many things to a good many people. Just as you shouldn't specialize in your practice, don't specialize in your marketing. Use the print media, pro bono work, the Internet, mailings, speakers bureaus, newsletters, publishing, trade associations, sponsors, products, and all other methods alive and working for you as your time and resources permit.

> *I'm not convinced that I can't be all things to all people, but I do know that I'm many things to a good many people. Do not delimit your own opportunities.*

The final point for advanced marketers is to beware of the rubric "find out what works for you." The point is to find out *what is likely to work for you in the future.* Beware of the success trap, in which past success ensnares you in a morass of the repetitive, noncreative status quo. I've sold articles, speeches, books, tapes, and my private mentoring services over the Internet. I've begun a newsletter which has created a steadily growing five-figure revenue stream that can easily go to six. I've both commercially published and self-published to meet varying objectives.

Jump into the biggest pond you can find and intend to become the biggest fish that the environment will accommodate. Avoid the hooks and lures that will attempt to divert you. Watch the larger fish, but don't follow them. Seek what they seek, but in your own way, using your own strokes.

6
Staffing and Supporting the Business

"I made 200 speeches last year."
"So, why are you so glum?"
"I lost my shirt."

Staff Is Not the Stuff of Life

Ever since the publication of *Million Dollar Consulting* in 1992, people have asked me if I *really* don't have a staff. After all, we hear advice for brand-new speakers about getting administrative help; we're told that we can't possibly market ourselves successfully without someone taking on that accountability; and there's no way, it would seem, to fulfill product orders without dedicated bodies. And then there's all that follow-up . . . and it does get kind of lonely . . .

So, if even modestly successful speakers need that kind of support, a seven-figure practice must require it, right? *Au contraire.*

Thank the fates that I didn't hear all that advice before I happily discovered that I'd much prefer to keep what I make. Ever since my wife first questioned—11 years ago—why I was considering renting an office for my nascent consulting/speaking practice, the two of us have rigorously resisted anyone else on the payroll other than the chairman, president, and CEO—all of whom happen to be me. (No, my wife isn't on the payroll, and she isn't my staff, except in her capacity as my chief advisor. She's strictly pro bono, and a bargain.)

I have this old-fashioned idea about not taking the risks inherent in running one's own business *unless* commensurate rewards are possible. Consequently, I want to keep what I make, and I've managed to keep between 80–90 percent every single year. I don't support other people on my payroll, and that's a large part of the financial success that places me in a tiny fraction of the general population.

How is it done? Here are my major tenets.

1. *Outsource absolutely everything possible.* I actually have a huge "virtual staff," in that I hire people on a situational basis to do my books, fulfill orders, respond to messages, produce correspondence, etc. The key point here is that all of them are *paid for performance.* They are compensated only for specific jobs of finite duration. I make certain that I am not their sole customer, so that there is no confusion about their being employees, and there are no benefits or fringes required. Thus, I can afford to pay very well, receive the best help available, and still save money over full-time resources.

2. *Do nothing other than what you must.* Most speakers and consultants I've observed perform too many minor tasks that have nothing to do with the client's need or well-being. (Ironically, this includes many of those who are "organization and time-management experts"!) I make it clear that the client is responsible for a great deal of the administrative and logistical work. I make liberal use of voice mail, fax, and e-mail, which are all quick and simple. And I never perform any task just because someone tells me "every good professional does it." I must see a demonstrable return for the client and for me. (For example, I've even stopped using the sacrosanct and overemphasized prespeech questionnaire, substituting the discussions I normally have with the client for the cumbersome paperwork and follow-up.)

3. *Use leveraged techniques.* For instance (hold on to your seats), I don't follow-up on every lead I get. I send out a press kit with a toll-free response number and add the name to my semiannual mailing list. I've found that people either hire me (or at least respond) based upon our initial contact, or they don't. Follow-up virtually never changes the dynamic, so I've stopped doing it (although I make certain I'm very user-friendly to contact). In addition, I invest in sources that get me all kinds of media attention because I want buyers to come to me, not vice versa. *This does not cost more in the long run because my time is highly valuable—too valuable to spend chasing prospects.* Yeah, I know: blasphemy. But I've been a heretic all the way to the bank.

4. *Exploit technological* and *nontechnological shortcuts and advantages.* I can touch-type 60 words a minute. I know the language sufficiently to write a letter or report one time—I never do drafts (this chapter went from my head to the keyboard to the editor). My phone automatically dials clients. My computers can do anything but cook me a meal. I carry a phone in my briefcase. I belong to every air club in existence. If you want to reach next door, don't go around the block.

I'd never advise you *not* to have a staff. There are plenty of people who are highly successful explicitly *because* of hard-working, loyal, full-time staffers, and we'll examine those options momentarily. I'm simply suggesting that lean, mean, and green (money) can work quite well also, irrespective of the size of your practice. Give it some thought the next time you have a hiring itch. Don't set "automatic pilot" for the staff destination. Give it some thought because the money you spend on staff must be returned several times over through increased business, or it's money you'll never see again.

If you already have a staff, think again about its size and even its necessity. I received a panicked e-mail recently from a colleague whose staff accountant embezzled funds, neglected to pay bills resulting in credit problems, and failed to follow-up on critical leads. His speaking topic is "hiring and retaining good people." I am not making this up.

If you're lonely, get a dog. By the way, you can write-off his expenses as part of the security system.

In my estimation, less than 15 percent of successful speakers—that is, those supporting their desired lifestyle through speaking and related activities—use full-time, paid staffs. So let's eliminate spouses and significant others, and let's place in abeyance for the moment those paid solely for performance, such as a marketeer who earns a commission only on speeches sold for you. (A little later in the chapter, we'll discuss contract players, who are people hired on a project or situational basis, and whom I don't consider staff.)

Five Essential and Legitimate Staff Functions

All right, let's assume that you need a staff because of the volume of your existing business or because of your understanding of your own marketing limitations or because all the kids on the block have one and you want one, too. Here are some criteria for staff acquisition.

Marketing Skills. The individual should be able to minimally handle passive marketing, which generally consists of calls made to the office while you're not there. There's a huge difference between saying, "Mr. Weiss will get back to you" and "What dates do you have in mind? What type of audience? It just so happens that Mr. Weiss is available on that date and has worked with those audiences as recently as last month. Would you like me to place a `hold' on that date, and send you specific information and a sample contract?"

Ideally, the individual should have assertive marketing skills and should be able to find prospects, respond to leads, initiate cold calls, and determine which contacts can be closed without your help, which can be closed with your help, and which should be abandoned (or merely placed on a mailing list). The individual should be able to identify and establish communications with the real buyer. Call these telemarketing skills.

Administrative Skills. The individual should be able to use standard office technology, including the creation of computer data banks, keyboard skills, professional phone manners, assembly of mailings, fulfilling of literature requests, product fulfillment, spreadsheet work, and travel scheduling. Routinely, I reach speakers' offices where the voice-mail recording is more professional and polite than the live administrative help at other offices. If someone's going to answer your phone, he or she should be nothing less than charming.

If you have a staff, "shop" your own office, or have a colleague do it for you. Test to see how rapidly literature is mailed, how quickly leads are followed and relayed, how a complaint is handled, and what general level of intelligence is conveyed about your practice. I told one highly polished speaker that his administrative assistant didn't have a clue about his speaking topics or background. He was aghast, but he had never educated her or tested her on the topics.

Judgment. This person is representing you to the world, and the world will have much tougher expectations and standards than if they were leaving a message with automated equipment. People are funny that way. Consequently, your office help must return calls received in their absence promptly—within 3 hours at the outside.[1] Complaints have to be assessed as valid ("You promised a press kit last week, and we haven't received it.") or invalid ("Why won't you send us a free copy of Mr. Weiss's materials so that we can evaluate them?").

Your staff should be able to schedule your time and travel in full conformance with your preferences, but without your active participation. They should be able to interact with colleagues, vendors, prospects, and clients professionally, articulately (after all, you do run a speaking business), and consistently with regard to your philosophy and manner. I fall down in amazement every time I meet a speaker's staff member who can't communicate well.

Innovative Ability. One of the primary reasons to have assistance in this lone-wolf profession is to get feedback and to challenge "the way we've always done it." Your staffer(s) should continually be able to recommend new, more efficient, and more productive methods to get results, ranging

---

[1]We return calls within 90 minutes with no staff whatsoever. If I had a staff, I'd demand that all calls be returned within 20 minutes. Often, merely getting there first is what lands the business, and the competition often doesn't return calls until the next day.

from mailings and new products to new speech topics and promotional literature. This is a person who should know your business intimately, perhaps even better than you do, since he or she is watching it every day from a wide range of perspectives while you're preparing for the next speech and a new audience.

So the staff person should be someone whom you respect and trust, *and to whom you'll listen when new ideas are explored.* If you find that new suggestions aren't regularly forthcoming or that you don't choose to engage in business discussions with the "administrative help," then you have the wrong resource. One of the results you're investing in with a staff commitment is innovation and new ways to grow your practice.

Leverage.   The investment in staff must result in leveraged growth *on the profit line.* If you're spending $45,000 a year in staff, enhanced revenues of $45,000 are woefully insufficient, and enhanced profit of $45,000 is break-even. My advice is that your total outlay for staff resources ought to be returned three times over in *profit* or the investment isn't worth it. That's because, in addition to the tangible and measurable outlays, there are the intangible and immeasurable outlays of your time, attention, focus, and energy. Those of you who have managed people know exactly whereof I speak. Even with one person on board, there will be personal issues, training and education time, debate, confusion, and meetings. Multiply that accordingly by the size of the staff.

Hence, staff has to leverage your profit potential in any combination of these types of interventions:

- acquisition of sales through aggressive cold calling and marketing
- acquisition of sales through more rapid and effective lead follow-up
- higher volume of mailings, client contacts, and responses
- increased speaker sales and delivery time through less office time
- improved visibility through increased interviews, articles, etc.
- more attractive offerings through new speech and product ideas

Let me state the obvious, in case you've missed it: If you are offsetting the bullet-point advantages through the investment of time required to manage, nurture, and otherwise tend to your staff, you are losing money hand over fist. You should be able to grow a successful practice by 10–15 percent a year *simply through your own momentum and referral business,* so a staff has to result in a 20–30 percent growth rate to make the investment worthwhile.[2]

---

[2]If your practice isn't successful, don't think a staff will change that. Lack of success in this business is due to poor business savvy (low fees, poor marketing) or poor performance (weak topics, lousy platform skills). It is not due to poor support work.

> *A general rule of thumb: You should be able to support your current lifestyle through speaking and related activities, and be growing the business by 10–15 percent annually on the basis of your own momentum and repute. At that point, a staff might make sense. Staffs can help leverage the success that you, first, have to create.*

If a full-time staff can leverage your success, it's a wise and prudent investment. However, if you're not at that level or, like many of us, have reached that level and don't feel the need to invest in full-time resources, then contracting is always a wise choice.

Acquiring Help When You Need It: Just-in-Time Speaker Support

Over the course of a year, I typically contract out for the following help related to my speaking business:[3]

- graphics creation
- mailing fulfillment
- mail list maintenance
- handout material creation
- test and survey creation
- product fulfillment
- phone response (especially client "hot lines")[4]
- audio/visual editing and dubbing
- phone interviewing
- newsletter formatting and proofing
- material and product storage

---

[3]By "contract," I mean that I hire talent for a specific project or duration. When I send my visual aids to a large audio/visual house for creation and duplication, I'm not contracting, but patronizing a retailer. But when I get a graphic designer to create slides by collaborating on a client project, I have contracted for help with that effort.

[4]As do many of you, I consult as well as speak, and "hot lines" are third-party, anonymous, toll-free phone lines that client employees can call to voice their opinions and/or complaints on company issues.

Call this "just-in-time support" if you wish, because I pay for performance when I need it and to the degree that I need it. In this manner, I can tightly control my outlays, have strong influence and priority with the contractor (I pay promptly and guarantee future work as long as my quality needs and deadlines are rigorously met), tailor to client need, and create, in effect, a large, talented staff that provides "heft" to my business in the prospect's eyes.[5]

> *I can respond as rapidly and at least in as high a quality manner as any speaker's operation that has full-time staff. That doesn't make my method better or worse, but it does make it a legitimate option.*

Acquiring the right contract people, I've found, is often a matter of balancing chemistry with talent. A graphics designer might have a bit of an argumentative edge, but I'm not trying to hire a full-time staffer with whom cordial relations day-in and day-out are a must. If the talent is there, I can tolerate a wide variety of personality styles and even quirks. (And I have no right to demand conformance to my particular behaviors since, like me, these people are all running their own businesses as they see fit.) However, I make no such allowances for quality, performance, and talent. No matter how well I might get along with, or even enjoy, someone's company, failure to meet quality requirements or deadlines is anathema. If you don't return my calls, meet my delivery dates, and have it right the first time, you don't work for me.

Most subcontractors I've encountered—and by "most" I'm talking upwards of 90 percent—charge by the hour, not by value. Consequently, they represent highly definable and fixed investments, and they generally undercharge for their real worth to you. It's not unusual to have a complete publicity piece designed, put through several iterations and edits, and formatted as camera-ready copy *with the first 1000 copies printed* for under $750. That's a nice payback on my investment, and it's

---

[5]Disclaimer: If you're uncertain, speak to your accountant, but subcontractors who do not rely on you for their sole income are not considered employees and do not require taxes to be withheld. However, at the end of the year, you will probably have to issue Form 1099 to those who are not incorporated businesses themselves. If payment is below a certain threshold—at this writing, $600—then no reporting is necessary. This is not meant to be legal or tax advice, and you should consult your CPA for definitive policies for your practice.

a spectacular return if you consider that doing it myself would have required about $20,000 of my time.

It often doesn't matter where subcontract help is geographically these days, since e-mail, fax, and FedEx can compensate handily for distance. Consequently, in my experience, the best ways to acquire contract help are:

- Ask other speakers whom they use for what purposes.
- Ask *other practitioners* (lawyers, accountants, consultants) whom they use for similar needs.
- Network through your local printer, Rotary, stationery supplier, chamber of commerce.
- Place an ad for your needs in the local weekly newspaper.
- Post your need on the appropriate Internet bulletin boards.
- If you see something impressive, ask for the source (which is how I acquired my web home page designer).
- Watch for ads in association newsletters (or place an ad yourself).
- Chat with neighbors who may be interested.[6]
- Investigate local college work-study and intern offerings.
- Investigate local students seeking research projects.

I've found that subcontractors are a cost-effective, highly leveraged technique to grow your business. The stereotypical test to determine if I'm ahead of the game is when another speaker compliments me on my visuals and asks if I used PowerPoint™ software.

"No, I have the slides created for me."

"Don't you realize that with the right software, which costs less than $500, you could produce these yourself?"

"The fact is that it would require about $30,000 of my time to learn and use that software, and it still wouldn't produce the creativity I get for a $2500 investment in their design and creation."

We both walk away scratching our heads, except my colleague is getting into a Volvo while I'm getting into my Ferrari.

---

[6]Cut me some slack before you call the gender police, but I've found that neighborhood homemakers often have college degrees, are at home raising the kids, and have free time and lots of talent. They are very receptive to the idea of such contract work. I've used these superb resources for mailing, phone work, order fulfillment, and a myriad of other important needs.

> *The IRS generally considers someone to be an*
> *employee, not a subcontractor, for tax purposes if they*
> *meet the following criteria:*
>
> - *comply with employer's instructions about the work*
> - *receive training from or at the direction of the employer*
> - *provide services that are integrated into the business*
> - *provide services that must be rendered personally*
> - *hire, supervise, and pay assistants for the employer*
> - *have a continuing working relationship with the*
>   *employer*
> - *must follow set hours of work*
> - *work full-time for an employer*
> - *must do their work on the employer's premises*
> - *must submit regular reports to the employer*
> - *receive payments of regular amounts at set intervals*
> - *receive payments for business and traveling expenses*
> - *rely on the employer to furnish tools and materials*
> - *lack a major investment in facilities used to perform*
>   *the service*
> - *cannot make a profit or suffer a loss from the services*
> - *work for one employer at a time*
> - *do not offer their services to the general public*
> - *can be fired by the employer*
> - *may quit work anytime without incurring liability*
>
> *From the General Accounting Office publication NO.*
> *GAO/T-GGD-96-130,* **Tax Administration: Issues in**
> **Classifying Workers As Employees or Independent**
> **Contractors 5** *(1996).*

Advisors and Mentoring

None of us in the speaking profession ever receives enough feedback. I know that's strange to hear, given the fact that we face audiences on a weekly basis who are usually encouraged to fill out the ubiquitous feedback forms. But there are two things wrong with using such responses as your sole—or even main—source of assessment.

First, the audience feedback isn't from the *buyer*. That's like Mercedes asking the family members how they liked the ride, but neglecting to ask the purchaser, who is the person most likely to buy again in the future. Since buyers used both rational and visceral impulses to hire you (logic impels people to think, but emotion galvanizes them into action), it's important to hear what that person's reaction is. Speakers whose feedback loop ends at the "smile sheets" completed before the audience leaves the room seldom have comprehensive information and rarely make improvements based upon the real buyer needs.

Second, with the best of intentions, the audience seldom knows what to look for.[7] The buyer's objectives might have included that they be shocked or provoked or driven to action, and not entertained or comforted or made to feel safe. Every audience member reacts slightly differently to what's heard because unconsciously each is seeking to establish relevance with his or her background. That's why (good) speakers use multiple stories and examples to try to appeal to a gamut of experiences and perspectives.

The advice that we tape all of our speeches and listen to them is among the most simplistic and specious. Our frame of reference is severely limited. Hearing ourselves and trying to decide how to improve is like asking the famous question, "What's different about a duck?" Well, a duck has feathers, but so does a goose. A duck has webbed feet, but so does a frog. A duck can swim, but so can a fish. A duck can quack, but so can a duck caller. Perhaps there's no such distinct animal as a duck, then? The point is that the question is wrong. It should be, "What's distinct about a duck as *compared to what?*" (It's smaller than a goose, frogs can't fly, fish don't swim on the surface, and duck callers can't mate with another duck.)

> *We need independent feedback that includes external frames of reference. Otherwise, we keep getting better at what we already do, and what we already do might be the problem.*

---

[7]Audiences are famous for feedback such as "the room was too cold," "the food wasn't good," and "the chairs were uncomfortable," as though they're attending a learning experience for the culinary or comfort factors. I ignore smile sheets completely because they reflect agendas which often have nothing to do with the quality of my work. There is a speaker I know in a local association who praises colleagues to their face and then writes devastating, anonymous feedback on the forms. He's a therapist's dream.

As a business requisite, you need support in the form of qualified, external advice and mentoring if you are to grow as a professional. You trust your finances to the advice of a CPA, your health to your personal physician, your corporate status to your attorney, and your graphics to a designer. Why wouldn't you trust your professional development to equally qualified sources?

If you do record your speeches, *send the tapes to trusted confidants whom you know will give you candid, blunt reactions.* If you want to feel warm and loved, watch any show in which Richard Simmons appears. But if you want to know if you're growing as a speaker, find people who can provide honest feedback and advice and not worry about your sensibilities. These people can be other speakers, but shouldn't be limited to them. Here are some sources for your mentoring and feedback needs.

Five Sources of Professional, Honest Feedback

1. Recruit an **advisory team** of people whose judgment you respect and who are familiar with the type of business you are in. These folks might include your financial planner, a colleague on a civic association, another entrepreneur (e.g., the person who owns one of your supply sources), a local politician or school board member, a business consultant, your attorney, etc. They needn't be geographically proximate because this can easily be done via e-mail or fax.

Tell them that you'll ask their help no more than two or three times a year. On those occasions, send them a tape (or invite them to hear you if you're speaking in their neighborhood) and ask them for their assessment of how you should reach the next level of the profession (larger audiences, larger companies, media work, high-visibility keynotes, etc.). Ask them what you do well, what should be further developed, and what underwhelms them, which might be abandoned. Don't react to stray comments, *but if you see a pattern emerging, take action.* (If one person says, "I didn't like that story," ignore it. But if five people say, "You seem to have no energy in those stories," then you know you've probably told them a few times too many.)

In return for their kindness, take your team out to dinner, offer to reciprocate for them, and/or provide a gift. You don't have to accept their advice, but you won't have it at all if you don't ask.

2. Seek out **other speakers who are successful.** Note that I didn't say, "whom you like," or "whom you respect" because that leaves the door open for the mutual admiration society. There are a lot of speakers who don't make more than they do because they spend so much of their

time telling each other how good they are and bestowing awards on each other.[8]

Find exemplars who represent success with which you can identify. Don't be taken in by the publicity klaxons, wailing away. Everyone lives in an "oceanfront home" and drives a "foreign car" and is "a prolific writer." (When I was helping someone else in this capacity and critiquing his promotional literature, I was compelled to remind him that Peter Drucker and John Updike might be among "the world's most prolific writers," but he, certainly, was not, despite the claims to that effect in his press kit.) Take the time to develop relationships with those whom you see addressing the organizations you want to address in the capacity you want to assume. Or find someone with a platform presence you admire, a visibility that impresses you, or a business acumen you'd love to acquire.

Develop a network of several of these people whom you can access just a few times a year. *Don't try to emulate their style or attributes.* Simply obtain frank feedback on your style, business, and direction that you can use to critically examine your progress. What's good for them might not be good for you, but their insights are from a highly valid frame of reference.

3. Invest in a **formal mentoring relationship.** There are some of us who are called upon so frequently for advice and guidance that the relationships have to take the form of formal consulting. In general, these relationships are focused and directed toward specific growth goals. You can stipulate what you want to tackle: penetrating the corporate market, using more humor, publishing, ancillary products, raising fees, etc., and you can determine the duration. In my experience, you need at least 6 months of regular contacts with a mentor—which, again, needn't be in person—in order to create the follow-through and discipline to reach your goals.

The characteristics of a professional, effective mentor who will provide you with the proper ROI include:

- success as a speaker, *not just as a mentor* (a "doer," not an "expert")
- unlimited access during the period, not designated days or times
- "real time" help with actual prospects, fees, presentations, etc.
- requirements for action and follow-up on those actions

---

[8]Beware of organizations that provide you with "certifications" and honorifics—and, sometimes "guaranteed" leads—after completing their seminar and/or sending in your money. They are a scam and worthless unless there are truly tough criteria to earn your designation and buyers accept the designation as a legitimate criterion of quality.

- contacts provided, such as book agent, speakers bureau principal, etc.
- solid references from other speakers

Mentors can be highly effective and well worth the investment if they can focus on your particular needs and offer specific, pragmatic techniques to grow your business and meet your personal objectives. Always eschew a "blanket" approach. This must be an individualized process.[9]

4. Choose **an association of professionals** that is geared to provide feedback. At preliminary levels, Toastmasters[10] is a good alternative because it offers (predominantly amateur and/or infrequent) speakers the opportunity to hone skills in front of a supportive audience. There are also contests run by the parent organization on local, regional, and national levels which provide the opportunity to perform in front of judges. The disadvantages of Toastmasters are that the feedback won't always be crisp and honest (I'm the next one up there, so I'm going to be kind) and the criteria for speeches are narrow and somewhat passé.

The National Speakers Association (NSA) has a membership of about 3500 speakers, ranging from the highly visible, professional keynoters and high-income training professionals to entry-level and aspiring speakers. It's a good vehicle to meet potential colleagues, advisors, and mentors, and the local chapter meetings provide "spotlight" opportunities to make a brief presentation and receive feedback from the audience. Some chapters provide videotaping and much more personalized feedback, as well. Although NSA considers itself the voice of the profession and provides various levels of accomplishment, its membership represents a minority of actual professional speakers and it's hardly known beyond the meeting-planning industry. Nevertheless, its conventions and meetings can provide camaraderie and an excellent feedback source for those disciplined to use them as such.

Similar associations include the International Platform Association, Professional Speakers Network, and the National Association of Parliamentarians.[11]

---

[9]A word on another type of help, the coach. This is a person who charges for a seminar or for a consulting relationship on such technical needs as platform skills, gestures, elocution, dramatic impact, etc. Many of them have background in the theater, and some speakers swear by that type of help, while others claim that coaches have ruined more good speakers than they've helped. We'll discuss them in Part 3 under "platform skills" because I don't consider them career advisors.

[10]See the appendix for contact information for all associations noted.

[11]Consult *National Trade and Professional Associations of the United States,* Columbia Books, New York, for more sources.

5. Seek help on **the Internet.** There are numerous speakers' chat rooms, home pages,[12] association listings, and similar sources. Allocate a morning to using the relevant search engines to generate alternatives. The beauty of the Internet is that you can exchange visual aids, speech transcripts, actual recordings, and on-line discussion, if you have the proper equipment and software.

You're able, through the miracle of cyberspace, to access a network of self-selected advisors who can provide you with downloadable examples of promotional literature, critique of your speeches, advice on your business plans, opportunities internationally, and a host of other potentially useful feedback. If you're technologically able and individually willing, you can find a trove of help sitting right at your desk.

The truth will inevitably and eventually seek you out and find you. You might as well solicit it and obtain it on comfortable grounds.

No matter what method you choose, find a source of direct and honest feedback: those people who will tell you the truth and not simply stroke your ego. "Care more for the truth than what people think." Aristotle said that, and he wasn't a bad advisor.

Things Better Not Left Unsaid

There are some random issues that don't belong in Parts 2 or 3 of the book, and haven't smoothly fit in to this point. So this final section of Part 1 will deal with the things I need to say somewhere. There's a chance that not all will apply at the moment, so I'll use bold headings to facilitate your selections and provide for referencing if and when the time comes for their application.

Incorporation

By all means, incorporate your business, no matter what size. (Whether as a C or an S company makes little difference, so consult your financial advisor. I've chosen C because I want to look like my corporate clients.) Incorporation affords the following benefits:

---

[12]Mine has an "article of the month" and archive posted at http://www.summitconsulting.com. There is also "real sound," enabling you to hear 30 minutes of one of my speeches.

- a legal entity which can borrow money, sue, or be sued (so that your personal assets are safe—this is a litigious society)
- a professional status and sometimes a preferred status, that is, as a small business, when seeking contracts or responding to RFPs (requests for proposals)
- corporate benefits written into your bylaws which may (consult your attorney) include a health plan, company car, retirement plan, board of directors meetings, directors' fees, and other corporate amenities and perquisites
- Payment of all reasonable business expenses from before-tax funds

Incorporation can be accomplished painlessly by any competent attorney for several hundred dollars or so, depending on your state's requirements. (You will probably get a nifty corporate seal, which I've had occasion to use exactly three times in the past 12 years!)

Insurance

Aside from the basic lifestyle insurance you should carry—health, life, dental, umbrella liability, whatever suits you—there are two other types you should be absolutely certain to obtain:

1. *Errors and Omissions.* This is typically called "E&O" in the insurance industry, and "malpractice" by the rest of us. It protects you when being sued by a client for purportedly providing bad advice that has injured the client's firm. (Accidents such as someone tripping over your projector wire are covered by general liability insurance, which you should also carry.) This type of suit has actually become *more* of a likelihood, given the increasing litigious remedies that have replaced discussion and debate. Theoretically, if you gave a speech on strategy that included warnings or opportunities for the audience, and the company acted on them and lost its corporate shirt, some legal beaver on the client's staff might advocate a suit against you. Consulting firms are sued with increasing vigor, and a speaker's advice can be construed as consulting (and many of you are consultants, as well). Do not proceed in this business without E&O coverage. Do not pass "go." Do not collect your next fee without investing it in such protection.[13]

2. *Disability Insurance.* There is a far, far greater chance of being disabled than of dying during the most productive aspects of our

---

[13]Fees are usually based on practice volume, but can be mitigated if you join a trade association or similar organization which offers group coverage. On an individual basis, plan to pay anywhere from $1000 to $3000 annually, which is probably equal to or less than one speaking engagement.

careers. Yet few speakers comprehend the importance of disability coverage. Choose coverage which pays you for as long as you cannot return to your full and normal type of work (some coverage applies only as long as you can't be employed, irrespective of whether it's your normal type of work). The law and insurance company procedures usually dictate that you can carry total coverage equal to some percentage of your normal income, generally about 80 percent. As a speaker, you'll need to work with brokers or companies which are sensitive to the swings in potential income in this profession and can arrive at equitable average earnings in deciding about policy coverage amounts. As with any insurance, group plans are less expensive than individual plans, and a wide variety of trade associations—not necessarily speaking associations—offer the former with a variety of options (e.g., the longer the "waiting period" before the insurance kicks in, the less expensive the premium). You cannot afford not to have disability insurance, even if it means taking less life insurance for the moment.

Financial Planning

For many speakers, financial planning means whatever is left after the checks are deposited and the bills are paid. That's not financial planning, but there is a name for it: bankruptcy.

It's silly and irresponsible to take the risks associated with any entrepreneurial business such as this one and not reap the rewards. While some of the rewards may be in instant gratification (especially for those of you from California), and you may feel that you can speak until you drop (and some people are apparently continuing to speak *after* they've dropped), you should have an intelligent long-term financial security plan.

Consult a first-rate financial planner—*someone who charges a fee for the advice, not someone who earns a commission by selling you securities*—set up a plan appropriate for your circumstances and objectives, and contribute to it faithfully, as though you're paying off the mortgage or the local utility. There is a variety of options and the laws change frequently, so keep abreast of what's best for you. Just one example: An SEP, which is like a corporate IRA, at the moment allows up to $22,500 a year to be contributed by your corporation, tax-free, to your retirement account. There are other goodies like this, so invest in professional help.

Banking Relationships

My preference is to have a professional, as well as personal, relationship with a bank. Especially as your business grows and prospers, it makes sense to arrange for credit lines, references, advantageous interest rates, and all the other perquisites that remain unhidden until, magically, they appear when you ask about them.[14]

My personal banker is on my mailing list, I meet with her once or twice a year, and I keep her highly informed about my work and its impact. (For example, she gets a copy of every book I publish.) Every so often, a new client's purchasing department will ask for a bank reference, and a new vendor requests them all the time.

One other perk of this relationship: If you can become a "private banking customer" or whatever the euphemism is in your area, you can short-cut banking lines, obtain easy overdraft protection, and even have the bank cover an inadvertently unsupported check (or allow you to draw on uncollected funds). Banks do a lot for good customers that they obviously don't choose to advertise. If your bank is intractable about affording reasonable benefits, find another bank while saying a silent prayer for the competitive benefits of deregulation.

Motivational Summary

How many of you couldn't resist this heading? My final point is a simple but often ignored one. You are as successful as you position yourself to be.

As your business takes off, don't continue to regard it (or yourself) as the same enterprise it was when you received your first $100 check for speaking to the local trade association that couldn't find anyone else. The people who reach out to you usually want something—your dollars, your advice, your support, your repute. You have to reach out to make certain things happen *on your terms*. I'm astounded by the people who try to sell securities over the phone, since that seems to me to be the ultimate personal, relationship business. But someone must be buying that way. Don't purchase insurance, vendor services, retirement plans, advice, or even pencils from just anyone who offers—and I'm someone who has seen speakers choose their attorney from the Yellow Pages of the phone book.

You're a success. Act like it. Choose your help carefully, but choose it now. The savvy of this business is in carving out your own route. Only the lead dog ever sees a change in scenery.

---

[14]This might be of at least footnote interest: I recently lowered my interest rate on my major credit cards simply by asking the head of those operations and pointing out that I am constantly appealed to (as are you) by their competitors with offerings of better rates. Since I use credit lines extensively for funding certain ventures and sybaritic inclinations, that successful inquiry saves me thousands a year in interest charges.

PART 2
Steak

7

Choosing and Broadening Your Topics

"What do you speak about?"
"What do you mean?"

Establishing Your Playing Field

Without spending any time at all thinking about it, and before doing anything else, write in your response to the question below as quickly and honestly as you can:

What Do You Speak About?

The worst question in the world is the one most often asked by colleagues in the speaking business: "So, what do you speak about?" The question is dreadful because it immediately places you in a box.

"What do you speak about?"

"I give dynamic, high-content talks on customer service."

"For what industry?"

"Primarily for financial services, usually mortgage lenders."

"For what duration?"

"Typically, workshops of 3 hours."

"And where are your clients?"

"Mostly in the Dallas/Fort Worth area."

"So, you do a half-day workshop on customer service for mortgage lenders in the Dallas area. I'll let you know if anyone needs that."

Here's the same encounter, but with different responses:

"What do you speak about?"

"I help to improve the client's ability to meet business goals."

"In what area?"

"A wide variety of areas."

"How do you do that?"

"It depends on the client because each one is different. Why don't you tell me something about yourself and your operation, and I'll be happy to provide you with some examples of how we'd work together."

Your playing field needs to be as large as possible. In the first example, we're talking about a playing field the size of a postage stamp—one type of format on a particular, specific topic for a narrow group of potential customers located in one area. In the second example, the playing field is as large as all outdoors. You might be most comfortable with something between the two, but err on the side of the outdoors, not the stamp.

Many of you are thinking, "But I have my particular content expertise and subject knowledge. How can I speak on just anything?" The answer is you can't speak on just anything, but you can speak about a heck of a lot more than you think *if you look at your ability to help the client from the client's point of view and not from your own pride in a certain presentation.* Always put yourself in the client's shoes and ask what would help the client make the connection between his or her need and your ability. This seems like a marketing factor, which it is and was covered in Part 1, but it's also a primary consideration in determining your topic areas.

> *Always seek to maximize your playing field and thereby increase your number of "plays." Don't be afraid to test the boundaries regularly.*

Let's say that your topic has been "negotiating." Your talks have focused on enabling people to better influence others, obtain their objectives, avoid being overwhelmed or tricked, prevent succumbing to aggressive behavior, etc. I would suggest that with those kinds of skills and knowledge you could also speak on any or all of the following:

- conflict resolution
- setting objectives
- influencing those outside your direct control
- presentation skills
- building consensus
- telephone techniques
- understanding nonverbal behavior
- setting priorities
- dealing with difficult people
- effective listening
- how to say "no"
- power speaking
- responding to questions
- providing feedback

I've named 14 possible topics that could be addressed with workshops, training sessions, seminars, keynotes, after-dinner speeches, facilitation sessions, and other means. Perhaps you're not comfortable with all 14, *but I'm willing to bet that you can embrace at least half of them,* which improves your possibility for connection with additional buyers by at least sevenfold.

Here's another example with "team building" as the topic and the playing field expanded:

- setting priorities
- coaching and counseling
- interpersonal communication
- assigning talent to tasks
- one-on-one coaching
- establishing objectives
- hiring and selection
- providing feedback
- establishing rewards
- running meetings
- conflict resolution
- building consensus

- measuring results
- presentation skills

There's another 14 options. If a client were to express a need for coaching and counseling individuals, you wouldn't want to be overlooked because you were considered someone who does only "team-building" sessions. The abilities you apply in team-building work can certainly be applied to individuals in coaching sessions. Again, you might not be comfortable with my 14 options, but you're certainly going to be able to choose at least half (or perhaps develop 25!).

Take the phrase that you wrote in at the beginning of this chapter and place it on top of the Expansion Worksheet. Then expand your playing field by completing as much of the worksheet as you can in the next few minutes.

You might not have filled in every space, or you might have overflowed the available room. But in the space of just a few minutes, you have begun to expand your playing field considerably and enlarge the types of groups to whom your topics will appeal. If you apply this expansion process with some discipline on a regular basis, you'll find that my original response, "I help the client to achieve business results," is one that you'll be getting quite comfortable with.

In Figure 7-1, I've provided a simple example of taking a single business topic, "decision making," and expanding it by layers until the playing field includes organizing and planning both work and life goals. In my opinion, all of the layers simply build on the processes of decision making: setting objectives, generating alternatives, evaluating risk, test-

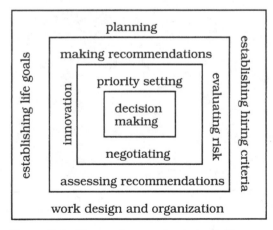

Figure 7-1. One way to expand a playing field.

Expansion Worksheet

What do you speak about (conventional reply)?_____

What type of group do you usually speak to?_____

Fill in each of the lines below with topics that answer each question.

■ What components of your topic could form separate talks (e.g., listening skills are a component of "effective communications")?

_____   _____

_____   _____

■ What aspects of the talk involve results that are independent of the talk (e.g., higher close rates are a result of a talk on "sales skills")?

_____   _____

_____   _____

■ What questions usually arise from participants that you have to anticipate and constantly answer (e.g., "How do I influence my boss?" is always a question demanding careful response when delivering "how to set priorities")?

_____   _____

_____   _____

■ What visual aids do you use that most intrigue participants (e.g., your chart on the differing roles we play at home and at work is part of your work on "managing time")?

_____   _____

_____   _____

■ Now, reviewing your responses in the categories above, list four kinds of groups that can profit from these topics in addition to the one you listed at the top.

_____   _____

_____   _____

ing your decision, etc. You might use different words, sequences, or topics, but that's not the point. The point is that anyone who speaks strictly on decision making will be attractive to only a fraction of the buyers who may be interested in those on the expanded playing field.

Your playing field is the size you construct it to be. However, once you define it, the prospective client will not attempt to enlarge it. If they've come to play soccer and only find a tennis court, they're going to take their ball and go home.

The Secret Leverage of Process over Content

The key to expanding our playing fields and appealing to increasing numbers of potential buyers is to understand that *we build content around process.*

Process. A sequence, system, design, model, or approach that enables the user to achieve a given, desired result. For example, a decision-making process provides the individual with the ability to arrive at an alternative which will meet his or her objectives. A sales process will allow the salesperson to more quickly and efficiently generate new business.

Content. The particular environment, surroundings, subject matter, or specifics within which one applies processes. In other words, the sales process at Chrysler involves selling cars, but at Northwestern Mutual it involves selling insurance. The basic process of selling—identifying buyer objectives, demonstrating value versus investment, etc.—is the same, whether one is selling cars, insurance, or lawn fertilizer.

We should identify what processes we are adept at and then build content around them which relates to particular buyers, industries, audiences, and conditions. For example, I deliver a keynote speech called "Capturing Opportunity" that deals with the processes of innovation, empowerment, and relationships. I've achieved great success with it in front of everyone from top-level executives to front-line supervisors, from aerospace to newspapers, and from American audiences to Asian audiences. Remember, I believe in huge playing fields.

The following "topics" are really examples of process, applicable to vast arrays of people, places, organizations, and conditions:

- networking
- decision making
- time management
- spirituality

- speaking skills
- team building
- customer service
- motivation
- humor
- ethics
- negotiating
- problem solving
- planning
- substance abuse
- writing skills
- technology
- sales skills
- use of media
- futurism
- health/wellness
- building self-esteem
- priority setting
- image building
- change
- listening skills
- creativity
- productivity
- leadership
- diversity
- career management

I could go on, but in these 30 I've probably covered most of you. The critical issue is that "planning," for example, is the same process whether used in a legal firm or a pharmaceutical company, although the content "plugged-in" to the planning process will be very different. However, I can successfully make these content adjustments as a consultant working on long-term projects, and I can easily make them during the course of a keynote or workshop. So can you.

Content follows process. In the Expansion Worksheet, you were asked

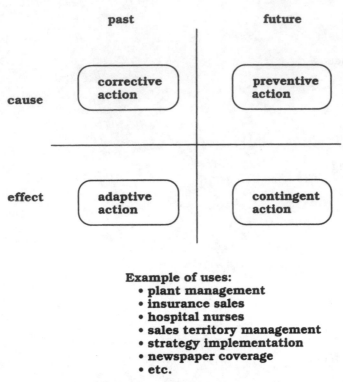

Example of uses:
• **plant management**
• **insurance sales**
• **hospital nurses**
• **sales territory management**
• **strategy implementation**
• **newspaper coverage**
• **etc.**

Figure 7-2. An example of a universal process.

to cite a visual aid popular with your audiences. In Figure 7-2, I've presented one of mine that is process oriented.

In this example of effective actions, I've used a traditional two-axis chart to show that cause and effect are intertwined with past and future time frames. If you're trying to remove the cause of a current problem (upper left), corrective action is necessary (e.g., fix the hole in the tire). If you merely want to circumvent the effects of the problem and not fix it (bottom left), then adaptive action is required (e.g., ride with a friend or use another car). If you want to prevent such a problem from occurring (or recurring) in the future, you take preventive action (upper right) intended to avoid it (e.g., check tires periodically, buy new ones when appropriate, keep correct inflation). However, should all your plans fail and you have to deal with the effect of the problem in the future (bottom right), you'd want a contingent action in place to remove the effects (most probably a functioning spare tire in the trunk).

This relationship, among cause and effect and the past and the future, is applicable to virtually any personal or professional environment. In the figure, I've listed some of the environments in which I've applied it, ranging from plant managers to hospital nurses. (In manufacturing plants, engineers provide preventive maintenance on the machines; in hospitals, nurses constantly check vital signs to prevent complications; and in newspapers, reporters validate facts from several sources to avoid errors in news stories.)

Choosing your topics as a speaker is a self-limiting and arbitrary exer-

> **All of us can readily describe our content. Sadly, that content is a minuscule portion of the total value we're capable of delivering in our processes.**

cise based upon what you think you know about your abilities. The real issue is broadening your appeal. If you're relatively new to the business, ironically you're in a stronger position to identify broad processes because you probably have less to "unlearn." But if you're a veteran, you should invest time "deconstructing" what you do to broaden its appeal.

I have a colleague in New England who listened to me speak on the value of processes and later told me that it had been a revelation.

> "I had been doing a seminar on customer service for 10 years," he said. "I could do it in my sleep. It was well-received, but I hadn't had the success in my business that I'd hoped, and frankly, my heart wasn't really in that speech anymore. Having heard you, I realized that I had been 'insisting' on delivering it in one format to one kind of business because *I had begun using it in that kind of format and that kind of business when I was first hired a decade ago!*"

People hire you to speak to their circumstances, on their turf, to their people, to meet their objectives. That makes sense. But since those circumstances, turf, people, and objectives differ widely from client to client, refusing to change the content of your talks to better convey your valuable processes makes no sense at all.

The Myth of a Speech's "Shelf Life"

I had delivered a highly successful series of engagements around the country for Coldwell Banker on innovation and creative thinking. After the final one, the president of relocation services told me how much his people had benefited from the approaches.

"But tell me," he said, "what kind of 'shelf life' do these speeches have? I imagine you must have to change them fairly frequently to keep fresh. That's a pretty heavy investment for professional speakers, isn't it?"

I stammered out some reply which glazed his eyes over because I wanted to avoid the cold, harsh truth: I had been delivering that speech in one form or another for 10 years, and I fully expect to continue to deliver it for another 10 years. Oh, my specific examples change with each client, and my generic examples change to reflect timeliness (you don't want to use tape cassettes as an analogy when everyone is listening to CDs). He had found it fresh and timely. Isn't that the only test?

Processes don't change. There are speakers who make their living doing character portrayals of people such as Mark Twain, Albert Einstein, Abraham Lincoln, and Benjamin Franklin. One of the central reasons for the appeal of such historical figures is that the wisdom, wit, and lessons they provide are as applicable today—if not more so—as the day they were first uttered. There are really relatively few things new under the sun. But the application of traditional ideas in the face of a changing world, new demographics, novel environments, increased stress, and new technologies is a constant challenge for the innovative speaker. Interpersonal sales skills were once a part of the repertoire of the Fuller Brush or Avon door-to-door salespeople, who have disappeared in the wake of dual-career couples and locked doors. But those same skills in varied forms are still applicable for retail salespeople, telemarketers, and assorted others. Conditions and environments change, but basic processes and skills do not.

Shelf life becomes a problem only when topics are inextricably entwined in some fixed event. If one's topic involves quality and is woven around the space shuttle *Challenger* disaster, it's going to suffer from the disinterest caused by distance. However, using the current problems with the MIR space station would solve that handily (as would examples from the client's actual environment). We'll talk more about this in terms of specific construction for speeches in the next chapter.

Why You'll Seldom Get Tossed Out for Using Common Sense

For several years early in my career, I was regularly worried that approximately 10 minutes into my speech someone from the audience would stand and shout:

"Why that's totally obvious! Why are you wasting our time with things we know quite well? Don't you have anything new to say??!!"

After a few years of sharing what I came to believe were concepts and principles that everyone should already know, and not having been confronted or pulled physically from the stage, I learned a valuable lesson: Most audience members don't always know what you think is obvious, and even if they do, *they don't mind hearing it again.*

In the series of Coldwell Banker keynotes I mentioned earlier, it was inevitable that some people showed up more than once because they carried dual titles, had qualified to attend the conventions several ways, or were changing roles. I tried to keep my material fresh and varied,[1] but there was some unavoidable repetition. Yet no one ever said a word, nor did I or the buyer ever detect the inattention that follows "having heard this song before." Finally, toward the end of my series, participants taught me an invaluable lesson.

After the keynote, several participants approached who had heard me before.

"Why didn't you tell the story about how you avoid speaking to people on airplanes?" asked one.

"Yeah, and you skipped the one about the time you couldn't get room service."

"I have to admit," I said, "that I recognized some of you and wanted to eliminate some of the things you'd heard in prior sessions."

"Don't do that!" one shouted. "Those stories are what really make the points work. Every time we hear them we get something new from them."

Imagine, people asking me to repeat stories that they had heard before! In my arrogance, I thought that I knew what was best for their learning and that it did not include repetition. I saw my job as having to be constantly fresh and entertaining. I was working harder than I needed to and achieving less than I wanted to.

When prospects watch videos of my prior speeches, I often expect them to say, "Do the same for us, but make the following adjustments for our industry, audience, and culture." They usually don't. They usually say, "If you can do that exact same thing for us, it will be terrific!" They expect that I have the native intelligence not to open a steel convention by saying, "It's a pleasure to be here with so many accountants" just because that was the group on the video. Clients expect common sense, *both in the content and in the process.*

---

[1]More about this later, but every example, story, or anecdote that makes a certain point should have another two or three "backups" reinforcing it for precisely these circumstances.

Of course, everyone knows that you should set objectives before considering alternatives in decision making. Yes, it's obvious that you should only handle most items once if you're trying to be effective at time management. We can all agree that self-esteem is based upon our achieving an accurate view of ourselves and not a distorted picture caused by old "baggage." But apparently, we can't hear any of that too often, particularly if it's integrated into presentations that are unique, energetic, dynamic, and interesting.

Here are my guidelines for avoiding overcomplicating your topic and preventing "fear of shelf-life burnout":

Do Not

- hitch your topics to the latest fads
- depend on highly industry-specific examples
- radically rename the topic for each customer (modifications are okay)
- use convoluted charts and diagrams
- portray it as the "only" way to achieve the result
- assume that the audience doesn't know it or doesn't already do it
- pretend that you invented it
- acknowledge that some of it may not be applicable to this audience
- confuse your ego needs with audience learning needs

You won't get tossed out on your ear if you're honest about your work and your intent. There *is* little new under the sun, but you are in a position to help reinforce some important processes for talented, interested participants by presenting them in an engaging way which is relevant for their environment and circumstances.

Although I tend to use the corporate world as a frame of reference, note that the premises we're discussing apply to education and youth, volunteer organizations, nonprofits and charities, international audiences, public seminars as well as in-house groups, short keynotes and lengthy seminars, and virtually all other combinations of speakers' "gumbo."

Common sense is in amazingly short supply. You will rarely get in trouble for suggesting that people ought to use their heads.

Prognosticating: 10 Sources of Expansion for Your Consideration

Every speaker or prospective speaker reading these words has at least one of the following concerns confronting them right now:

1. What areas should I be developing for future speeches (what playing field should I create)?
2. Into what areas should my current offerings evolve (how should I expand the playing-field boundaries)?

A great many ideas for topics come from clients and prospects, themselves; bureaus can tell you what appears to be on the horizon; colleagues in trade associations and through networking will share ideas; and the daily news provides a surfeit of provocation about what may be affecting your present and potential clients.

Incredibly, even veteran speakers fall victim to the success trap—or simply get extremely lazy—and tend to rely for too long on material and topics that are dated and passé. Speakers continue to use hackneyed, generic examples (e.g., the starfish story and the lighthouse incident) that most of the audience has probably already heard in one version or another. I've seen speakers talk about assessment and learning technologies without attribution (e.g., social style theory, right-brain/left-brain thinking, personality profiling), which are not only very dated, but aren't even their own work. Some of the audience knows that they're seeing a tap dance, and smart buyers know that they haven't received much value. (And many of us in the profession know that we're seeing unethical behavior.)

We tend to feather our own nests and become highly comfortable and lethargic in our success. Thus, it's often harder for an experienced speaker to expand the playing field than it is for a relative newcomer. But we all must investigate the need to do so periodically.

Here are 10 sources for playing-field creation and expansion. They are probably not all what you'd expect to pursue. They are generic in that they apply no matter what your current focus or strengths. You can use this list as a reference when you feel you need an organized approach to expanding your focus or finding a new one. You might well find yourself leaning more heavily toward some than the others, which is all the more reason to ensure that you deliberately examine them all. *The categories can apply to you, personally, or to others in the business.*[2]

---

[2]Note that these categories are not "pure" and that the same idea can emerge from several, for example, high growth and unexpected success. They are meant to be triggers and not separate, discrete silos.

1. Unexpected Success

I'm not referring to the successful speech with the audience's and the buyer's plaudits. I'm talking about the truly unexpected success that caught even your own ego by surprise.

Several years ago, I was asked to make an after-dinner awards presentation honoring humor in speaking for a trade association of which I was a member (I had won the award the prior year). I was given 15 minutes for the introduction and presentation to the winner, who, unfortunately, was ill and could not attend. The recipient was a friend, everyone present knew him, and I created a funny piece that I knew was being captured on video to be shown to him. The audience loved it.

When I reviewed the tape later, I found that it was much better than I had ever imagined, I had loved doing it, and it might represent a new area for me. I sent the brief video to my bureaus, added after-dinner speeches to my materials, and in the next year, delivered five of these for 30–45 minutes each *for my full keynote fee*. What have you done that's worked surprisingly well that you can formalize as a topic or an offering?

2. Unexpected Failure

You're thinking that any failure is unexpected, in that no one plans to fail. But I'm talking of the whopper—the failure that was so overwhelming and swift that you lost your breath (or someone else did) sliding down the slope.

I saw another speaker fail dismally trying to use a management approach to strategy with a human resource convention audience. Her attempts to talk about "driving forces" and "core competencies" fell on deaf ears because she hadn't adapted her examples to the very real differences (and perceived lack of empowerment) in these staff positions. Nor was she talking to the same high-level people her material targeted. Most human resource professionals are midlevel managers without the ability to influence market strategy.

I saw the need to align myself with that audience. One of my playing fields deals with consulting skills and entrepreneurship within organizations. I adapted it to take the position that there was little difference between me, as an external consultant, and human resource people, as internal consultants, other than the manner in which we acquire business (and even that is sometimes similar). By creating a collegial approach to this market segment, rather than a threatening one (external consultants are often called upon because internal people don't have the requisite skills and/or credibility), I was able to expand my audiences and became a keynoter at several human resource conferences, as well as a professional resource for consulting skills. What are you doing to expand your audiences?

3. Unexpected Events

This is an easy one. Read the newspapers, trade association journals, and weekly magazines. Attend association meetings. Network with your usual contacts. Something always changes suddenly.

Cable companies are receiving permission to enter the phone business. That creates certain customer service demands not encountered before. Airlines are enjoying renewed business, requiring them to hire large numbers into that industry for the first time in a decade, without the large training staffs they once employed, creating a need for external trainers.

Changes in governments or altered trade conditions create the need for acculturalization for managers suddenly sent to the far corners of the earth to transact business for their organizations. Downsizing creates a need for people to hear information about how they can master their own fate, not merely meet corporation objectives. The increase in teams and the deemphasis on hierarchical control provide for a demand in facilitators and team-building experiences. What are you doing to exploit change, instead of being buffeted by it?

4. Technological Change

The Internet alone has created a wealth of expanded opportunity for those whose specialty was restricted to technological companies. There is a growing, almost desperate, need for technologically adept people *who can express themselves in normal English* and help managers understand how to use e-mail, the Internet, search engines, and so forth without becoming consumed by them.

Virtually every technological presentation I've ever seen has been undermined by some technological glitch (best captured in Apple's classic commercial demonstrating the futility of trying to rely on Windows at huge conferences). For anyone who understands both technology and the needs of the adult learner—and who can present even technojargon in an engaging and comfortable manner—the potential is vast.

Similarly, I'm now being booked for teleconferencing and satellite learning events. The presentation skills for these broadcast options are somewhat different from regular platform work. What are you doing to explore and prepare for these additional outlets for your talents?

5. Process Weaknesses

Where do things consistently fail or fall apart? I've found, for example, that strategy formulation is almost always completed as planned, attested to by thick three-ring binders filled with the strategic wisdom of the senior executives. The problem is that, a year later, few of the strategic initiatives have been launched, let alone realized.

That's because the process breaks down at the implementation stage, when the idealistic conceptual plans have to be translated into tangible operating realities by a lot of people who weren't privy to the plan formulation in the first place. Rather than compete with a gigazillion people speaking on strategy formulation, which I could do, I've focused on strategy *implementation*, which most people either can't or won't do.

Consequently, I have positioned myself in an area where organizations can readily identify past failure, but can't quite put their finger on why it happened and don't trust the people who helped with the formulation because they didn't provide sufficient help originally with the implementation.

These process weaknesses abound, and they're usually processes that can be applied to any organization (e.g., lousy sales forecasting results in incorrect inventories, missed profit, etc.). Have you studied them at all?

6. High Growth

The incredible acceptance of personal computers influenced a wide array of seemingly unrelated industries. For example, furniture makers started to produce "ergonomically correct" products. Publishers began to produce magazines and newsletters dedicated to a single platform and even a single application.

How should people and organizations handle high growth, be it their own or the effects of someone else's? If you speak on customer service, is there an expansion that might involve customer service during peak growth periods? Or if a competitor is growing voraciously, what about customer service aimed at retaining every current customer? (A vice president once asked me what the proper ratio should be of repeat business and retained customers. I told him 100 percent and that, if his people had any other goal, the number would plummet to near zero. I got the job.)

If you speak on quality, what's the difference in behavior, communication, reward, etc. in times of very high growth? This is a mild expansion of the playing field, but one that provides for great timeliness and relevance. Are you taking advantage of this and similar opportunities?

7. Market and/or Industry Structure Change

Cable television has reshaped an industry. So has telephone and airline deregulation. Healthcare will never be the same, for better or for worse. The armed forces have moved to all-volunteer fulfillment. What will happen tomorrow?

I moved my talks on improving sales and more aggressive marketing to the financial services industry, which had never seen a marketing department prior to deregulation. I've spoken on managing rapid change to cattle ranchers and meat processors, once among the most conservative and unchanging of all industries. Once I methodically turned down offers from farm groups. Not anymore. They need to hear my messages about change management and strategic profiling, which I easily adjust for their environments and concerns.

Whenever an industry or a market is shaken out of its prior status quo, it becomes receptive to ideas it wouldn't have considered before. What new areas are opening for your skills and talents that might not have been approachable last year (or last month)?

8. Demographic Change

This is the area in which diversity and gender topics have grown extraordinarily. Managers—irrespective of industry—who have to lead and work with people who are no longer photocopies of themselves are experiencing everything from mentoring help to sensitivity sessions. A great deal of it is schlock and has been repudiated. What are you doing to create assistance in this area tied to the legitimate business goals of the client?[3]

My approach was to eschew the dreadful "managing diversity" (as if we should all work to look alike and act alike) and develop an approach called "embracing diversity." Since a great deal of the existing work was being done by minorities and women, I was a relative exception as a white male, yet important because white male role models were needed on the platform and in the workshops. I also had the business skills to make a case for diversity's importance in meeting pragmatic business goals.

Dual-income families continue to increase in number. English as a second language is a growing issue. Remedial reading, writing, and speaking skills are required in business because our secondary schools

---

[3]For example, case studies in the literature have demonstrated that heterogeneous teams actually work better and produce superior and faster results than homogeneous teams.

are often failing to create competence. Basic business etiquette and image issues need to be addressed. Networking becomes an essential skill to acquire in a world of layoffs and downsizings. Are you adapting to the demographic changes around you?

9. Perception Change

Do you remember when cigarette smoking was considered so suave that you could barely see the stars for the smoke in movies from the fifties? Do you recall the "drunk comics" on television in the sixties and seventies? Do you remember when it wasn't unusual for programming to include ethnic, racial, gender, and other stereotyping?

Today we see concerns about health and the environment, quality of life, and animal rights. What will we see tomorrow? I'm not advocating that we leap aboard every fad that sails under the window, but I do suggest that legitimate trends deserve our full attention.

Wellness in the workplace, as an alleviation of stress and improvement in productivity, is an important evolution from solely individual health concerns. The perception that the organization no longer reciprocates employee loyalty and hard work has prompted many companies to demonstrably invest in their people's learning and well-being, perfect potential areas for speakers and trainers.

Perception is reality. People don't operate based upon some reality they can look up in the back of a book, but on the perceptions they develop every day through the stimuli of the job and their environment. Organizations have to manage perception, internally and externally, just as they manage their bottom line. Who is better to assist in that management than master communicators?

10. New Knowledge

This is the "patent office" of concepts. We do sometimes develop new insights and even new technologies, in exception to "nothing new under the sun." Lasers and biotechnology are industrial examples; teamwork and participation supplanting militaristic hierarchies are humanistic examples.

I've developed a few concepts I'm rather proud of (i.e., value-based fees in consulting and speaking, the product/service/relationship matrix in strategic thinking).[4] You might have done the same, or per-

---

[4]See, respectively, *Million Dollar Consulting,* McGraw-Hill, New York, 1992, 1998, and *Best-Laid Plans,* Las Brisas Research Press, Shakopee, MN 1994 (originally published as *Making It Work,* HarperCollins, New York, 1990).

haps you will once you put your mind to it and develop the needed experiences.

Are you in a position to develop competencies and skills for those who work at home; for those moving from organizational life to creating their own businesses; for those who will be competing globally for the first time; for those who will allow teams to do their own hiring, firing, and rewarding; and for those seeking to spend more quality time with family and achieve more fulfilling work/family balance?

Only you can keep broadening your playing field—or creating new ones—to match your market savvy. Let's turn now to actually creating the specifics of what you do "on stage."

8

Creating a Speech

"Good morning . . . no . . . wait . . .
that wasn't right . . . "
The Five Rules and Eight Steps for
Writing a Speech

Use Original Sources Because a Lot of "Truths" Aren't

Some people never write a speech. They inherited, stole, purchased, cobbled together, or winged something quite some time ago and are still doing it. When accompanied by poor platform skills, these people are invariably unsuccessful. When accompanied by superb platform skills, these people are inevitably not as good (or successful) as they could be. They're getting by on sizzle without steak.

There are five simple rules of excellent speech preparation:[1]

Rule One: The Originality/Validity Rule. The speech should be yours.

Rule Two: The Relevance Rule. Stories and anecdotes should be germane.

Rule Three: The Perspective Rule. People learn best when they are comfortable.

Rule Four: The Outcome Rule. The buyer's condition should be improved.

Rule Five: The Adult Rule. People learn in different ways.

---

[1]I'm including here training program, workshop, seminar, presentation, etc. For simplicity, let's just consider them all a "speech."

Rule One: The Originality/Validity Rule

I once traveled a long way to Lake of the Ozarks, Missouri, to keynote a senior executive conference for corporate giant Unisys. About 70 of the top-level executives were present, and the senior vice president of marketing rose to introduce me. He quickly moved into a story, which became alarmingly familiar. It was one of my real-life experiences, which I had planned to include that morning.

At first, I thought he was using the story to introduce me, but it quickly became apparent that he was using it to get some laughs. He merely substituted himself for me and told it verbatim. He had stolen it from one of my tapes and had forgotten the source, creating the Kafkaesque situation of relating it prior to introducing the person he had stolen it from!

This happens all the time, and too often among speakers. I've heard enough variations on a single theme from scores of different speakers to make the various parts of *Bolero* seem like Ravel had an independent thought for each movement.

There are two reasons not to steal from others:

1. Personal stories are just that, and it's unethical to use them unless they're your own.

2. A lot of what you steal simply isn't true.

The first reason shouldn't require a whole lot of explaining. I've occasionally heard my own "stuff" regurgitated by another speaker who had been in one of my audiences previously. It's never as powerful, questions from the audience can't be handled well, and sooner or later, word always gets back to the originator. If we can't act like ethical professionals, then we have no right to call this a profession. If a journalist or writer uses someone else's materials, it's called plagiarism. If a company uses another organization's proprietary creation, it's called patent infringement. If an employee who moves to a competing company uses confidential, classified information from the former employer, it's called theft.

When a speaker takes someone else's materials, it's no less a crime and no less dishonest. Corporate audiences can often spot it, since they're exposed to so many speakers, and they will always react negatively. Buyer's will not invite you back and may not even pay you the balance of your fee.

> *If you have to steal to get material, go into computer hacking or hold-up convenience stores. The rewards are more immediate and at least your comrades will readily admit to what they're doing.*

The second reason not to steal is more subtle, and it's the primary reason for The Originality Rule. A great deal of what you hear from the platform is simply not true. For example, I've heard at least 30 speakers claim during a variety of different presentations that "less than 7 percent of the impact on an audience is based upon what you say." They claim that over 90 percent of the audience impact is based upon how you say it, and they quote the work of a Dr. Albert Mehrabian, who did some psychological studies, as the source of the statistics. The speakers then proceed to make their point, which is that *how* you present something is more important than *what* you present.

There are only a couple of things wrong with this. The first is that Mehrabian did his work over 30 years ago, far too long to still have credence in a society as turbulent as ours. The second and even more important, however, is that his work (if anyone bothers to actually read it) is based upon social situations and people standing in line, waiting to be served, etc.[2] About 10 years ago, a speaker at a national convention cited this work incorrectly, and hundreds of others simply incorporated the nonsense into their "act." Anyone who knows psychology realizes it's false, and anyone with a decent brain realizes that great, captivating speakers such as Franklin Roosevelt, William F. Buckley, Peter Drucker, and Henry Kissinger have relied almost exclusively on the beauty of their words, not their platform skills.

Let's end the madness.

It's important to be original for the sake of professional ethics, but also as the basis of your own competence. You can't rely on random "facts" just because they're spouted from someone holding a microphone. As Casey Stengel used to say, "You can look it up."

Pictures Are Worth, Literally, 1546 Words

Rule Two: The Relevance Rule

Try opening a conversation with two different sallies:

- How was your vacation?
- Would you like to hear about my vacation?

Now, which do you think will elicit the warmer, more attentive response? If you think it's the second one, then you're Donald Trump.

---

[2]For example, he used assistants who attempted to break into lines at a post office, some cordially smiling and others rudely assertive, to see how patrons responded. See *An Approach to Environmental Psychology* by A. Mehrabian and J.A. Russell, MIT Press, Cambridge, MA, 1974.

It's vital to make your speech as relevant and comfortable for the audience's frame of reference as possible. If that means *your* discomfort, so be it. It's far better for you to be uncomfortable in alien territory than for your audience to feel that way. The absolutely best way I know to accomplish this is to talk to some of the potential audience members well ahead of time.

Ask the buyer if it would be permissible to call a random selection of the audience.[3] So as not to take too much of either their time or your own, tell them that you simply want to ask them three quick questions to better prepare your remarks *and be sure to offer the options of a voice-mail, e-mail,* or *faxed response* so that you don't have to play telephone tag with busy people and you can shorten the process.

Ask anything you like to gain relevant input for your speech, but here are my usual three questions with my permission to steal them:

1. What's the biggest challenge you are facing on the job?
2. If you could change just one thing tomorrow, what would it be?
3. What advice would you give to a new person in your position?

I modify these as needed, but they basically stand up well in a wide variety of environments. I use the results at various junctures in my speech, so that perhaps three times during an hour's keynote I'll refer to "what you've told me." Doing this in advance provides the luxury of incorporating the feedback into visual aids if desired. Never mention how many people you spoke to, even though small random samples are generally quite accurate, but merely cite "those of you with whom I've spoken over the past several weeks."[4]

My experience is that virtually no one refuses a request to help a speaker tailor remarks for their company if the request is polite, personal, provides choices in the means of response, and is brief.

> *Don't tell them everything you know. Tell them everything they need to know, and then try not to blatantly tell them.*

---

[3] I typically use 5 percent up to 500, so I'll call a dozen people in a 250-person presentation. My maximum is 25, no matter how large the audience. If it's a small group of two dozen or fewer, I try to call at least half.

[4] If you're doing a longer presentation, you can even create a survey response sheet and/or comparisons with other companies if you use the same questions. The key is to include more than just the people in the room in your sampling.

A "verbal picture" is a story, anecdote, experience, or metaphor that captures a point for the audience prior to beating them to death with it. For example, the number of people who die of tobacco-related illnesses annually is equal to 3 fully loaded 747s crashing into the earth *every day for a year.*

That's enough said. The point doesn't require lengthy citations from mortality tables or three-dimensional charts and graphs (visual aids are not always "pictures" in my sense, but are too often simply more extended verbiage). The metaphor is powerful.[5]

A verbal picture is worth 1546 actual words. So if your keynote is an hour, and that involves about 10,000 words, you can knock that off with just 6.468 stories or anecdotes. How did I come up with these figures? Someone told me that Albert Mehrabian did this study . . .

There's Nothing Funny About Humor

Rule Three: The Perspective Rule

There is nothing like self-effacing humor to help an audience become comfortable. Comfort is a key aspect of adult learning. If I'm uncomfortable, I'm resisting, not focused, diverted, and looking inward. If I'm comfortable, I'm receptive, open, outward-focused, and "present." The trouble is that most speakers consider comfort to be external, and therefore focus on the room temperature, the seating, refreshment breaks, and a host of other tangential environmental factors. There are actually some self-appointed "coaches" who specialize in external surroundings. (I've spoken in rooms with power outages, failed sound systems, adjacent to gospel meetings, next to street construction, with panoramic views of the Rocky Mountains, with simultaneous translators in the back, with wait staff constantly bussing dishes, and with participants hustling in from other late-running events. Such is life, and I've managed to engage almost every one of those audiences, although the bomb scare was difficult.)

In fact, comfort is *internal,* and that needs to be our primary focus, not how much water is in the water glasses. People are relaxed by humor, but since most humor is based upon someone's discomfort, it's best to ensure that the humor is self-effacing and directed solely at the speaker. People will tend to commiserate and sympathize ("I've been there!") and identify not merely with your situation, but with the ensuing message.

---

[5]One of the classics is the college admissions officer who tells new freshmen some variation of, "Look to your left, look to your right, and then consider that two of the three of you will not be here in 4 years."

There are two basic types of humor: generic and specific. Here's a rule of thumb: Don't use the former.

Generic humor is embodied in these classic puffballs, one of which I actually used myself early in my career (it didn't occur to me that others had already stumbled on to it, even though I read it in a national magazine). I'm presenting both here in the hopes that such exposure will ruin their utility forever:

The Naval Ship Story

The huge naval ship pounded down the coast during a dark and stormy night. Conditions were horrible, visibility severely limited. Suddenly, a light through the haze. Another ship, collision course!

A message was sent: "We're on a collision course. Change your heading 20° north." A reply, "Collision course acknowledged, change your heading 20° south."

A second message from the massive ship: "This is Rear Admiral Harvey Johnston. Change your heading 20° north." A second reply: "This is seaman fourth class Arnold Jones. Change your heading 20° south."

A third message: "I am standing on the bridge of the largest capital ship in the navy. Every gun and missile is pointed directly at you. Change your heading 20° north."

The final reply: "I am standing in a lighthouse..."

The Sand Dollar Story

A little boy was moving down the beach, stopping frequently to toss sand dollars, washed ashore in the tide, back into the ocean. A person approached and asked what the boy was doing.

"I'm saving the sand dollars," said the boy.

"But look at the thousands on the shore," said the adult. "You can't possibly make a difference."

Throwing another back into the ocean, the boy replied, "I certainly made a difference for that one."

After the second story, I'm prompted to say that the sand dollars are being eaten by barracuda stationed just off the beach, which is why the sand dollars had deliberately flung themselves onto the safety of the beach, where they can live quite comfortably and someday build condos, but that's still another story.

Use humor that is specifically yours. Not all of us are comedians or humorists, but that's not what I'm suggesting. Every day we laugh and experience irony. Write it down, make a note, record the occurrence. Then rework it into your material. Here's an example I use to reinforce my point that there is too much of a "that's not my job" attitude in organizational America. It really happened, and almost exactly as I describe it:

The Hyatt Hot Line

I'm staying at a Hyatt Regency Hotel and on the end table is a card that says in bold letters *Hyatt Regency Hot Line.* **"No problem too big or too small, available 24 hours a day. Call the Hyatt Hot Line with any request."**

I had no room service menu. I said, "This is a job for the Hyatt Hot Line."

I dialed and a woman answered, "Hyatt Hot Line! How can I help you?"

"This is Alan Weiss, room 734, and I have no room service menu."

She replied, "I'm sorry, we don't handle that."

I go on to relate that I asked if they handled nuclear war, since I needed to know what the criteria were to qualify for the Hyatt Hot Line assistance.[6]

Carry a notepad or recorder wherever you go. Keep it in the car console, on the night table, in your briefcase. When something funny, ironic, frustrating, or bizarre occurs, make a note. Someday you'll find the perfect place for it.

Here's another tip for adding relevant humor and stories to your work: Always have two in reserve for every one you intend to use. This is because:

1. Participants will sometimes ask for additional examples if they didn't get the point. (People learn in varying ways—see Rule Five: The Adult Rule.)

2. You sometimes unexpectedly find past participants sitting in the room who have heard your primary stories.

---

[6]All humor is based upon discomfort. In this case, it's my frustration of not being able to get the help I expected.

3. Even a proven story might not work. You can be interrupted by an equipment problem or other distraction. Or a story involving an airplane may be inappropriate if there was a recent air disaster.

4. A story can be inappropriate for a particular audience. I'm not going to tell that Hyatt story to a hotel convention because it would embarrass Hyatt in front of their peers (although I'd readily tell it to a Hyatt in-house meeting).

Build humor into every speech you give. I'm not of the school that says "don't try to be funny unless you're a comedian." Adult learning relies on comfort, and properly directed humor creates instant comfort. By using actual occurrences, striving for self-effacing humor, and telling true stories in a practiced, articulate manner, anyone can insert humor into almost any speech (I've seen it excellently done in eulogies and courtrooms).

Now That You've Been There and Gone, So What?

Rule Four: The Outcome Rule

Every valuable speech, training session, workshop, seminar, facilitated meeting, and emceed affair should have an outcome. A humorous after-dinner speech, for example, should leave participants in a positive frame of mind and feeling good about their circumstances at the moment. A training program on time management should leave tangible organizational skills with the audience. A workshop on diversity should leave attendees with an appreciation of cultural distinctions and the harmful effects of inappropriate language.

If you want to be rehired by the current buyer—or at least acquire a golden reference for future buyers—you must provide results *appropriate to the topic and environment* which remain with the client. There's nothing wrong with getting people fired-up briefly if that's the buyer's aim, but there's even more power in providing skills, techniques, and approaches that people are demonstrating to the buyer every day long after you've spoken.

Outcomes originate with the economic buyer. Ask him or her what's to

---

The more distinct and enduring the outcomes, the greater the probability that you will be both rehired and referred to others. Standing ovations don't last longer than a minute and don't increase your fee by a cent.

be achieved.[7] If the buyer says, "Well, I'm not certain," or "We just want to have a good time," always ask "*why?*" The responses will be revelations such as, "The conference was dull last year, and we thought an energetic speaker could liven things up," or "Our people have had a very rough year, performed admirably, and deserve to be told how good they are," or "We see our mission as educating the people who come to these meetings, both in terms of their professional and personal lives." You are then in a position to ask, "If they leave with this (skill, technique, attitude, awareness, etc.), will that contribute toward your goals?" Simply keep this up until the buyer says, "That's exactly what I'd like to see happen."

I know a great many speakers who don't bother to find the real buyer (they're hired by a meeting planner or placed by a bureau) and/or don't bother to understand what the desired outcomes are. They see their job as delivering a keynote or presenting a workshop. They collect their check and leave. This is equivalent to a salesperson making sales calls and considering the job well done. Salespeople should bring in new business, and speakers should meet the buyer's objectives by achieving agreed-upon outcomes.

How much repeat business do you received *unsolicited?* How many times does the buyer call you and say, "We've got something coming up that you would be just perfect for"? (Or how often does a new client call and say, "I was referred to you by a colleague who told me I couldn't afford not to hire you for our meeting"?) Most speakers struggle because they labor to make new sales to new buyers under new conditions for far too great a percentage of their available time. They have references, but they don't have *referrals*. They have client lists, but they don't have *relationships*.

Begin your speech preparation with the outcomes to be achieved. If you don't know them, go find the buyer and develop them.

People Learn in Different Ways: Not Everyone Is As Smart As You Think You Are

Rule Five: The Adult Rule

People learn in different ways. Not better or worse ways, just different ways. I'm not talking about esoteric (and highly dubious) right-brain/left-brain codifications, not about labels like "driver" or "INTJ," or other such nonsense. I'm talking about observable behavior.

---

[7]Even if you're not introduced at the buyer level, find your way to that person. Refer back to Chapter 2 for help in getting there.

Some of us prefer visuals. Some of us like sequences. There are those who rejoice in group learning, but others who prefer solitary absorption. There are as many people who shun volunteering for role-plays and demonstrations as there are those who rush to the stage to take part in them.

Adults make their own decisions. It's always permissible to present options and even to challenge assumptions, but it's never a good idea to assume that your alternative is the best for everyone. Quite a few speakers who really ought to know better demand that audience members touch the people next to them, often in the form of a neck rub or a hug. For many people, this is an intimacy that is completely inappropriate. Some speakers become apoplectic when they ask the audience to sing or dance or otherwise engage in physical activity and then find some holdouts. This is seen as a personal affront. It isn't. It's merely a personal choice.

The best speech preparation embraces the philosophy that people are diverse and learn in varying manners. This means at least three things for the speaker and his or her preparation and attitude:

1. Provide for varied sources of input. For example, use visuals as well as text, have workbooks as well as slides, provide a summary sheet as well as detailed text, use interaction voluntarily but also use lecture to summarize key points.

2. Never demand participation in any activity that even one person would find demeaning. If you want to role-play, explain the situation and ask for a volunteer; don't nail someone in the back row (that person, unless a latecomer, is sitting way back there for a reason). Don't ask people to touch or to reveal an intimacy: "Tell your partner something you've never told anyone else before." (I've actually been present when this directive was given. My partner said, "It's only 10 minutes into the workshop and I already hate this speaker, and I've never had to say that before this morning.")

3. Always give the benefit of the doubt and never take anything personally. I've had people leave my talks within 90 seconds of my saying, "Good morning." I assume that they had a good reason, such as a sudden call of nature, the realization that they were in the wrong session, or the body odor of the person who sat next to them. I embrace every question as honest and sincere, unless I have incontrovertible proof to the contrary. "I don't agree with you. Can you give me a better example?" is a legitimate and valuable question. "I don't think a woman has any right to address us on a management topic. What do you think you're doing here?" is not.

> *Adult learners invariably give the speaker the benefit of the doubt. It's the fault of the speaker, not the audience, when credibility is lost.*

Speakers are vested with tremendous credibility and support when they ascend the platform. The audience wants to be part of a success. Fewer than 5 percent of your attendees (that's 10 people out of 200, 1 person in 20) suffer from the kind of personality disorder that impels them to crave someone else's failure. People may slow down to see a traffic wreck, but virtually no one would want to contribute to one.

Pay your audience the same respect when preparing your speech or workshop. Don't insert stories or exercises that merely make you look good and lack any kind of learning point or relevance for the audience. Build in backups and alternatives if a given segment seems not to work or an example falls flat. Allow time for questions. You can always fill in with support material if there are none, but it's death to cut the audience short because you have too much mandatory material to cram in.

And despite what you'll hear from meeting planners who seem to feel they're evaluated by the quantity of time filled, no audience or buyer ever complained because a terrific speech ran 10 minutes short or an intriguing seminar ended 40 minutes early. But once you go even 5 minutes overtime, you'll begin to lose large segments of audience attention, not to mention the damage done to the rest of the agenda.[8]

Audiences are no different from you, except that you'll usually be speaking and they'll usually be listening, if you let them.

Now the Mechanics from Our Esteemed Service Technicians

This final section is for those of you who must have a formula or template for creating a speech from scratch. Fair enough. The previously discussed conceptual part above is the tough stuff. The next few pages are easy, but only if you've embraced what's preceded.

---

[8]As a closing keynoter for the International Human Resource Information Managers Association, I waited patiently in the wings while a director of a charity took all of his time and most of mine trying to solicit corporate donations. The meeting planner looked on like a mushroom. I had only 20 minutes left after my introduction. I opened with, "In view of the time, I will be brief," got a thunderous round of applause, finished in 20 minutes, and left, my full fee having been paid 6 months prior. I had one of the highest reviews of the entire conference.

There are eight primary steps to building a successful new speech:

Step One: Outcomes
Step Two: Time Frame and Sequence
Step Three: The Key Learning Points
Step Four: Rough Draft Assembly
Step Five: Supporting Stories, Examples, and Transitions
Step Six: Visual Aids and Handouts
Step Seven: Build the Opening and Closing
Step Eight: Practice the Speech and Adjust the Timing

Let's say that a client has asked you to speak to a management team of 50 people. It is a successful high-tech (or healthcare or automotive—it really doesn't matter) organization in a competitive marketplace. The vice president of operations wants to instill formalized techniques that people can use to constantly raise their own standards and outpace the competition. Your speech is the kickoff for the day-long conference. All of the other speakers and activities involve internal people.

Step One: Outcomes

You ask the vice president to specify the results (the Outcome Rule) he'd like to see in the aftermath of your speech. He says there are two short-term and one long-term. The short-term are:

- Prepare participants to "open up" their thinking so that the rest of the day can take advantage of innovative and "out of the box" ideas.
- Provide a few simple techniques they can use to keep them focused on new and creative ways to get the job done.

The long-term objective is:

- Instill a sense of pride that they, in fact, *have* been very creative, which is why the company is so successful, and they shouldn't become conservative or defensive just because the company has grown so dramatically.

Step Two: Time Frame and Sequence

You will have 90 minutes, including any question and answer time. You will kickoff the session after the vice president's brief welcome and introduction. There will be a 15-minute break after your talk, followed by break-out sessions to discuss the impact of what you provided on several key issues the company is currently facing. These will be facilitated by midlevel managers.

Step Three: The Key Learning Points

Ninety minutes is a relatively brief duration. At best, you'll want to stress only a few learning points around the three outcomes specified. You might choose different ones, but for the purposes of my example, I'll choose four:

1. Problem solving is the enemy of innovation and usurps its time and focus unless innovation is formalized as a process.

2. Organizations reward what they truly value, and people act in consequence of those rewards. Since managers are exemplars, they must continue to reward in the future the creativity and innovation that has marked the company's past and current success.

3. We mercilessly examine the reasons for failure, but seldom examine the causes of our success. This is a successful group. We need to articulate the reasons for our own successes to date so that we can replicate, communicate, and improve upon them.

4. There are generic sources of innovation that exist in most companies. Let's take a look at them and determine how to spot and exploit them in this company.

Note that the learning points combine the short- and long-term outcomes and also combine prescriptive (here are 10 sources) and diagnostic (Why have we been so successful?) processes. This is simply another illustration of varied learning—the Adult Rule.

Step Four: Rough Draft Assembly

I'd now place the learning points in the order that makes most sense from a flow and interest standpoint. My choice is to start with point 1 as a source of controversy and then go to point 2 to demonstrate that they control their own environment through rewards and examples. Points 3 and 4 will be virtually concurrent and will allow me to end on a "high" with praise for their successes to date.

Step Five: Supporting Stories, Examples, and Transitions

Support your points with stories (remember the Originality/Validity and Relevance Rules), examples, and transitions from one major point to the next. For my point about problem solving, I'll support it with:

- a definition of problem solving and of innovation

- an audience exercise to test whether they tend to be problem solvers or innovators (they'll be more innovative than they think, and be pleasantly surprised)
- an assessment of how much time the organization is spending on each pursuit
- examples of organizations which have problem solved themselves right out of existence (they fixed old things really well and created new things really poorly)
- a transition to conclude this section that will determine what organizational rewards have supported problem solving and which have supported innovation, and determine whether they should be fine-tuned to further accent the latter

Note that you don't begin with the stories and examples that you always use. Some of them might well fit, but if you begin with them and build the speech around them, you've merely duplicated someone else's presentation for a client who needs his or her own.

Step Six: Visual Aids and Handouts

Given your time frame, environment, major points, and supporting material, what is appropriate for visuals (computer-generated, slides, overheads, easel sheets, video, etc.), demonstrations, presession handouts, and postsession leave-behinds? Does the material have its best impact distributed in advance or provided as reinforcement? Vary your audio/visual/textual material given the Adult Rule.[9]

Note that you do not start with handouts or visuals that you happen to have around—even if you've spent a fortune on them—and determine how they fit. Many of them might, but if you start with these, you're starting with someone else's outcomes.

In this example, I'll use slides with 50 people if I can assure that the room will be lighted comfortably but still provide contrast on the screen.[10] I'm going to use a summary handout at the end of my session, but nothing during it, because I don't like people's attention divided between my message and interaction and their attempts to follow text in front of them. I'll recommend that people take notes if they so choose, because many people learn better by writing down key points.

If you opt for a separate question and answer session, build it into the latter part of the body of the speech; do not save it for the closing.

---

[9]And if any of you use those sophomoric, simplistic, "fill-in-the-blank" workbooks (e.g., "We must ____ the audience to get its attention."), then go back to page 1 and start reading this book more slowly.

[10]See the appendix for a chart suggesting strengths, weaknesses, and appropriate uses of different types of visuals.

Step Seven: Build the Opening and Closing

What you've worked on to this point is the *body* of the speech or workshop. Step seven is absolutely the most important—and the briefer the presentation, the more important it usually is—but it can't be effectively created until this point. Since the opening and closing are directly related, I find it best to create them at the same time, bearing in mind the Perspective Rule.

Look at your outcomes and key learning points and ask yourself how you can open your presentation and create this result: *The audience is motivated to listen intently.* This involves the following criteria:

1. There is a "hook" (the Relevance Rule) to gain their enthusiastic commitment (not merely compliance). A story, humor, a challenging fact about the company, citing your interviews with participants, a contradiction, or a provocation can all be used to set the hook. Use what's comfortable for you and most appropriate for the topic.

2. Apprise them of what's to come. Prepare the audience for the points you'll be making by *briefly* summarizing you route. This allows people to anticipate and begin to plan their own learning. (If you're using handouts in advance, this is a good time to refer to them.) Now's the time to "tell them what you're going to tell them," albeit with some flair and variety.

3. Make a smooth transition to your first point, and before anyone knows it, they're committed to listening and the process has begun.

For a keynote speech, a good introduction is usually no longer than 2–3 minutes.[11]

> *The opening and closing are the most important parts of any presentation because they inform the audience members why they are there, gain their commitment to learn, and then provide the outcomes in terms of key departure points and calls to action.*

---

[11]For longer presentations, introductions are often thought to include people introducing themselves to neighbors or even briefly explaining why they've come to the session. This is "icebreaker" involvement, but it's really about mechanics and comfort, not about learning objectives and motivation. Even with day-long seminars, you'll need an effective opening to the topic, or people may have become comfortable in the environment but still not know why they're in it.

My opening will begin with a funny story of bureaucracy I encountered with a client who wound up being unable to contact his own office because of the intricacies of his voice-mail system. I'll then talk about how this company's organization has managed to avoid such indignities and some of the reasons that I've seen and heard in the phone interviews (which will focus on the outcomes). I'll also plan to refer to one of the vice president's remarks from his brief opening to create a continuity of theme.

The closing (tell them what you've told them) should result from a review of the outcomes and points that have been raised in the body of the speech and contain two elements:

1. *Key Learning Points* (*KLPs*).   The KLPs are those points which you want the participants to retain. They are centered on the outcomes. You should formally summarize them at the end, and any supporting handout material or follow-up material should focus on them. There should be relatively few, since people's focus is limited. In my speech, the learning points might include:

   ■ With every new challenge, first try to innovate (not problem solve).
   ■ Choose the three sources of innovation most relevant to their jobs.
   ■ Reinforce and reward those behaviors they're already doing so well.

2. *Call to Action.*   This step usually isn't necessary in speeches meant to entertain or merely inform, but it's too often neglected in all others. What does the buyer want people to do when they leave the session? This is the most immediate of all the outcomes. In my speech, I'll choose only one call to action:

   ■ In the break-out sessions which follow, take an innovative approach to each challenge your facilitator presents and immediately try to raise the standard, not repair the damage. (Thus, my opening has carried forward a remark from my introducer, and my closing has transitioned into the following agenda item.)

Never end a session with questions and answers. If you don't take them spontaneously during your talk, then pause just before your conclusion to make the offer. Don't feel obligated to end with a funny story, although humor often works quite well in the closing. Finally, don't let your ego allow you to believe that the closing is about you, standing ovations, and ratings on "smile sheets." The closing is about *implementing the key learning points that will lead to the buyer's desired outcomes.* If you do that, you'll be rehired and referred to others. If you don't do that, your ovation and 10 rating will get you only a fleeting memory.

Step Eight: Practice the Speech and Adjust the Timing

Only after you're sure that you have the proper elements and outcomes supported should you adjust the timing. Practice the speech just as you would deliver it at the event, allowing for the introduction,[12] a few questions and brief responses, and a few seconds of laughs where you might expect them. (If you get laughs where you don't expect them, you've got more trouble than just poor timing.)

If your speech is too short, then add examples around each supporting point for the outcomes. A good example takes about 2 minutes and solidifies learning, so these are your best bet. If you're using visual aids, consider a couple of additional supporting ones. For longer presentations, consider more audience involvement in the form of role-plays, application, small-group work, and/or facilitated discussion.

If your speech is too long, then try to remove any superfluous stories or visuals that you've included for comfort or cosmetics that aren't really essential to the outcomes. If you've included a predetermined question and answer period, shorten it or eliminate it and offer to answer what questions there are as they come up *as time permits.* Consider shortening your opening if it contains icebreakers and logistics. (Most icebreakers are for the speaker's comfort, anyway, not the participants'.[13])

Remember, it's better to be slightly short than slightly long. If you find that you can't reduce the speech to the allotted time without gutting essential elements, then you've probably taken on too much topic for too short a time frame, and it's best to go back to the buyer and suggest either a longer time frame or fewer outcomes.

The practice and timing should also allow you to change stories, sequences, transitions, and other aspects of the presentation for maximum logic and flow. Record your practice and listen to it a day or so later. Ask others to comment. You'll find that you'll have a fine speech if you adhere to the simple criteria from the perspective of buyer outcomes and audience learning.

---

[12]*Always* provide your own introduction. Never send material and suggest that the introducer select what's appropriate, and never rely on the introducer having (a) received it or (b) practiced it. Call your introducer ahead of time. Bring an extra copy of the introduction to the event, because the one you sent will have been misplaced. Keep it brief, have it double-spaced in bold type on large paper, and then tell the introducer to be sure to read it as it appears. Sometimes a large calibre pistol helps.

[13]I kid you not, I once saw two "professional" speakers run a 90-minute icebreaker for 25 people before allowing the featured speakers to take the stage. Those of us waiting to go on roared with laughter, until we had to go up there and fix their mess.

The Five Rules and Eight Steps for Creating a Speech

The Five Rules

Rule One: The Originality/Validity Rule. The speech should be yours.

Rule Two: The Relevance Rule. Stories and anecdotes should be germane.

Rule Three: The Perspective Rule. People learn best when they are comfortable.

Rule Four: The Outcome Rule. The buyer's condition should be improved.

Rule Five: The Adult Rule. People learn in different ways.

The Eight Steps

Step One: Outcomes

Step Two: Time Frame and Sequence

Step Three: The Key Learning Points

Step Four: Rough Draft Assembly

Step Five: Supporting Stories, Examples, and Transitions

Step Six: Visual Aids and Handouts

Step Seven: Build the Opening and Closing

Step Eight: Practice the Speech and Adjust the Timing

9

Becoming a Star

"Hey, I've seen you someplace."
"Of course you have."

Refusing Business Is
Good Business

There is an anchor in the speaking business that drags along the bottom and impedes your progress, at times even leaving you dead in the water. The anchor is called "early success."

All of us can cite the first client, first paid speech, first opportunity to actually earn a livelihood as a professional speaker. The problem is that it is almost invariably business we wouldn't accept today. Here are 10 dynamics that tend to change as we gain expertise, confidence, and repute in the speaking business:

Topics Evolve. As we grow and learn, and as society and business evolve, we move to increasingly relevant and topical themes. We might have begun with "Improving Customer Service Impact" and grown to include "Managing the Customer Service Professional" or created "The Customer-Focused Organization." As our skills and learning increase, we might move into entirely new fields as well: "Embracing Diversity As Sound Business Practice."

Fees Increase. This had better be happening regularly. If you don't believe it, start the book again at Chapter 1.

Methodology Changes. We might begin with a heavy accent on lecture and full-group questions and answers, and later incorporate small teams and break-out facilitation. More commonly, we move from the "expert" position of newcomers to the "consensus" position of veterans, allowing key points to emerge from the group. Usually, as speakers grow, they become less "scripted" and more spontaneous, appearing to be less of a rehearsed performer and more of an extemporaneous authority.

Technology Changes. Many of us began with easels and whiteboards. Today, computer-generated graphics are common. Satellite transmission, video conference, and teleconference are all growing avenues of audience interaction.

Duration Shortens. What were once multiday seminars tend to shrink to single days because the client wants less time off the job or the work included as part of a larger conference. Speakers with the requisite skills will tend to move toward half-day workshops and keynotes because there are higher fees available for less time on-site. One sure sign of speaker growth is that we can make the same points we used to in a third of the time.

Buyers Change. We often begin working through a seminar house that employs us as subcontractors. Or we sell to training directors and meeting planners. But if we're any good, that sale should move to line executives and/or be made by bureaus representing us.

Industries Expand. Many people enter speaking through an industry that they had been a part of. An insurance agent adept at training becomes a speaker focusing on insurance sales. However, once positioned, that speaker can use the same sales expertise to address mortgage lenders, financial planners, and bankers. Eventually, our former agent addresses any sales group, regardless of industry.

Audience Level Increases. When we begin, both we and the buyer trust us with "safe" groups, usually front-line supervisors, new recruits, and/or low-paying customers. If we're good, we become comfortable addressing anyone, and there is a great need for talented, confident people who can address senior executives, "grizzled veterans," and tough, skeptical groups.

Additional Services Grow. The lateral moves to group facilitator, emcee, after-dinner speaker, panel moderator, consultant, speech coach, and related roles are relatively easy for highly accomplished, well-regarded professionals.

Products Emerge. From the first taped session that produced a small cassette album, the entrepreneurial speaker creates books, booklets, videos, performance aids, mentoring help, newsletters, hotlines, and a myriad of other additional revenue streams.

In view of these inevitable changes that affect good speakers, we have to be able to "let go" in order to reach out. This means that old business, no matter how instrumental to your early career (viz., you would have missed the mortgage payment without it) will serve as that anchor, snagging you on the bottom, unless you cut it loose. *At least every other year, you should abandon the bottom 10–15 percent of your business!*

Only by removing business at the bottom of your priorities can you gain the ability to reach out and embrace business at the top of your priorities.

I've met and mentored hundreds of speakers who don't have the "time" to expand their businesses. Their response is to hire marketers, subcontract business, turn down engagements, and generally, tear their hair and rend their garments. The problem, however, is always the same: They treat all business equally, no matter how much it pays or whether it is congruent with their own growth plans, and they cling to old business as though it were still an umbilical cord.

Every December, review your past year's business. Ask yourself these questions:

- Is it at the fee level I want, or even my average fee level?
- Am I growing, or can I do this in my sleep?
- Do they really require my talents, or can anyone do it?
- Is this adding to my image and repute?
- Would I be proud to cite this as a reference of my current talents?
- Have I been doing the exact same thing for over 2 years?
- Have I become a habit rather than a resource?

If the answers to the first five are "no" and the final two are "yes," get out now. In fact, if even half of these answers go the wrong way, give the business away. Talk to the customer and explain the reasons, refer a trusted colleague (someone who is where you were a few years ago), or offer to do a few more engagements and then gracefully bow-out in a smooth transition.

Every day I see people whose literature still reflects the fact that they began in the business 10 years ago as a ventriloquist, singing bus driver, car dealer, or beauty contest winner. But they've changed and could be proceeding at a much quicker pace if the anchor weren't still dragging behind them.

Avoiding Meat Markets

There is a pernicious trend in the industry, almost always by people who should know better, to create speakers in a single image, thereby establishing a commodity which buyers can readily choose from based upon price and, worse, appearance. I have heard meeting planners say that they demand demo videos because they want to make a selection based upon the speaker's "appeal" to the audience. That means, translated, their gender, ethnicity, race, physical attributes, and other traits that should never enter the decision. When I recommended a colleague for an assignment beneath my fee level at a Fortune 100 company, the meeting planner told me flat out: "We don't want a woman for this audience."

That, my friends, is not only unethical and moronic, but it also happens to be illegal. Welcome to the world of "speaker as commodity."

Fortunately, we control our marketing and our image, unless we surrender it. To make a million in this business requires a singularity, not a march into the crowd. So the following advice might be contrarian and countercultural, but the only people making really big money in this business are contrarian and countercultural by definition. Here's how to avoid being displayed in a storefront with the rest of the merchandise, often marked down by the end of the month. (In a classic movie scene, a character played by Bette Midler was kidnapped, but the abductors had to negotiate their demands because her husband didn't really want her back. Hearing the criminals haggling and their ransom demands plummeting, Midler screams, "Oh my God, I've been kidnapped by Kmart!")

- Eschew "showcases" and other "auditions" hosted by bureaus and third parties. Some bureaus will tell you that all successful speakers participate and will drop names of people you know and respect. The problem is that it's often not true (my name has been used, and I've never gone near one). These events will feature dozens of speakers, each doing 20 or 30 minutes over the course of a full day for "buyers" who usually aren't. Inevitably, low-level recommenders attend, and even legitimate buyers become glazed after the eighth or ninth consecutive spiel. Moreover, there is a charge to appear (plus your travel expenses), which means that the third parties are profiting, which also means that they accept almost anyone who will pay the freight. These showcases are therefore often filled with novices, neophytes, and people new to the profession (or who haven't been able to climb in the profession), which affects the total quality. I've never viewed appearing in a showcase as a high-value image for the participant and have often used the reverse psychology: "I don't appear in them because I don't have to."

- Be very selective about bureaus. We've alluded to this in earlier chapters, but I want to stress here that, while a bureau's interest seems like a sign from the gods when we're starting out, it can become an onerous relationship if it's not collaborative once we're successful. Bureaus that insist that they, not you, own the client, that insist on promotional materials that don't reveal your own contact points, and that present you as simply a body in their stable aren't bringing you any value, even if they place you a few times a year. You are the one paying the bureau *through your commission to them.* You are the one who should make demands, not them. There are some superb bureau principals in the field, all of whom I would trust with my wallet and, more important, my reputation. (I can always replace a wallet.) But there are some which, if you watch carefully, you'll see hiding in the bushes in *Jurassic Park* and *Lost World,* along with the stegosaurs and raptors. The profession has changed, but they haven't.

- Don't create a "canned" video. Demonstration videos can be quite effective. I've functioned well with and without them, and contrary to popular industry opinion, my corporate buyers only request them about 25 percent of the time. I find that executive buyers virtually never request them. Meeting planners (and therefore, bureaus) require them 80 percent of the time. I recommend that you don't use one of the mass marketers of these services to create one. Several of these production houses are excellent and provide near-flawless quality work. But that's the problem. The result is "perfect," and the products all look the same, no matter who is on them. I'd recommend that you hire a quality video production group that normally does industrial shows (the ones who provide the projection onto large screens at trade conventions are almost always excellent) or a local operation that shoots advertising and promotion spots. Have them capture a live performance with a client, using one or two cameras on you and another for audience reaction. The key is to show the "live," unadulterated quality of your work. My original demo video, which I continue to use, is taken from a cassette that was in the camera projecting me on one of those large screens. Neither the lighting nor the sound is perfect, but then neither is any speech I've ever delivered.

- If you're going to advertise or appear in listings, put yourself in the potential buyer's shoes. Advertising in magazines or "puff pieces" with a quadrillion other speakers isn't exactly singular. Appearing in a special "speaker's issue" or in the house organ of a speakers bureau is hardly distinctive. Advertise and promote in unique settings. In every airline magazine I've ever read, Chester Karras, the negotiations expert, has a multipage ad. Flying back from Barcelona on Iberia Airlines, sure enough, I found his ad in Spanish in Iberia's in-flight magazine! I'm not advocating this expense (though it reflects what you can do when you make a million in this business), but you might try trade association publications, business periodicals, and educational magazines if you want to stand out in the crowd. Some speakers swear by advertising; others (myself included) largely ignore it. My point is, if you're going to do it, don't do it like everyone else.

- Beware of coaches. There are a lot of speaking coaches who are not very good speakers. Okay, I'm willing to buy the fact that great sports coaches don't need to have been superb athletes. But I do want the person who taught my doctor how to operate to have been a hell of a good surgeon. Therein is my problem, and yours. I can generally tell a coached speaker from 100 yards. They exaggerate their platform movements and gestures. They articulate in ways not consistent with their meter and rhythm. They insert unnaturally long pauses. They overdo eye contact. They move around so much that they distract from their message. They appear to be delivering a piece from *Macbeth* and not merely a new sales technique. They artificially laugh (or worse, cry) at something they've obviously rehearsed and performed 4000 times. Coaches tend to remove the wonderfully imperfect distinctions about us and create smooth, unremarkable performers. I think most coaches are frustrated actors (or unsuccessful speakers). Stay away from them. We all need feedback. Buy a tape recorder and get a friend. This is neither rocket science nor Broadway. It's hard to accept, but when we're struggling in this business, the answer is in ourselves, not someone else.

Generally, a little judicious advice will improve anyone and retain their singularity. However, a great deal of paid "expert" advice will transform people into the output from a common cookie-cutter mold.

The Art of the Leave-Behind

Perhaps the single, elementary marketing ploy that both newcomers and veterans overlook is to leave behind some indication that you've been at the client. Now I know that sounds ridiculous after your dynamic, warmly received, exquisite presentation, but here is the normal sequence of events:

1. We're terrible at customer service. Get that Robert Leonard in here.

2. That Robert Leonard is a fabulous help in customer service!

3. Robert Leonard provides us with useful techniques.

4. Robert Leonard shows us why we're already good, which is nice to hear.

5. Leonard provides us with some tips.

6. We're really good at service. Why do we need Leonard?

7. Who was that guy who used to come in here for some reason?

8. No, we've never had customer service help.

One of the adverse impacts of successfully transferring skills and transforming organizations is that the learning becomes internalized, reinforced through continual application, and its sources quickly obscured. Such is the lot of effective speakers.

Even in organizations in which the buyer can readily recall your name, hundreds or even thousands of participants, who might recommend you (or in trade association audiences, be buyers themselves), will not remember your name a week later. A lot of standing ovations turned out to have been bestowed on "that speaker who kicked off Thursday morning" or "the presenter just before the dinner cruise." Don't kid yourself—you have to manage your own immortality.

Hence, the leave-behind. If you use workbooks, handouts, and other material for reference and support in your presentation, these are not embraced in my definition of "leave-behind" because, often, they're simply "left." People seldom refer to lengthy handouts and usually even disregard their own notes (the more copious, the greater the chance they'll be ignored).[1] You need something that is useful, either as information or diversion, and you need to be readily accessible. If people have to work more than a few seconds to try to remember you, they will abandon the pursuit.

People are asked for recommendations for speakers every day. They usually will cite someone they've personally heard. At that moment of recollection, you must be accessible.

---

[1]Many years ago, a consulting firm I was with by the name of Kepner-Tregoe conducted an informal study of how its clients retained information from its training workshops. We found that over 80 percent of the ensuing usage and application was purely from memory, without recourse to our substantive textual materials.

I use a plastic card. It measures $4\frac{5}{8}$ by $3\frac{1}{2}$ (I deliberately wanted it to be larger than a credit card) and looks like the illustration on the front and the back.

I placed my name on both sides, with full contact information on one side. I created this after seeing participants at a Hewlett-Packard speech take an easel sheet I had written on and hang it on the wall in their department. Not unreasonably, I figured I had made a few points of some practical use. But I also realized that no one was going to identify me or call me based upon an analysis of the handwriting on that sheet (which subsequently became typed and distributed).

The points on my card are those that I make in the majority of my keynotes. You might create different cards for different groups or provide a wall chart, memo pad, or calendar. The alternative is up to you (although I personally dislike coffee mugs, T-shirts, and toys because they don't provide the same image of practical application of ideas), as long as you leave *something*. And don't confuse product sales with leave-behinds. The former is a revenue stream device which may or may not create long-term recognition and may or may not be obtained. The latter is an attempt to provide a practical connection to your name for every participant at every speech.

Create a leave-behind now, no matter what your level of speaking, no matter what your fees, no matter where you are on the path to your million. It is an automatic marketing tool that has the potential to reach every single participant in every single engagement. You can't afford not to do this. In the worst case, begin with your business card distributed at every seat. It's not good, but it's something.

Years ago, I received a call from someone at Bell Northern Research who asked if I'd be available to speak at an upcoming conference. We closed the deal right there on the phone.

"How did you find me?" I naturally inquired.

"Oh, my predecessor left a set of your tapes in my desk. Apparently, he got them at a conference he attended at which you were the keynoter. I finally got around to listening the them the other day. You know, you're not bad . . . "

The ultimate leave-behind!

(side one)   *Focus on Five Factors*

1. **Keep raising the bar**
   Innovation over problem solving
2. **Achieve results and outcomes**
   Means are less important than *ends*
3. **Empower: power doesn't corrupt**
   Powerlessness creates bureaucracy
4. **People only believe what they see**
   Exemplars, not banners in the hall
5. **Perception is reality**
   Wear the *other person's* shoes

Thanks for attending!
Alan Weiss, Ph.D.
Summit Consulting Group, Inc.
Box 1009
East Greenwich, RI 02818
800/766-7935
Fax: 401/884-5068
e-mail: 71525.553@compuserve.com
home page: http://www.summitconsulting.com

(side two)

"Empowerment means being able to make decisions which influence the outcome of your work."

—Alan Weiss, Ph.D.

How and When to Raise Fees
(Boldly and Often)

We discussed how to set fees in Chapter 4, where many of you probably began this book. In a pleasant surprise for those readers, I'd like to briefly return to the topic here to deal with a very discrete and vital issue: When and how do you raise them *once you're successful?*

The conventional and mundane approach to raising fees is to do so when demand exceeds supply. Assuming that you can speak once every working day and on most weekends, that's about 350 engagements a year, taking holidays off and assuming you never want to see your kid's soccer game or go to the theater with a friend. Of course, if you were efficient with your schedule and specialized in keynotes, you could easily fit in two talks a day, which means that you'd have to reach about 700 engagements before demand exceeded supply.

There are only three things wrong with this philosophy:

1. Demand never exceeds supply, unless your fees are so low that you're irresistible. But even if you charged as much as $1000 an engagement and adhered to my fictitious schedule, you'd still be making less than I do working only 20 percent as hard.

2. This is a highly competitive profession in which overexposure can quickly kill you. You're not going to keynote at the major trade association 2 years in a row, and you're not going to conduct workshops in time management again for the same people you trained last month. New technologies and approaches often make "mass" fads obsolete. Transactional analysis, left-brain/right-brain thinking, and sensitivity training have all had their day. Value is in rarity, not commonality.

3. The objective is to enjoy life, not sacrifice it. Speaking is a means to an end, which should be the healthy, prosperous, and secure future for your family and loved ones. Ergo, especially once you've become known and successful, the idea is to get paid more for doing less, not less for doing more.

The key, then, is to boldly raise fees *whenever your value to the client (and prospects) increases.* This is a manageable process, which is part of its great allure. That is, value may be in the eye of the beholder, but you can help to influence what the buyer beholds. Here are 10 conditions for knowing when to raise fees. Note that many of them constitute strategies which you can initiate and propel. All of them assume that you are running a successful practice, which is growing in bookings, repute, and breadth.

10 Conditions That Support Raising Fees

1. A Major Publisher Has Published a Book You've Written

This has to be a known commercial publisher, not a vanity press or a self-published work.[2] Once you have a publication date, raise your fees—*this might be 6 months in advance of its actual release.* Cite yourself as the author of the book by title, to be released on January 23 of next year. Depending upon your existing fee structure, a significant hard-cover book should increase your fees by $1000 to $2500, and if it's widely reviewed and generates major media appearances, even more than that.

2. You Obtain Major Media Exposure

I'm not talking about drive-time radio here, but rather a spot on *Oprah* or *Larry King,* for example. You want to promote this as, "As seen on *Oprah Winfrey*" or "As interviewed by ABC's Ted Koppel . . ." This is not as difficult as it may appear. A friend of mine, Greg Godek, writes self-published books on how to be romantic (*1001 Ways to Be Romantic*). He's appeared on more major talk shows than Madonna (including a spot on *Good Morning America* with his 40-foot "love bus" tour). Another friend, Robert Siciliano, wrote a self-published book on how to be safe when traveling (*The Safety Minute*) and managed an appearance on the *Montel Williams Show.* They, and a raft of other people in similar circumstances, don't necessarily gain direct bookings from the appearance, nor even sell a great deal of product. But they are then able to place prominently on their materials, bureau packages, fact sheets, and mailbox: "As seen on the nationally syndicated *Montel Williams Show*" or "As interviewed by Joan London and Charlie Gibson on *Good Morning America.*"

3. You Develop Blue-Chip References

I carry my reference sheet right in my briefcase and include it in every press kit. I've never said to any prospect, "References can be supplied upon request." It sounds too much like I'd have to wake up my cousins

---

[2]Self-published books are fine as products with high profit margins, but they do nothing for marketing credibility or worth in the buyer's eyes. Ignore claims to the contrary by the vanity press people—only a tiny fraction of self-published books has ever achieved any note in the professional market. Self-published and commercially published are not mutually exclusive; I do both, with differing objectives for each.

and tell them to expect a call from a stranger asking personal questions about my past. I thrust my references into the buyer's lap because they reflect that buyer's peers (or superiors) in analogous organizations. I've placed 15 on a single sheet because they fill up the sheet completely, as if there are plenty more which simply couldn't be squeezed on (which happens to be true for any of us who have made it in this business). Their titles, addresses, and phone numbers are sitting right there, so accessible and so convenient *that the prospect virtually never calls them!* After all, who would have the chutzpah to cite these people if they weren't really enthusiastic supporters? The higher level and more known the people on your reference list, the better your position to charge higher fees representing the value you've brought to the buyer's peers.

4. You Provide a Rare Breadth of Talents

Clients have asked me to present the opening keynote and then facilitate break-out groups. They've asked me to modify a presentation so that it can be given briefly to officers, in more depth to middle managers, and be integrated into sessions delivered by in-house trainers for supervisors. I've been asked to address boards of directors, to deliver a humorous talk after dinner, and to emcee an awards ceremony. Buyers have asked me to design a brief test so that the audience can rate themselves against the attributes I'm presenting during the talk and have asked if I'd make the predominant part of my presentation a question and answer format. I've spoken in auditoriums with projection onto large screens, in amphitheaters, in classrooms, over board tables, and in cinder block, bunker-like, subterranean basements. I've spoken to international groups, people with varying English skills, and people who utilized simultaneous translation. Some of my colleagues have spoken on buses, trains, boats, and planes. The more you can do, and the more different the ways in which you can do it, the more valuable you are.

5. You Write a Monthly Column (or Are Interviewed Regularly)

Many speakers have been able to write monthly (or weekly) syndicated columns that appear in business publications all over the country. I once mentored a fellow who had the monthly last-page humor column in *Management Review,* the magazine of the American Management Association. He was unhappy about his fees not being higher! It had never occurred to him to leverage his extraordinary monthly visibility.

Other people are interviewed frequently because of the nature of their expertise (e.g., negotiating skills) or a set of accomplishments (e.g., writing humor for politicians) or because they have an aggressive public relations firm constantly presenting them to national writers. If you can get into the public eye to the point that you can cite the interviews and provide the tear sheets, you can raise your fees because of your repute. (It doesn't matter whether the buyer has read the piece; it only matters that you can show the buyer the piece.)

6. Your Business Has Been Growing and Your Fees Haven't Changed for 2 Years

This is an arbitrary measure, but I've found it to be a very powerful one. If your bookings have been increasing over a 2-year period (and you're following my earlier advice about eliminating the bottom 10–15 percent) at a constant fee level, then you can safely raise your fees in the third year without fear of losing potential customers.[3] My practice is to raise fees for all new clients, but honor the old fee structure for existing clients (with the exception of point 7 below) because existing, valued clients shouldn't subsidize new ones by paying higher fees than they are (which is why I'm outraged when publications provide better subscription deals for new customers than for their renewal customers).

7. Your Existing Clients Ask You to Do Something New and Different

The one exception—and opportunity—to raising fees with existing clients is when they ask you to do something novel. For example, I've been asked to provide feedback to management on the results of speeches across the country, to design programs specific to a given organization, and to learn technical aspects of a company's operations in order to create relevant applications. Others have asked for a transfer of copyright for the program or have wanted to create audio- and video-tapes to incorporate into their training programs after I've concluded the assignment. All of these "one-off" requests allow you to structure a proposal above and beyond what you've normally provided in return for

---

[3]You won't lose current customers because you should never raise fees for current customers for identical work. However, you can ask for concessions: "I'll honor my past fee arrangement even though my fees have increased. However, I would ask that the entire fee be paid in advance to secure the date." If you don't want to honor past fees because they're simply too low, then either raise the fee or abandon the work.

the clearly enhanced value the client is requesting. If you feel you have
to do these things merely to retain the customer, and therefore cannot
charge for their value, then there is something seriously wrong either
with the relationship or, more likely, with your perception of how much
value you're providing.

8. You May Be Asked to Do Something You Can Do, but Don't Like to Do

I despise full-day sessions. I find them labor intensive, long, and unin-
teresting (for me). However, some clients rightfully demand them to
take advantage of the expense of bringing their people together off-site
(and others demand them incorrectly because the equate length with
worth). My response was to develop a tiered fee structure that was extraordinarily expensive at the full-day rate. However, occasionally a client
says, "Just do it. The value far exceeds the cost." And you know what? I
find I really enjoy doing it at that rate of pay! Whether it's the length, as
in my case, or the type of audience (salespeople) or the environment
(after dinner) or the geography (more than a 2-hour plane ride) or the
circumstances (three identical concurrent sessions in a row), you have
the right to charge very high fees for things you're capable of doing but
don't like to do.

9. You're Asked to Do International Work

My feeling is that you should always charge a premium for international
work (and, no offense meant to anyone, you can easily include Alaska
and Hawaii in this category, but rarely Canada). Trips to Europe, Africa,
and Asia are especially grueling in terms of time changes, and South
America is little better even though the clocks don't change as radically.
I've found that I need a full day of acclimation, on the ground, prior to
the session, and for my own health, an intelligent return, which isn't
always the first flight out after the applause ends. In addition, logistics
are difficult: Paper size is often different, electrical current varies, words
and phrases must be altered, examples changed, delivery modified to
accommodate language requirements, customs paid on materials
shipped, visas secured, money exchanged, and so on. Even for existing
clients, and certainly for new ones, a significant premium is appropriate
for international assignments. My suggestion is to take your existing fee
structure and charge a 50–100 percent premium for international

assignments, depending on your confidence level and the other factors noted here.[4] Beware of the people offering you a "tour" of multiple bookings in their countries for a package deal. You'll lose your shirt. Once you board the airplane they've got you, unless their check has already cleared your bank.

10. You Are in a Nondifferentiated Fee Range

Let's say you're charging $3500, working frequently, and growing your business. However, you know that you're in a fee band ($2500–$4000) that contains 90 percent of your competitors at your level of expertise and success. My suggestion is to get out of there because you have to become more distinct. *Buyers believe they get what they pay for.* Their expectations (and their egos—"I hired a $10,000 speaker for our conference") are greater for a $5000 speaker than for a $2500 speaker. No buyer I've ever met said *before the speech,* "This is $5000 worth of talent, and we're getting it for only $2000!" I believe that you can increase business by increasing your fees. Yes, you read that sentence correctly.[5] (I don't believe, by the way, that you create differentiation by doing bizarre things like charging $4800, which some "experts" advise, as if the buyer is too stupid to know that it's an attempt to be sneaky-close to $5000.) If you're good at what you do and in the midst of a crowd, step out by raising fees to escape the masses. The only people who follow will be the buyers.

> *Make no mistakes. Buyers believe they get what they pay for. Your fee actually creates an expectation range and ties-in to the buyer's ego as well.*

[4]By the way, *always* get paid in U.S. dollars drawn on U.S. banks, preferably in advance. There are laws against taking too much currency into and out of some countries (including the United States), and exchange rates will often kill you. In addition, U.S. banks charge a premium to cash and convert checks drawn on foreign banks, sometimes as high as 25 percent of the total. Attend to this contractually in your proposal.

[5]You can easily increase *wealth*. Speaking 10 times for $7500 is much more lucrative than speaking 20 times for $2500. But I'm also talking about increasing *business*, that is, speaking 20 times for $7500.

Let's take a final look at my 10 conditions for boldly raising fees:

1. *A major publisher has published a book you've written.*
2. *You obtain major media exposure.*
3. *You develop blue-chip references.*
4. *You provide a rare breadth of talents.*
5. *You write a monthly column (or are interviewed regularly).*
6. *Your business has been growing and your fees haven't changed for 2 years.*
7. *Your existing clients ask you to do something new and different.*
8. *You may be asked to do something you can do, but don't like to do.*
9. *You're asked to do international work.*
10. *You are in a nondifferentiated fee range.*

How many of these conditions are you actively managing? Points 1 through 6 are certainly within your direct control to influence, points 7 through 9 require a sensitivity to the environment on your part, and point 10 demands an ongoing scrutiny.

No one grows by correcting weaknesses. We grow by building on strengths. If you've reached the levels of success in this business that this book is meant to engender and support, it's remiss not to "turbocharge" your continued growth and prosperity.

How and when do you raise fees? Boldly and often. No one else, you see, is looking to do it for you.

PART 3
Sizzle

10
Platform Skills

**"Your speech lasted 3 minutes.
There were dull stretches."**

The Medium Is Not the Message

First, a definition: "Platform skills" are those techniques you employ as a speaker during your delivery to enhance the receptivity of your message. Most of the books on speaking and many of the "authorities" will attempt to convince you that these techniques are the most important part of the profession and that their mastery is essential to becoming a successful speaker.

They are wrong. We've already raised the errors in citing Mehrabian's work as supporting this view. The key to successful speaking *is to be able to make a living at it,* which means that marketing and content are the two most important aspects. You do not improve the client's condition with delivery techniques; you mostly improve your own.

Then why do so many people advocate and focus on the acquisition and development of platform skills as the key to success? The answer is simple: That's the area where money is to be made as a coach. There aren't many people adept at coaching in marketing (although there are some very good ones), and there are even fewer skilled in advising on content and developing presentations. Those are tough areas, but the critical ones, which is why the prior nine chapters of this book have focused on them. Platform skills, however, can be taught by anyone, partly because they're relatively simple and partly because they're highly subjective. A great many unsuccessful speakers, bureau principals, consultants, and sundry others have found that it can be lucrative to teach people speaking mechanics.

But the medium is not the message in this business, Marshall McLuhan notwithstanding. No one has ever walked away from a speech saying, "Get that speaker back next month. Did you see how well she used hand gestures?" or "That was the most important speech I've ever heard. Did you notice how often he asked us to raise our hands?" People remember a speech by commenting, "I'm still using that planning technique he showed us a year ago," and "I refer to her notes on reducing stress at least once a month."

> **Content is audience-centered; platform skills are speaker-centered. The only function of the latter is to enhance the former.**

The techniques used on the platform are important insofar as they augment the content of one's presentation, thereby enhancing the client's condition. This applies whether the presentation is an hour or a day, a keynote or a seminar, upbeat or serious. Even for humorists, the nature of the story is everything, although it can be augmented through physical technique. Yet, I've seen humorists who had me rolling in the aisle while they never moved from a fixed microphone.

Having said all that, there is a place for the development of platform skills, but my belief is that it demands a chapter, not a book. I had to put it someplace, and it seemed most appropriate here in the "sizzle" part of the book. Herein, then, a relatively few pages on those techniques which require attention in order to enhance the receptivity of your message to the client.

10 Interpersonal Techniques (and Expert Devices) to Engage the Audience

1. Eye Contact

Look audience members in the eye. Even in large halls and auditoriums, you'll find that you can establish eye contact with people seated at quite a distance.[1] The more intimate the group, for instance, 20 people

---

[1]The exception occurs when you are spotlighted, making it impossible to see the audience. In this case, look at the room from the stage prior to your presentation and remember the seating layout. During your talk, keep your eyes moving to the seating arrangement as you recall it.

around a U-shaped table, the more important it is to establish personal eye contact.

In general, hold eye contact for 2 to 5 seconds. Less than that creates distracting movement, and more than that can make people uncomfortable. If someone doesn't return the contact, move on but return to them later. If they look away after two or three "invitations," then don't look at them directly again and respect their discomfort.

Eye contact is not merely to create a more direct link with the listener. It is also a primary source of nonverbal feedback for the speaker. If people are eager to return your glance, including smiles, head nodding, and similar reinforcers, you know you're striking a chord. But if people are reluctant to return the glance and are sitting dead still, then you are making them intensely uncomfortable.

> Expert device: If possible, prior to the speech, chat informally with some participants, particularly in smaller groups. Use these people as your "friendlies" and first establish eye contact (and a smile) with them. Their nonverbal behavior (return smile, nod) will quickly increase your comfort level.

2. Gestures

I once watched a speaker deliver a 90-minute speech on the distinctions between men and women with the sole aid of moving her hands to illustrate the differences between how men and women viewed life. It was extraordinarily effective.

Avoid the overly dramatic (and banal). There's seldom, ever, a need to sink down to one knee or rend one's garments. If you use a lavaliere mike, you'll have both hands free to use for illustration and support. With a hand mike, you usually can use just one. Specify which you'd prefer, but be prepared for either. The larger the group, the more you can exaggerate your gestures, since they need to be seen in the back of the hall. The smaller the group, the more you can get away with nuance and subtlety. But avoid most drama coaches' advice to make every gesture into a sweeping panoramic ballet movement. It's terribly artificial and detracts from the message.

A highly effective technique is to acknowledge the gesture itself. For example, by using your hands or arms to portray a grand event—an airplane's takeoff, bridge building, or tidal waves—you can also state, "We spare no expense on visual aids for the Acme Company."

> Expert device: Always try to practice your speech with the gestures and movements you intend to use dressed exactly as you'll be during the speech, complete with anything that will be on stage with you.

I've seen otherwise carefully prepared speakers get ties caught in mike cords and high heels caught on projector wires.

3. Inflection, Intonation, and . . . Pauses

There are actually approaches that stipulate that there are nine different pauses and conditions under which they should be used. Maybe for Al Pacino playing Hamlet, but for speakers there's simply one pause, and it occurs when they are not speaking. The only question is: How long should it be?

There are only three reasons I know of to pause, two of them deliberate and one accidental. In the case of the first two, you either want to dramatize a point or allow people some time to think. Pauses are wonderful for people who need some self-correction in their pacing because they tend to speak at full tilt. (One participant told me once that I was speaking faster than he could think, which is not exactly a condition that's going to thrill my buyer.) The third reason is that you've forgotten where you are, and at that moment, you literally have nothing to say. That's all right. Take a moment to think or return to your notes (or say to the audience, "Where was I?"). Don't fill the silence with "ums" and "ahs" and grunts. I know a fine speaker who includes a great deal of extemporaneous material in his presentation but fills every silence, while he thinks, with a loud "ummmm." I think he loses 20 percent of his effectiveness when he does this. Pauses should be brief, in any case, unless you're waiting for laughter to subside. For dramatic purposes, however, 3 to 10 seconds should do it.

Inflection and intonation concern emphasis and volume. Varying your pitch and speed are important techniques to keep the audience involved. Lowering your voice to a whisper or raising it to a shout can be very effective if you do so judiciously. Even high-volume, dynamic speakers need to learn this lesson. A colleague told me that a speaker he had invited was so fast, so dynamic, and so high-octane that no one really understood him or retained his message. "It was like a midwesterner trying to understand someone speaking Cajun," he explained. "It took so much energy just to try to listen and sort out the facts that we were too exhausted to learn anything." The best practice is with a tape recorder. Listen to your speech devoid of any visual accompaniment. Are you interesting and easy to listen to orally, or are you monotone, too fast, too slow, and/or too consistent? The "tape test" is an excellent self-assessment.

Expert device: When you are introduced to the audience, try beginning your talk with a pause. Simply establish eye contact and smile.

The room will settle down, people will be interested in what you're up to, and you'll quickly establish a locus of attention. Hold the pause for about as long as one deep breath. You'll find it focuses both you and the audience.

4. Audience Participation

Audience participation (not "involvement," since every audience had better be involved) has been transmogrified from a rarely used device in an era of "podium lectures" to a trite affectation in an era of "feel good" speeches. It makes sense to include the audience only if it enhances their receptivity and acceptance of the message, and not as some ego device for the speaker.

The very worst technique I've seen over the past several years is that of repeatedly asking the audience to raise their hands if they've shared a certain experience or if they agree with the speaker. It's one thing to say, "How many of you work directly with the customer?" in order to get a sense of the audience's disposition if you don't already know it, but it's another to say, "Raise your hands if you think I'm right," and "Raise your hands if you've been to Texas, if you like fried chicken, or if you breathe oxygen." After a second or third request, only about 10 percent of an audience will respond to this stuff, and small wonder. Unless you're trying to get some legitimate feedback or information to help guide your comments, don't do this—it's the sign of an ego-centered speaker. (Right next to it in amateurville is the instruction to the audience, "Give yourselves a nice round of applause.")

Occasionally, a presentation requires a volunteer or direct input from the audience. For example, in training sessions and workshops, it's much more common for participants to present their work, raise interactive issues, and take a significant role in the proceedings. But it's relatively rare in keynotes (and should probably be outlawed).

Depending on the nature of the presentation, the audience can be embraced through the use of handouts, brief exercises (either completed alone or, preferably, with a colleague or small group), question and answer periods, and similar exchanges. As a rule, the longer the presentation, the more critical the audience participation.

Expert device: The rhetorical question is an ideal way to increase the psychological participation of audiences. Ask a general question such as, "Think about it—how many of you have actually wanted to tell a customer to take their business elsewhere?" Or you can present a model and ask, "Where would you place your department in this grid and where do you think it should be?" These challenges create active, individual emotional participation and can be used repeatedly during even brief speeches.

5. Visual Aids

Some speakers are superb with just a mike. Others are superb with a sound and light show rivaling Disney World. The criteria are twofold: (1) what will be most effective for the audience and conditions and (2) what is most effective for your personal style.

There's a speaker who goes around claiming that "in 5 years you won't be hired if you don't have extensive, state-of-the-art visual aids." He's been saying that for 15 years, and I think most people may finally be wise to him. I've delivered the exact same speech with visual aids and without (because the conditions wouldn't permit them), and the result was virtually identical. The 10-percent effectiveness I lost without some of the visuals was regained due to the poor conditions in which they would have been shown (low ceiling and a virtual blackout to create visibility).

Everyone knows how impressive computer-generated graphics can be, but only if they make sense for the topic. (One client told me, "Don't use them. They're too distracting.") I've seen videos that show a person using an easel and marker *on the video!* Hardly a state-of-the-art usage. I've seen overhead transparencies which are simply copies of memos and reports that people already have in their materials. I've seen slides which don't relate to the topic but which were obviously included and tap-danced into the presentation because the speaker had them in her "kit." At one meeting, we had to pay to rent a slide projector so that the speaker could show three slides for a total of less than 2 minutes during a 90-minute presentation.

We are not facing nonvisual Armageddon, no matter who claims it. Use those visuals that help make your point, are friendly to the environment,[2] and are comfortable for your style. They are not a prerequisite, particularly in shorter presentations. As a rule, try not to use visual aids in an after-dinner speech. The full meal (and sometimes alcohol), the end of the day, and the presentations and conversations which no doubt have preceded you will have created high fatigue levels. Focusing on visuals, especially if lights have to be dimmed, is the equivalent of taking sleeping pills.

> Expert device: If you don't like to memorize your speech (which is fine), don't like to read from notes (which is fine), and are afraid about forgetting your material (which would not be fine), use the

[2]As a rule, slides require very low lighting, unless you can arrange for rear projection. Never shoot slides up a center aisle, or you'll be unable to stand there without being in the line of fire. Overheads have limited visibility over certain numbers of participants. Easels can be wonderful in small groups and are virtually essential for workshops. *Always* have a spare bulb, a spare easel marker, and a contingency plan if the equipment fails.

visuals as your frame of reference and outline. In 90-minute presentations, I frequently use slides that serve as my total outline. I simply speak from each visual, incorporating the current group's dynamic and relevant examples about that client.

> *If you have to explain a visual aid, you're working backwards. A picture is supposed to be worth a thousand words, not generate another thousand words.*

6. Handling Questions

There are three elements to effective question and answer sessions, whether formal ("I'll now take questions") or informal ("I see you have a question in the back").

1. Repeat the question. This allows everyone to hear it, any taping to pick it up (since you have the mike), the audience to reflect upon it, and you to think about a logical response.

2. Respond. Provide your answer. Don't be afraid to say, "I don't know" or "What do the rest of you think?" Never view a question as a sign of hostility. Even an objection, after all, is a sign of interest. Treat every question with respect. Don't be afraid to disagree. Don't begin with, "That's a good question" every single time, because it gets hackneyed (although using that phrase occasionally, contrary to conventional wisdom, can be effective to highlight a crucial point raised by a participant). Don't think you have to play baseball (hit a home run every time). Play volleyball and throw the question back (over the net) to the audience. "Would someone like to comment on that from a sales perspective?"

3. Review the response with the questioner. Ask, "Did I answer your question?" "Does that address your point?" "Is that something that may be useful?" Don't assume that you've answered satisfactorily. More times than I care to admit, a participant has said to me, "That was an interesting response, but it wasn't what I was asking you." Oh.

When you solicit questions, wait in silence for at least 20–30 seconds if none is immediately forthcoming. Don't worry; people won't get up and leave. Allow time for people to think and to gather their nerve. It's better to wait in brief silence than to continually badger the audience with, "Come on, *somebody* has to have a question!"

Never end a presentation with a question and answer session. It's not appropriate in terms of participants leaving with a call to action or an uplift. If you do take questions near the end, make it clear that you'll then have a brief summary after the question period. This will keep people in their seats and create the right expectations.

> Expert device: If you get a clearly hostile question and you want to avoid confrontation and/or a prolonged debate with the questioner, only use elements 1 and 2 from the list. Repeat the question, respond to it, *but then* move your eye contact elsewhere in the room and ask, "What other questions do you have?" or state, "I saw some-one's hand up over here." That will enable you to move away grace-fully and also allow the group to help change the focus.

7. Errors

If you make an error, admit it and move on. Neither try to ignore it nor fall on your knees begging forgiveness. If it's a modest error, humor often helps. I was once referring to the hostess of a party when I real-ized in midsentence during the story I was relating that the term "host-ess" might not be *au courant* in terms of gender equality. So I wound up stammering, "The hostess, er, wife of the host, er, person who . . . well . . . the woman who owned the place . . . " The audience laughed, a woman said, "We get the point!" and I moved on. I've since included the "error" as a standard part of that particular story.

There are stock phrases you can use to cover generic errors. If a slide is upside down, you can always say, "I've changed my view on this point." If a bulb blows, you can comment, "Well, now you're in the dark along with me." However, if someone points out that you've confused return on investment with return on equity, you should immediately correct the point, apologize for the error, and ask if there are any further ques-tions or comments.

I once spelled a client's name wrong on handouts that were already distributed prior to my speech. I apologized at the outset, told people a corrected set would be sent to everyone, and that I was waiving my expenses for the trip as a gesture of my regret over our own inattention to detail. The audience immediately forgave the error, and I went on with my normal presentation. As in the "hostess" dilemma, we can often turn an error into an opportunity.

> Expert device: If you're comfortable, use the error to point out that we live in an imperfect world and the point isn't to be *flawless* but to be *accountable*. Tell the audience that, as in their professions and

jobs, you'd rather be able to correct an error than be unaware of it, and anyone who points out an error is always exhibiting an interest in your work. Customers who complain should always receive a polite and careful hearing because, not only might they be correct, but they are invariably potential long-term customers.

8. Disruptions

Let's call a disruption an error that's outside of your control. These range from a wait staff clearing dishes to participants talking to each other loudly enough to interfere with your communications. There are two kinds: major and minor.

Major disruptions are fire alarms, blizzards, loud noises, and so on. Every speaker eventually experiences the room next door with a sound system that overwhelms their own. Or the snowstorm that causes participants to begin worrying about getting home. I've been in two sessions, as an observer, in which medical emergencies occurred.

In the case of major disruption, stop what you're doing. Confer with the buyer or coordinator. *Inform the audience about what's going on.* "I see the snow accumulating steadily outside, and I'm going to pause to allow Charley and Joan to decide what we should do. Let's take a 5-minute break." "We've had a medical problem occur here in the first row, and if all of you would please keep your seats, we'll be able to help the individual with a minimum of commotion. Could I ask that you chat with your colleagues for just a few minutes?"

Remember, you have the microphone and the attention. You cannot ignore your surroundings and you should never assume that an alarm is anything less than it is. It's better to evacuate for a false fire alarm and lose 20 minutes of your presentation than it is to suffer a single injury during a real fire.

Here is the ultimate approach to minor disruptions: *Never make them into major ones.* Ignore the wait staff. If they become overly noisy, don't pick on them. Ask a coordinator or manager from the platform, "Could we ask whomever is responsible for the staff, who are only doing their jobs, if the rest of the work could wait until we're through here?" Don't blame anyone; simply try to enlist help in correcting the situation. If another meeting's noise level is interfering, raise your own volume and ask someone if they can work out an accommodation. If it's so loud you can't be heard easily, then take a short break while you work out the problem.

Never embarrass a participant. If two are talking, try walking in their direction while talking to the group. That will often squelch it. If it's chronic, ask them during a scheduled break if they would stop, since it's tough for you to concentrate. You might ask them if there's a question you can respond to in the room, but don't use that technique more than once. The onus is on you to overcome disruptions. They are not a personal affront.

Never assume that someone leaving the room is making a statement about your presentation. They may be visiting the rest room, making a critical call, taking a breather, or maybe they really have no interest in what you're saying. None of this matters. Your obligation is to those still sitting there. This is about them, not about you. If everyone gets up and leaves, you're in the wrong business.

> Expert device: Work with either your client or directly with the banquet manager when speaking in conjunction with a meal to arrange for tables *not* to be cleared after the final course if you will already have been introduced. It's the bussing of tables that creates the worst noise and most movement. Either have the dishes cleared before you speak or after you speak, but not *during* your speech.

9. Use of Humor (Assuming You're Not a Humorist)

There are two kinds of humor: planned and unplanned. In my opinion, everyone should build some planned humor into their talks. Unplanned humor—ad libbing—is much more problematic because it can backfire.

I've touched on this is an earlier chapter, so let's simply cover the basic rationale for using humor:

- make the audience comfortable
- create a congenial learning environment
- make a point
- take yourself off the "pedestal" (self-effacing humor)
- break tension
- put an error or disruption into perspective
- begin or end on an upbeat note

The safest humor involves personal stories, because they are guaranteed to be original and unheard, they can be practiced and perfected, and they are highly personalized to your style. Unplanned humor can be safe if it's aimed at you, for example, when you can't get the computer to work and comment, "I'm in the breakdown lane of the information superhighway." If you're quick and very good, unplanned humor can create bonding with the audience that is invaluable. A participant who was

an avid fisherman once said to me that, when I was asked a question, my
face seemed to go through all the expressions that a fish does when he
pulls it toward the boat. "Yeah," I replied, "but I always get off the hook."

> Expert device: Talk to the client in advance and find out something
> you can safely use that the group would find funny. For example,
> there's usually a story about a golf outing, a trip, a sales meeting, a
> retirement, or some other company legend that can be incorporat-
> ed. I found that one participant, in a prior session, had actually gone
> onto the stage to draw a picture of his point. I began my speech by
> introducing myself and then asking if I could just turn my segment
> over to Joe, as I pulled an easel forward.

---

*Don't laugh at your own jokes. Everyone knows that
you've told them and heard them 10,000 times. People
will wonder if you think that little of their intelligence.*

---

10. Theatrics, Music, and Effects

To each his or her own, I guess, but I'm underwhelmed by the attempt
to create a "mood" in the room. I know a speaker who specifies that certain music be played as people enter and depart. He is certain that it
adds to their receptivity as they enter and their memory as they leave. In
my observation, it just makes them speak a little louder as they converse
on the way in and out.

Music can set moods and make dramatic points, as can various the-
atrical effects, such as lighting, sound, and multimedia. But the basic
question remains: How are we improving the client's condition? We are
not in the entertainment business; we're in the learning business. I'd
never suggest to a singer that he or she refrain from using music, but I
have suggested to several that they stop giving speeches. Their skills are
in entertainment, not learning.

If you do use existing music, you must have permission to do so, usually from ASCAP, the licensing body. All commercial music and lyrics
belong to someone. You must pay a royalty to use them in public, no
matter how briefly.[3] You can purchase "generic" music, especially creat-

---

[3]This is the law, and it's enforced. Even if you were to play a short segment of Billy Joel at a
local trade association chapter meeting, you need permission, which almost always requires a
fee. In the same respect, no one can record your speeches and use them without your permission. It's just that Billy Joel has wider play than you do.

ed to be sold or leased for these purposes. Or you can have your own original music created, which is then your property. The same rules pertain if you use tapes or slides that are proprietary, such as a segment of a television news broadcast or a clip from the Super Bowl.

Do not ask people to touch other people. Sound elemental? Well, it seems to be an increasing affectation among speakers who must mistake themselves for therapists or masseuses. Many people do not like to touch or be touched, gender issues aside. Asking people to rub each other's shoulders, hug, or even hold hands is a very basic infringement on their personal comfort and is totally inappropriate for any speaker to request.

I've seen speakers cry on stage, as if they'd never done it before. Yet everyone in the audience knows full well that the speaker cries at precisely that point in every speech on that topic. It's phony and manipulative. (As one participant remarked during stirring music and the speaker's tears, "Ah, it's the obligatory call to patriotism and false tears.")

Finally, never, ever sing unless you're a trained musician and it's an integral part of your act. Singing is virtually *never* done to improve the client's condition. It's always done out of the speaker's ego. No one pays to hear a speaker sing, just as no one pays to hear The Rolling Stones or Madonna give a speech. Sing in the shower if you must, but keep the door closed and the shades drawn.

> Expert device: The client will often have a theme for the conference, a logo, or even music that they've rented for the event. With moderate advance planning, you can place their logo on your materials, incorporate it into your slides, use their music in your opening, cite their theme in your points, etc. This creates a highly customized approach which buyers truly appreciate.

Five Environmental Techniques (and Expert Devices) to Engage the Audience

1. Handouts

There are three options to use in distributing handouts:

1. *Prior to the presentation.*   This enables participants to arrive at a common level of understanding about your topic and to prepare themselves to learn by determining what aspects appeal to each of them. Participants can use them to track your presentation. Downside: People often lose them, they aren't distributed correctly, or if they're

not clear and concise, they can be a "turn-off." If you change your sequencing, people can become confused and unfocused.

2. *During the presentation.* This is a dynamic method to enable people to reinforce what they've just learned. People will use them to make additional notes in the margins. You can also use them as an interactive tool, asking people to complete certain portions. Downside: It's often time-consuming and disruptive to pass things out, especially during briefer presentations. Not everyone likes to complete questions or write in personal responses.

3. *After the presentation.* This can serve as a powerful reinforcer and provides a rationale to contact participants again. The materials in this case will reflect exactly what was discussed in the proper sequence, since alterations can be made. Downside: Many participants don't like to take notes anymore and prefer to use handouts as a "crutch" during the presentation.

If you use visual aids, faithful copies of the visuals should be included in the handouts. You can also use the handouts to provide extra value, for example, include a bibliography at the end for further reading. Handouts can also include tasteful offers to purchase your products.

Try to avoid the juvenile approach favored by many speakers, which is to utilize handouts that include "fill in the blanks" that are supposed to pass for audience participation. Unless you're dealing with participants below the fourth grade, it's embarrassing and sophomoric to ask the audience to follow you as you demonstrate what should appear in: "To manage time effectively, we must put things in the order in which they should be done by setting P _ _ _ _ _ _ Y."[4]

> Expert device: Always put your complete name and contact information on every page of the handouts. It's not overkill. Sometimes pages will be photocopied or torn apart for use. Place a copyright on every page. Place a toll-free number on them for people to call for more information. Use the handouts as a marketing device. This is why I like to provide something 30 days after the presentation, even if we provided something at the time of the speech.

2. Room Set-up

There are actually people who make their living trying to coach speakers on how to establish the room environment. But the fact is that poor speakers will die in Carnegie Hall and terrific speakers will knock the

---

[4]No, I'm not giving you the answer.

audience's socks off in a dungeon. Having said that, here are some safety tips.

Try to arrange for a center aisle so that you might walk down it, if appropriate. As mentioned earlier, don't shoot a projector down a center aisle, which will put you in the line of fire. Shoot it at an angle or use rear projection.[5] If you're far removed from the overhead projector, arrange for someone to change slides for you on your cue. Ensure that the slides can be seen from all points in the room while there is also sufficient light on you.

Visit the room far enough in advance (usually 45 minutes to an hour) to make changes, if necessary. If someone is using the room prior to you or if you're following other speakers without a break, make sure that whatever you need is provided prior to the program's start (e.g., have yourself "wired" with a lavaliere mike well before you're introduced). Test the mike for dead spots and feedback. There is sometimes unavoidable feedback below ceiling speakers. Practice your movements to avoid those spots in advance, not while you're delivering your key learning points.

If you hang things on the wall, make sure that the facility and the wall texture allow for it. Ensure that there is a table for your notes, handouts, and/or products. Check the sight lines—can everyone see you if you move around? If there's a follow spot, let the operator know what your likely movements will be and check the limitations of the lighting range. If you won't be able to see the audience because of the lighting, memorize the seating arrangements so that you'll know where to look, particularly if you'll be addressing certain people. ("I'd like to thank the sales vice president, C.K. Jones, for inviting me here today.") If there's a timer, find out where the timer will be sitting and what cues he or she will be providing. Practice how you'll ascend and descend the stage, especially if there is an introducer you'll be passing. (I've seen speaker and introducer get into a traffic jam on a single set of stairs.)

> Expert device: Call the facility a week in advance and ask to speak to the banquet or meeting manager (or call the client's production company manager if a third party is running the meeting). Specify what you need. You may find that the ceilings are too low to show slides, the front of the room can't be darkened, or there are no break-out rooms available on the day you intended to use them. You can always alter your presentation to fit less than ideal circumstances, but you can seldom alter the circumstances to fit an inflexible delivery plan.

---

[5]Rear projection, unless done with a mirror, requires that the slides be reversed in the carousel. This is not something you want to accomplish 2 minutes before your introduction.

3. Pre-presentation Participation

While this is highly interpersonal, I've included it here since it's not something that occurs during your presentation.

Many clients will offer the opportunity to participate in a dinner or social event the day or evening prior to your presentation. Unless your schedule prohibits it, such participation is always a good idea. You'll be able to meet participants and become a known entity. You'll be able to pick up recent developments about the client which may be included in your talk ("I understand that your field force has just expanded by 50 percent, which makes my talk today on retaining good people more important than ever!"). And you'll be able to chat with company officers and prospective future buyers on a casual, unhurried basis.

My feeling is that dinners, recreational activities, and sightseeing activities are all fine opportunities. But card games, barhopping, gambling,[6] and insider "political" meetings are not. Also, never drink alcohol at these events, no matter how convivial and informal. You never know what you might say after even a few beers, and you're also not going to hear all that you should. I was once called in on an emergency basis by a client who "fired" the scheduled speaker after first meeting him the day before the presentation at a company picnic and disliking the way he conducted himself.

> Expert device: If you have a spouse or significant other, and there are presession events that he or she might be invited to, bring them along. It's a wonderful way to cement relationships and become part of the "family." It's also a great way to spend more time with special people in your life and share the travel experiences that the profession affords.

4. Product Sales

There is not a thing wrong with selling products in conjunction with a speaking engagement. Here are some tips I've found effective:

- Give one of your products away while on the platform. I ask for a volunteer, reward them with "any book on my table over there," and move on. You can also hold the book or tape up and present it at the moment.

- Have the introducer mention your products and how to acquire them while at the conference. It's a good idea to include that "Ms. Jones

---

[6]More and more conventions are being held at or near casinos as they proliferate around the country.

has kindly provided a 15-percent discount to conference participants while she is here."

- If there is a convention bookstore, arrange to have your products displayed with you advertised as a featured speaker.

- Have someone staff your table. It's awkward to do this yourself. I try never to exchange products for money personally. If you need someone from the association, facility, or client, make arrangements to provide them with a commission or a flat fee.

- Accept all major credit cards. This can be arranged easily through your local bank or American Express.

- Create a "package" price, for which someone can purchase every product on the table at a discount. If it's not there, no one can take advantage of it. If it is there, someone will almost always do it, and you get a several hundred-dollar sale from one person.

- Give every visitor to the table a catalog of your products, whether they purchase or not. You may want to stamp the conference or client name on them and indicate that there is an XX-percent discount in effect for 30 days.

- Present one set of your products as a gift to the trade association library, client library, or a charity supported by the client.

Here's the real key: View your product sales as something that will help the audience to learn and improve the client's condition, not as primarily a revenue stream for you. If you can't make the first statement credibly to yourself, then you need different products.

> Expert device: Always inform the client of the availability of your relevant products and provide options for their inclusion. Some clients will purchase in bulk if you sign each book, send one to participants' homes, etc. If your books are commercially published, local bookstores will often agree to provide them at large discounts.

5. Personal Preparation

You have to be in the "right place and time" if you're to be effective for a client. An audience can sense uncertainty and/or distraction, and they get restless if a speaker is tentative or scared.

- Focus on the speech in front of you. Don't worry about the one next week or next month (or even tomorrow morning).

- Practice not to be *perfect* but to be *comfortable*. Audiences don't care if you're perfect, but they will only be comfortable if you are.

- Understand that this is not a turning point in Western civilization. The world will continue unimpeded tomorrow, no matter what happens today on the platform.

- View the audience as mature, intelligent, constructive adults who want to see you succeed.

- Your job is to please the buyer and meet the buyer's objectives, not to receive a standing ovation or perfect scores on rating sheets.

- Don't try to "outdo" the prior speaker or to latch on to something that seems to be working for everyone else. You are unique. Use only your strengths.

- Be provocative. No one is roused to action by platitude and repetition. Force your audience to think, and make them feel an urgency. Logic makes people think; emotion makes them act.

    Expert device: Prior to your speech, do something that makes you laugh. Listen to a humor tape, watch a funny movie, chat with good friends by phone, call your kids (provided they make you laugh!), or just think about some good times. No matter what your topic or audience, you want to be having fun just before you hit the stage.

The Six Great Myths of Professional Speaking

I've tried to place platform skills and related concerns in their proper perspective. I thought we'd conclude with what I consider to be the great myths of the profession.

Myth One. *You should always get nervous "butterflies" before you speak.* I don't know about you, but if you're still nervous about speaking after scores, hundreds, or thousands of talks, you ought to get some Valium. I get an adrenaline rush, and I can't wait to go on, but I don't get nervous. Anxiety will kill your timing, deaden your reflexes, and paralyze your movements. Athletes who perform well under pressure don't get nervous. They get good. Get some DDT for the insects.

Myth Two. *You should always prepare for a talk for at least three times as long as the speech itself, no matter how many times you've given it.* Well, perhaps you should do this if you're a fish, since fish have a measured attention span of 4 seconds (which is why the same fish keeps getting hooked—it forgets everything it ever learned 15 times a minute). This is utter malarkey. Prepare, perhaps, for the nature of the new audience, a new environment, and some contemporary delivery, but if you still need to rehearse your signature speech for 3 hours every time, better check for gills around your throat.

Myth Three. *If you have a speech, you have a book.* This should be restated as follows: If you have a speech, you have an excruciatingly tiny book. Speaking and writing are discrete skills, sometimes synergistic but not at all equal. Don't give the published work short shrift: Books require extensive research, tight, Jesuit-like logic, brilliant metaphors, and immaculate construction. If that sounds like it doesn't resemble a lot of books out there, that's because most are not very good. (Maybe they ought to be speeches.)

Myth Four. *Carefully study your platform skills and get coaching.* A speaking colleague, Jeff Slutsky, has observed that nothing has ruined more good speakers than speech coaches. Content and knowledge are what carry the day, and if you have those, decent platform skills will get you through nicely. If you don't have those, superb platform skills simply put the icing on a house of cards. I find that speakers spend inordinate amounts of time on delivery mechanics and not nearly enough time on research, new ideas, client familiarization, and spontaneity.

Myth Five. *Track your audience evaluations more carefully than you'd check your stock listings.* Dr. Albert Bandura, whom I've had the good fortune to meet and work with at one point in my career, is one of the preeminent psychologists of our time. His work on self-efficacy raises an interesting aspect for speakers: People with low self-perceptions of their knowledge and abilities put a premium on external performance standards to reassure themselves of their accomplishment. People with high self-perceptions of their knowledge and abilities place the emphasis on personally established learning goals and—his words—self-mastery. Think about that.

Myth Six. *Our self-worth is based upon our success and accomplishments on the platform.* I don't think so. Our self-worth ought to be based upon our contributions to the environment and society around us, to our families and friends, and to our own vision for our futures. Speaking is simply a means—one of a great many—toward that end. People who tell me that all of their friends are speakers frighten me. We need a broad perspective, big gulps out of life, and a diverse variety of experiences. Those are what make us vital people, and better speakers in the bargain.

As usual, other than that, I don't feel strongly about it. Now let's take a look at how to make still more money with some legitimate sizzle.

11
Passive Income

"Good morning. How much did we make last night?"

This Is the Information Business

Every morning, including holidays and weekends, my e-mail, voice-mail, and/or post-office box will contain orders for books, booklets, tapes, and newsletters. Sometimes I'm more productive sleeping than I am when ambulatory.

For a long time, I was not a supporter of product sales. I felt that hawking products from the platform was sleazy, and even the speakers most adept at it couldn't hide what they were doing. Holding up your own book and quoting it or announcing that you'll be happy to stay after the presentation to "personalize" books had the subtlety of a train wreck. If you were perceived as a huckster, it had to detract from your message.

I still feel that way and never, ever, promote products in front of a corporate audience. However, I've learned that the objective is quite legitimate and that there are means which make me quite comfortable. I also realized that I was ignoring my own message: First and foremost, help to improve the client's condition.

Whether a corporate, educational, nonprofit, civic, general public, or pro bono audience, some of its members will want to continue their growth and education beyond your session. The best way to provide for that need is through personalized learning options. My awakening came when I realized that we're not in the "speaking" business or "seminar" business or "training" business or "keynote" business.

We're in the information business, and information can take many forms.

The good news is that additional information in varied forms is an extremely natural aspect of our business. The bad news is that too many speakers see it as a primary, and not secondary (follow-up), role and create products that are arbitrary, of low quality, and/or obviously nothing more than revenue generators. The more a product possesses inherent value and perpetuates the learning experience you began on the platform, the more likely it is to be seen as a natural—even required—continuation of the improvement process.

I've said earlier that not everyone has a book merely because they have a speech. But I do believe that everyone should have products if they're speakers. A book simply may or may not be the right alternative, and fortunately, there are a great many alternatives to choose among. There are at least eight solid reasons for creating and marketing products:

1. They enable the participants to continue the development begun at your session.

2. They provide the buyer with the opportunity to supply additional value to the audience.

3. They create a lingering presence and visibility that can lead to additional business.

4. They provide revenues from people who have never attended (or are unable to attend) your sessions.

5. They provide promotional opportunities among the media.

6. They provide (in the right context) credibility.

7. They help to differentiate and distinguish you from competitors, including those in similar geographies, topic areas, or industries.

8. They generate income that can be vitally important during arid periods in your speaking schedule.

There are also downsides to products which can't be ignored:

- If promoted crassly, they detract from professionalism.

- If poorly created, they detract from credibility and professional image.

- If created in isolation without a marketing strategy, they will result in a net loss on the bottom line.

- If overly specialized or dated,[1] they will become obsolete rapidly, either requiring abandonment prior to realizing full potential profit or more investment for updating.

The benefits clearly outweigh the risks if the products are carefully developed, intelligently marketed, and professionally sold. So if you have the inclination at all, products are a natural and lucrative offshoot of your involvement in the information business. The driving force of your business is your speaking, however, and products ought to remain in a secondary position. That means that speakers must first focus on developing a successful speaking career. A premature investment of time and money into product will cripple the locomotive, even as you're perfecting the observation car.

As a rule of thumb, it's probably wise to have been supporting your current lifestyle solely through your speaking activities for at least a year before trying to develop products.

I know speakers who are struggling to make a living, working a day job, delivering most of their work pro bono or at very modest fees, but who are also busy churning out self-published books and creating audiotapes. This is not bold business. It's egregious ego. If you want to tell the world you have a book or tape album because it makes you feel better, I can guarantee there's at least one organization that won't be interested: the bank that supplied your mortgage.

---

[1] I don't mean "dated" merely in the sense of chronology and old examples. Business and society change faster than printed inventories do, and terms such as "sexual preference" give way to "sexual orientation," not a minor matter for those in the diversity arena. Just as no one should be talking about "left-brain/right-brain" thinking anymore today, "reengineering" will indicate a passé reference tomorrow.

Five Ideas for Product Revenue Generation

Here, then, are five sources of the most lucrative products and services. The list isn't meant to be exhaustive, but I believe it does represent the most propitious areas for any speaker, whether 2 years or 20 years on the platform.

1. Books

The moneymaker here is self-published books, and we'll focus on them. (For those who, as do I, also publish commercially, see the footnote.[2]) There are two flavors of self-published book:

- Make an arrangement with a publisher/distributor who might or might not share some of the production costs, and who will publicize and distribute the book in return for a (sometimes substantial) share of the revenues. I don't favor this approach, although it's proved successful for some people, because it involves many of the disadvantages of a commercial publisher (shared revenue, concessions on titles, covers, and even text) and few of the advantages (promotional campaigns, major bookstore chain sales, caché of the major publisher's name).

- Locate a good graphics designer and printer who will work specifically against your specifications on a book, which you totally control. The advantage is that you'll reap far more net profit and produce exactly what you intend with flexibility and timeliness. The disadvantage is that *all* of the marketing and promotion is in your lap. People do not knock your door down as soon as word leaks out that you've published something. In fact, word doesn't even leak out.[3]

You can self-publish hard-cover or soft-cover, lengthy tomes, or booklets. I've found that a booklet of about 60 pages covering any one of my

---

[2]There are three primary ways to make money with a book from a major publisher. One is through the royalties gained on book sales, per your contract. A second is by buying your own book through a major discounter, such as Ingram, at better than 40 percent off, and reselling it at retail price (or at a more modest discount). Finally, you can print the book yourself when it goes out of print (under a standard contractual term called "reversion of rights") and sell it as a self-published book, which leads you back to the paragraph above.

[3]Case in point: The outrageously successful *The Celestine Prophecy*, which has been on *The New York Times* best-seller list for over 150 weeks at this writing, was originally sold out of the trunk of the author's car to individual bookstores two or three at a time, until word of mouth took over. It required fanatic devotion and the abandonment of virtually all else in his life at the time.

speaking topics (or even a portion of the topic) is a very good investment. Of 60 pages, there are only about 30 pages of text. There are
another 20 pages or so of highlighted points, quotes, and learning aids.
The remainder is autobiographical materials, information about other
products, and order forms. I invest a lot in the cover art and quality of
the paper. The cost is about $2 per book for a 2000-copy initial run
(including the one-time costs of the artwork, typesetting, etc.), and $1
per book for each successive 2000. I keep the runs limited, even though
larger amounts would generate additional savings, for two reasons:

1. Inventory requires both room and expense.

2. I want the freedom to update easily without worrying about 10,000
   books stored in someone's basement.[4]

On the initial sales of 4000 booklets, for example, at $6.95 each, I'll
net $21,800. At the moment, I have five booklets in my catalog. If I sell
one press run of each every year (2000 × 5 × $6.95), the net is $59,500.
That pays the mortgage.

Create books or booklets that are easy to read, contain a multitude of
graphics and models, and are *attractive* to the eye (Figure 11-1). That's
why you'll need both a professional designer and printer, but those
costs are minimal in today's competitive marketplace. Use a sliding
scale for multiple purchases—it's common for clients to buy hundreds
of copies of my leadership or innovation booklets at a time for distribution well beyond the immediate audience.

Books and booklets can be produced during "downtime" and can be
used as value-added for the presentation (purchased in conjunction
with the speech), follow-up sales either in the back of the room or by
mail, and/or as opportunities for others who haven't been able to hear
you personally.

One final note that applies to all product sales: If you're going to sell
products at the presentation site, have someone other than yourself
staff the table and handle the transactions. You can always sign books
for people off to the side, but it's a better idea to remain "aloof" from
the actual purchase. And it's far, far superior to have your *introducer*
and the program's written publicity stipulate that your books have been
made specially available for the audience, rather than for you to do it
from the platform.

---

[4]I'm not kidding. I rent part of a neighbor's climate-controlled basement and store all of
my inventory—for over two dozen products—down there. I don't want to rely on distant
warehouses, and I want the products in a safe place.

Figure 11-1. One of the author's self-published booklet covers.

2. Audiotapes

These are very popular because they can be used in cars where a large number of people do their learning and self-development. You can sell these singly or in albums of two or more tapes. There is a plethora of production houses that specialize in everything from the artwork to the album configuration and from the tape editing to the duplication.[5]

I've found the best audiotapes to be "live." They should be made at your sessions and include the audience reaction and questions (so there has to be appropriate microphone placement). When you record in a studio, expressly to make a tape, there is a stilted, sterile nature about it. Moreover, your listening audience will be far more flexible about gaffes and errors (and even sound quality) if they know they're listening to a live event.

All of my tapes are either the result of recorded platform deliveries or radio interviews, in which the interaction with the interviewer compensates for the lack of audience participation. I try to keep them between 30 and 45 minutes per side. I sell some singly, some in sets of three, and some in sets of four which include two 40-page workbooks in the album. Generally, single tapes sell at retail for anywhere from $7 to $12, sets of three or four from $25 to $45, and tape albums containing multiple tapes and significant textual material anywhere from $50 to $150. The price ranges will depend on the nature of the topic, the depth of the materials, your credibility, and . . . your moxie. Value is in the eye of the beholder.

> *The price you set for a product should be based upon the buyer's perception of value. Use that as your criterion in design and promotion. I've seen virtually identical products sell for starkly different prices because of the perceived value of one over the other.*

---

[5]As with book publishing, there is commercial audio (and video) published through organizations such as Nightingale-Conant. Like a publisher, they will pay for production and promotion, and provide a royalty to you. The advantages and disadvantages are about the same as in book publishing.

Have your tapes edited by a professional. If the introducer at the event did a poor job (not at all an uncommon phenomenon), have a new one dubbed in. Remove extraneous noise and dead spots, such as the 5 minutes of an audience exercise. Create a professional voice-over at the ending (including how to purchase additional products) and a "turn-over" cue at the conclusion of side one. If you've used any dated references ("Last year, when Hong Kong reverted to the Chinese . . . "), try to edit them out to prolong the relevance of the tape.[6]

The more the tape is live and spontaneous, the more you can live with minor sound problems. You'll find that high value and strong content will overwhelm technical imperfections.

You can obtain tape editing, duplication, labels, boxes, and ancillary services for extremely good prices in what's become a hugely competitive industry. Shop around and ask other speakers what their experience has been. Despite economies of scale, I recommend creating and maintaining relatively limited inventories until you can project sales reliably. That might mean an initial run from a few hundred to 1000, and reorders of 2500.

To create a four-cassette album with two workbooks, including all artwork, editing, reproduction, and packaging, would probably cost about $3500 for an initial run of 100, and $1500 for subsequent runs. That product could easily sell for $120. That's a profit of $8500 on the initial run and $10,500 *per hundred* on subsequent runs. If you sell a thousand a year, that's a six-figure profit product. (Even if you're not as bold with your pricing, it's still serious money.)

Self-published tapes face the same challenge as self-published books: marketing. We'll talk about that in more detail later in the chapter.

3. Videos

Videos must be done professionally. I'll never forget the guy I saw standing in front of a camera drawing on an easel sheet. His video price was only $10. It wasn't worth it.

The best alternative for video as a product is to collaborate with a client to help produce one. That means that the client allows a production crew to shoot both you and the audience, and to light and mike the venue as required for top quality. In return, you provide the client with the option of free copies of the video, a reduced fee, and/or video of the remainder of the conference for the buyer's purposes. Many clients will graciously

---

[6]Obviously, the best method is to refrain from using such references when you know the session is being recorded for these purposes.

consent to such a quid pro quo, which is more than worth it in terms of the live audience and professionally equipped environment.

You must adapt your presentation to your video product intent. That probably means refraining from citing the client or specific client examples during the talk, avoiding time-related examples, including devices (humor, questions, requests) that generate audience involvement and responsiveness, and the use of only those visuals that will tape well.[7]

In my experience, videos for sale as products should be no longer than an hour and can be as brief as 30 minutes. Retail sales prices vary from about $15 to $95, depending on the factors we cited earlier. The production expense, however, can be substantial (unless you're crafty enough to work out some reciprocal arrangement with the production house, such as internal training, references to other speakers or clients, etc.). A professional two-camera production, with all related equipment and editing, could cost anywhere from $5000 to $10,000. The good news is that video duplication, like audio duplication, is very inexpensive, and can be as little as $5 to $10, depending on quantities.

A taping that costs $5000 to produce final product, and 100 copies at $10 apiece, results in an initial investment of $6000. If the product sold for $60, that would create a first run that broke even, and I'm being kind in the cost and the price. Video products are best created either with a producer/distributor who will underwrite the costs and pay a royalty *or* when your name and repute will produce enough momentum to drive sales. Typically, videos are a product that makes sense for established speakers who can rely on past book and/or tape sales for repeat business for new products.

4. Newsletters

I'm not talking about the blatantly self-promoting, mostly free fliers that many speakers distribute. I'm talking about a monthly, bimonthly, or quarterly publication of from four to twelve pages that people actually buy.

This is a tough market, but also a lucrative one. The ability to create periodic contact with constantly new information *and be paid for it* meets every criterion mentioned earlier for the success of a product. If you're in a position in which you constantly receive new ideas and information or are crafting new approaches and techniques or have responses and resolutions to ongoing issues of interest, then you might want to consider publishing a newsletter.

---

[7]You can add later, at additional expense, separate shots of slides and charts done at the studio.

One of the great disadvantages is the pressure on people's time to read a myriad of sources related to their work and interests. One of the great advantages is the nature of renewal subscriptions: If people like the product, then the original sale will result in annual business, which is a powerful revenue generator.

An eight-page, two-color, professionally designed and printed newsletter can be produced for about $500 an issue, with postage dependent on circulation size (after an initial, one-time cost of perhaps $2000 for design, plates, artwork, etc.). If your newsletter is a quarterly that sells for $45, and you attract 300 initial subscribers, then your first-year profit is $9500 (300 × $45 − $4000). If you grow to 500 subscribers in your second year, your profit is then $18,500, less postage ($45 × 500 − $2000). I run a bimonthly for $98 and attracted over 500 subscribers in my first offering.

You need to have the organizational skills, inclination, writing ability, and time.[8] Most of all, however, you need the readership. Newsletters are ideal when they are highly targeted on specific skills (mine is focused on consulting in the corporate market; others specialize in mortgage banking practices or employee incentive techniques), are backed by a credible name in that skill, and contain high content. Newsletters of this kind are not the place to promote your latest book, your speaking schedule, or your awards and honors. Focus on bringing value to the buyer. No one wants to pay to read your own promotional propaganda. They can do that for free.

I think that newsletters are highly specialized products that are probably best for speakers who have a customer base which has purchased other products. However, they are also overlooked products that are the perfect vehicles both to generate annual revenues and softly promote your credibility and stature. By sending the newsletters to publications such as *Bottom Line Business, Training Magazine,* or the local newspaper, you'll find that excerpts will be printed citing the source.

5. Advice and Counsel

Most speakers' most valuable asset is their intellectual property. Unless they are simply parroting someone else's ideas, such as "social style" personality grids first introduced 30 years ago, they provide an expertise and unique source of ideas. Those qualities are salable beyond the platform.

---

[8]Don't let the last factor fool you. I run a seven-figure practice which includes major consulting projects and about 50 keynotes a year, and I put out the bimonthly with no problem and no staff except for the actual printing. Drop me a note at *The Consultant's Craft,* Box 1009, East Greenwich, RI 02818 and I'll send you a complimentary copy.

Several years ago, I appeared at a series of presentations for Coldwell Banker. The buyer found that my approaches to consulting were of far more than mere informational value to internal service people and wanted to provide "real-time" help for those people around the country. As a result, a toll-free number called "Ask Alan" was established, and those service people were encouraged to call at any time to leave a question about a client situation they were currently facing. They were guaranteed a response within 24 hours.[9] In return, I received a retainer for the 3 months that the program was in effect. Next year, I'll be appearing on interactive television *originating from my home* and administered completely by a third party. Who knows what happens the year after that?

I don't refer to postplatform advice as "consulting" because the objective from an income standpoint is that it be remote and *not* dependent upon being on site.[10] It's passive in the sense that it can be recorded, requests can be received but not answered until later, and/or it provides access to you. Some clients will want their executives to be able to talk to you prior to their own presentations to obtain some presentation tips, some humor to insert, or some techniques to involve the audience.

If your relationship with the buyer (not the meeting planner and not the audience) is solid and if you've intelligently planned to talk to the buyer both prior to and after your platform work, then you're in an ideal position to pursue an advisory and counseling role. These should never be based upon a time unit, but rather should be fee based. For example, if the agreement is for people to call you for help for a 90-day period, don't charge by the phone call or the day; charge $25,000 (or whatever represents your value to the buyer) for the project.

How to Maximize Profit from Product and Service Sales

The five examples just presented don't constitute the only products, services, or passive income ideas available. But they are the most common, lucrative, and professional. I know you can point to someone who's selling other things and doing well, so please don't bombard me with cards and letters.

---

[9]Without evolving technology—in this case, voice mail at both ends—such services are impossible. This is another reason to embrace those aspects of technology that suit your clients' needs.

[10]And besides, too many speakers call themselves "consultants" when in fact they are not, and they shouldn't be confusing the issue. Speaking, training, and facilitating are noble callings in their own right.

I have seen speakers who sell sunglasses, bumper stickers, mugs, clothing, clever (and not so clever) aphorisms on cards, ties, games, wall hangings (dream catchers seem to be quite popular here), athletic equipment, and jam. I recall reading one e-mail message from a member of a speaker's group who went into great detail about how to procure and sell mugs to maximize profit, and the best profit she was able to generate was about $1 a mug. That means if she's selling 1000 mugs a year (which she isn't), she thinks she's making $2000 (which she isn't), and it isn't worth the trouble.

Before we delve into the realm of profit, let's be clear about one issue: Products are meant to satisfy the criteria mentioned earlier, not to solely and at any price generate income. Your products must represent you well, be of some inherent worth to the purchaser, and be professionally suited for the client. If you're going to be something other than a novelty shop or speaker's yard sale in the back of the room, then your products should professionally convey your ideas and values to the purchaser in a professional manner. That manner will be different for the humorist, business speaker, image consultant, and trainer. One size does not fit all. I don't expect a humorist to sell a booklet on corporate strategy, and I wouldn't sell someone a mug even if coffee were falling from the sky.

No matter what you intend to sell, here are some ideas to maximize your profit. Remember, it's not what you make; it's what you *keep*. You're primarily a speaker, one would hope, and product sales should be a profitable, ancillary business that takes little time but generates large profits, which result when you take in more money than you spend. And don't forget, *time is also money.*

The best products are those that "sell themselves" with little involvement from you. The worst are those that take your time away from speaking, developing new clients, or sitting at the pool. Time is money.

---

10 Tips to Maximize Product Profits

1. "Bundle" your products. Whether you have two products or twenty two, provide a single price for someone who wants to buy everything at once. Provide a nice discount for doing so (e.g., 20 percent off the total). Psychologically, people don't think about making such a purchase unless you offer it, and once offered, some people will make it. Be

sure the offer is clearly stated in print, either in your catalog or on your sales table.

2. Create a product catalog. Use this as a handout for people who merely stop by your table, as an audience handout if the buyer doesn't object, and as a mailer. Spend some money on this. Have pictures of your products, descriptions, *and testimonials from people who have used them.* Include an order form that takes only a half page. Don't allow your ego to defeat the purpose: You don't need your picture or paragraphs of text on how great you are. You need to relate what the products can do for the purchaser's needs.

Note: Make yourself "purchaser friendly." Get an 800 number and create a "branch" that allows the caller to hear a product description as well as place orders. Enable people to buy from your Internet site. Advertise your fax line. I receive an average of 20 orders a week on my 800 number, which is by far the most popular method my buyers use. Second is fax, third is conventional mail, and fourth is the Internet.

3. Accept all major credit cards. About 60 percent of all my sales are by credit card. You can easily establish these with your bank and/or with American Express directly. Get an electronic terminal for your office use for mail orders, which will provide authorization immediately 24 hours a day, and therefore instantly credit the revenue to your bank account. This also reduces the commission you pay to the credit card companies and eliminates the need to take these receipts to the bank.

4. Place your product catalog in your press kit. Whenever I send out an information kit, my catalog is included. Some people don't hire me; nevertheless, they buy books and tapes. Not only does this provide an ongoing contact for my lists, but it creates a "presence." Books and tapes are used and reused, and they can generate future interest in you.

5. Keep a meticulous list of product purchasers. Keep this list separate from any others (i.e., clients, key contacts, references, etc.) even if some people are duplicated on the other lists. Prior purchasers of your products constitute the most highly qualified list you can create, and they should be contacted at least annually with offers for additional products and/or new products. Create a brief form for every purchaser to complete (this is done automatically with any mail sale or credit card sale, but not always if someone buys in the back of the room). You need to mail to the list at least annually to keep it updated, if nothing else.

6. Obtain someone to staff your table. When selling in the back of the room, you can't be signing books, encouraging people to buy, and making change. Nor should you. Besides, it's more professional for you not to be handling money and to be a short distance away chatting with audience members. If your spouse or significant other is tagging along,

that's a good role for them; if not, sometimes a trade association will provide a staffer; if that fails, call ahead and hire someone, either for a flat fee or a percentage (e.g., 7 percent up to $1000, 10 percent above $1000 or more in sales) to handle sales. Sometimes, trade associations have a bookstore. In those cases, talk personally to the staff to explain how your materials should be sold, to arrange for attractive placement, and to offer to host a book signing if appropriate.

7. Include your products as alternatives at the proposal stage. It doesn't matter if they haven't been discussed to that point. When you submit your proposal, explain to the client what products might be germane to the session, include complimentary copies, offer special services (i.e., personalized, shipped to participants' homes, company logo inserted, etc.), and provide various discount options in addition to your speaking fee. Some clients will order in bulk; others will accept a discount for anyone who wants to buy individually and will publicize that in the program literature.

8. Ask the introducer to mention your products. This is *far* more professional than your doing so, and it carries more weight. Ideally, the introducer should make the reference and display the products sometime during the introduction ("Among Sandy's accomplishments are these three books and a cassette album, which she has made available to us today at a discount. I've read and listened to them all, and they are excellent.") and refer to them again when thanking you ("Sandy, that was great. I want to remind all of you that you can gain more of Sandy's wisdom by reading . . . "). If done as described, product sales will increase by at least 50 percent in the back of the room.

9. Provide discounts for large purchases. I recommend "break points" at 100, 500, and 1000; otherwise, you're giving away too much for too little. Think big, and the purchaser will tend to think big.

10. Give away smaller net profits to make larger net profits. When I sell my newsletter, which is $98 for a year's subscription, I provide a complimentary copy of one of my booklets which retails for $6.95. When someone purchases a 2-year subscription for $181 (note the discount), I provide an additional hard-cover book, which retails for $24.95. The key is that the booklet costs me only $1 to print, and the hard-cover books are free, from the oversupply of a colleague.[11] The purchaser should see benefit in terms of retail savings, while you should see maximization of net profit. The net profit on the $98 newsletter is well worth the money spent on the free books.

[11]Sometimes I provide one of my own, but that book only costs me about $4 to print.

Staying Out of Jail

There are some increased levels of vigilance and liabilities present when you go into the product business. And I want to emphasize that, just like speaking, this is a *business,* not an avocation or hobby. This is not a bake sale for the local Little League team nor a fund-raiser for the local school. This is a business, and as such it requires tax payments, record-keeping, and other adherence to the laws of the land.

Tax Issues. You must, obviously, pay federal taxes on product sales as part of your general income. You can also properly deduct all expenses incurred in the creation of, improvements to, and distribution of your products. At the very least, have your accountant separate out product sales from other revenues and similarly isolate expenses. This will also serve to inform you as to whether the product part of your business is profitable and prevent the real results from being buried in general income and expense. I advise most people to actually keep a separate bank account for product revenues and expenses, for both tracking and convenience.

You must also collect and pay applicable state (and/or local) taxes, depending on the locality. I won't go into the complexity of the tax laws state-by-state here, but you must find out the proper procedure from your financial advisor or attorney. You will sometimes be required to collect taxes, and sometimes not. Some states have reciprocity agreements, some do not. Find out what your responsibilities and liabilities are. Ignorance is no defense if a tax agency comes after you for 8 years' uncollected taxes. Penalties can be severe.[12]

Sometimes people will pay you in cash. Treat it religiously as income on deposit slips and tax records. When applicable, I add the appropriate taxes to my retail prices—I do not absorb them. People are accustomed to paying tax. Don't disabuse them of that notion.

Quality Issues. Be prepared for some errors and rejections. Printers routinely produce about a 10 percent excess to compensate for this. If you're doing a lot of business with one source, you can usually accumulate the quality rejects and return them for credit against your next print run. Inspect your stock. The only thing worse than your finding a quality error is a paying customer discovering a quality error. Never knowingly decide that something is "minor" and allow it to be sold. Use minor defects (e.g., a tear in a dust jacket, a missing cassette label) as giveaways for publicity or in response to requests for sample copies.

---

[12]By the way, inventories of unsold product are assets and subject to taxation. Check the rules carefully with your financial advisor.

Returns.   My policy is to accept any return without question and without
penalty. If someone says, "I was disappointed," I refund the money and say,
"Please accept my apologies," even if I feel that the person would have
been disappointed in the Sistine Chapel or desperately needs what I've
written. When a caller says, "The book arrived chewed up by the mail system," I say, "I'll send out another immediately," without asking for or
expecting the damaged merchandise to be returned. If I'm ripped off
occasionally by a scammer, it's still better than disappointing one real customer. This is simply a cost of doing business.

---

*Never view a product purchaser as a one-time cus-
tomer. View that person as a long-term repeat buyer.*

Liability and Plagiarism.   Odd fellows, perhaps, but I thought I'd
include them here. If you've developed your own product from scratch (a
pair of sunglasses or a balloon with your sayings on it), then it must meet
safety standards. If the glasses can shatter and damage the eye or if the balloon is prone to blowing up in one's face, you have a serious liability problem in a very litigious society. On such products, check carefully with an
attorney skilled in these matters to ensure that your materials, construction, and instructions for use pass muster.

   In terms of written words, simply heed this: They should be your own.
There's a distinct lack of attribution that goes on from the platform
(I've heard Goëthe, Henry Kissinger, Henry Ford, and Damon Runyon
all cited as if the speaker had just experienced a revelation on stage).
You can get away with a missed attribution—sometimes—during the
ephemeral delivery of a speech, but you can't escape notice in print.
When you create a written product, ensure that attributions are correct
and that anything you state is either yours or clearly referenced.[13]

Timeliness.   Written words, techniques, and aphorisms obsolesce.
Frisbees and Hula-Hoops had their day, and so did transactional analysis
and T-groups. Create your products to be enduring but flexible. Don't create so large an inventory—no matter what the producers tell you about

---

[13]I recently received a commercially published book, using decades-old technology and
approaches to human behavior, which didn't contain a footnote, bibliography, index, or reference to the originator of the approach. As the doctors say, "There's a lot of that going
around lately."

the economies of large press runs—that you're forced to sell old stuff just to recoup your investment. If you produce workbooks and binders for sale, keep them modularized so that you can change a page or a section without reprinting the entire product. Conditions change, and a casual reference to the Iron Curtain will create credibility problems for anything sold in the aftermath of its destruction.

If you find some of your product becoming dated, give it away for free as a promotion, as a two-for-one sale, or as goodwill. That way, you're still getting some benefit from the investment.

Failed Payment. You will occasionally receive a credit card number that isn't accepted or a check that hops around the landscape. Don't panic and don't get nasty. First, always get a phone number on every sales transaction (most checks include them anyway). Second, try resubmitting, at least once. Third, if still not accepted, call the purchaser and politely explain that the same thing has happened to you many times, and you would like their help in straightening it out. Now hear this: In 12 years of product sales, I've never had a single purchaser fail to pay, eventually. In 99 percent of the cases of failed payment, the credit card number was incorrect or the check cleared on a second try. *As a rule, I will invoice corporations if they request it, but I will not invoice individuals. Individual sales are by check, money order, credit card, or if in person, by cash.*

Theft. When you ship product to a site for sale, you are vulnerable to theft en route, at the scene, during the sales process, or after the fact. I have had products "walk away" from untended tables. If 5 percent of the general population has shoplifted, then 5 people out of every 100 in your audience might be so inclined. To safeguard:

- Ship insured, via FedEx, which tracks shipments meticulously.
- Ship to a specified person responsible for safeguarding your product.
- Never leave the sales table untended, even during speaking sessions.
- Have limited sample copies visible, marked "sample," and sell from an inventory behind the table.
- Carry a FedEx airbill with you to use to ship unsold materials back. Try not to ship excessive product to begin with (you can always accept orders if you're sold out and absorb the shipping costs).
- If you suspect theft, don't take action. It's not worth it.
- If you see theft, approach the person and ask if you can be of help with processing their sale. Never accuse anyone, especially in a client setting.

If someone other than you fulfills mail orders, and they're not your lifelong best friend, create a careful accounting system and frequently match revenues against inventory, something I do even though we fill our own orders.

Finally, store your inventories under your control. Don't leave them with the printer or publisher, where controls are notoriously lax. Pay to rent space if you have to, and make sure it's minimally climate controlled.

Every morning, I awake to find orders in my voice-mail system, e-mail, post-office box, and fax machine. It's not a bad way to have spent the night.

Epilog: What It Really Means

"What have I done?"

This Is No Business Like Show Business

Several years ago, I was speaking in Philadelphia, which is about 90 minutes from where I was born and raised in northern New Jersey, just across the Hudson River from Manhattan. During the 90-minute keynote, I had related to the audience of 35 people that I was raised in the most densely populated city in the United States and had grown up playing stickball on the streets amidst the traffic, for which the prerequisites were to steal a broom and to fish old balls out of the sewers.

"A couple of the stronger kids would prize up the sewer grate," I explained, "and then we'd hold the lightest, a kid called Berger, by the ankles and dangle him down the duct until his head was just above the horrors and he could reach the balls. We'd wash them in some rainwater and get on with the game until the cops chased us."

I was speaking on the subject of entrepreneurial success and establishing one's own business. Afterward, while signing some books, a man approached and asked if he could speak to me privately. He told me his name was Henry Johnson and that he had been talked into attending by a friend. He was very slim, somewhat shy, inexpensively but neatly dressed, and was missing a front tooth. Henry, it turned out, was 29 years old.

"In 2 hours you've changed my world," he stated simply.

Being a middleweight cynic, I replied, "I don't think I can change your world, but if you got a few useful ideas today, then it was probably worth it."

"No, you've done more than that. I've had a string of bad breaks and I'd given up. My plan had been to work with young people in the inner city, to help them get jobs, to stay in school, to take pride in who they are. I felt that way until I got out of the army, and couldn't get work myself. Friends have been pushing me to start something on my own and not rely on the city agencies. They want me to shape up, get my teeth fixed, develop a business plan, and go after private money. I've decided this morning to do it."

I had a feeling he was putting me on, or maybe repeating something he said after hearing anyone speak.

"Henry," I pointed out, "you're black and I'm white. I've been speaking for 20 years to corporations, and you're thinking about beginning to speak to youth groups. I live in a suburban New England town and you live in the heart of Philly. If I've helped, I'm honored to have done so, but what on earth did I do or say to cause you to feel this way?"

"I was Berger," he said. "I was the kid who had to go down the sewer and under cars and into yards patrolled by huge dogs to find the lost balls. I know exactly what you were talking about, because I was there. And if you could leave that behind and succeed to the point where you're invited to speak to us today, then I can surely get my act together for my dream and for these kids. There are kids out there like us, and I'm going to help them. You helped me understand that I can."

Like us. That was an amazing moment. Henry shook hands and walked off before I could even offer him my card. I never found out what became of him. But I do know what became of me.

I learned again—and perhaps most profoundly—that what we do as speakers has impact far beyond our understanding. Henry happened to choose to talk to me that day, but he might not have if there had been more people in the group milling around, and he could not have if I had made one of my customary dashes to the airport after I had finished my talk. It's not critical to talk to the Henry Johnson's each time, but it is essential to know that they are there. Our behavior, our words, our examples, our *presence* provide a powerful model to people.

What is the model you are creating?

Like a surgeon, hairdresser, psychologist, or teacher, we are capable of creating changes in people. But unlike those others, we are almost never in a position to understand the impact, appreciate the extent, or see the result. We don't receive the results of tests, observe changed behavior, or usually, hear about new successes. We trust something has happened, but we can never be certain. Rating sheets and accolades are worthless because they tell us more about the event and the environment than they do about the audience and the aftermath.

> *I really don't care if you like me; I care if you learn. I*
> *don't care if you applaud; I care if you think. I don't*
> *care if you're entertained; I care if you act.*

What is the example you're providing for people? That example is the sum total of what they see on the platform, in front of the room, behind the lectern, on the stage. It's a combination of your words, actions, attitude, spontaneity, examples, humor, materials, ideas, and emphasis. Are you extemporaneous, "in the moment," interactive, and honestly enthusiastic? Or are you rehearsed, choreographed, superficial, unoriginal, and "falsely authentic," shedding phony tears and sharing contrived laughs?

No one believes what they read or what they hear. They believe what they *see*. When people watch you, what are they seeing? Ironically, and wonderfully, the road to success in this business is paved with honesty, not subterfuge. All of the coaching and specialized platform skills in the world can only dress up a shallow message and an insincere delivery. They are contrivances which cannot lend weight, depth, or meaning. Superficiality and dishonesty will eventually collapse under the weight of the camouflage.

This profession is not like selling ice cream or televisions. The audience doesn't decide upon the flavor. They can't test the picture before buying or call for repairs after they've bought. Our responsibility is immense. Our accountability doesn't always measure up.

Ethical Considerations: A Speaker's Creed

There is no government agency, trade association, or consumers group that monitors what we do. While a given client can make the decision to rehire us or never to cast eyes on us again, that is after the fact, and there are always other potential clients who have never heard of us. We have to be self-governing. After all, anyone can hang out a shingle that says, "Professional Speaker, Inquire Within." In fact, most of us have done exactly that. Let's not kid ourselves—we didn't pass any rigid qualifying tests to enter or remain in this profession.

But my contention is that the more ethically you act, the more successful you are. "Doing the right thing" is not so much an abstract nicety as it is a pragmatic business need. Integrity, in this business, outshines glossy marketing brochures. Honesty counts for more than slick graphics. Your word is more important than your résumé.

Speakers gather frequently for formal conventions and informal meetings. I virtually never hear discussions about the ethics of our business. I know of no other professional group that so consistently ignores this aspect of its profession.

Here, then, is my nomination for a speaker's guidelines for correct conduct. I think it's a pretty good test for any of us and an excellent way to comport ourselves in a profession demanding high values and self-discipline.

A Speaker's Creed

- I will use predominantly my own ideas and experiences, and will credit others when I refer to theirs in support of my own.

- I will be honest on the platform and never make a statement I know to be untrue.

- I will approach my work with the intent of meeting the client's objectives through my involvement with the audience.

- My fee structure will reflect the value I bring to the client, and that client will feel that the investment was exceeded by the results.

- My intent is to help people learn, think, change, and act, and my real impact occurs well after the audience has left the room.

- I will never deliberately manipulate emotions through stories or actions that are unrelated to the client's objectives.

- I will never use material or actions with the intent of building my own ego or image irrespective of my topic and the audience's needs.

- I will refrain from proselytizing and respect the diversity, varied beliefs, and private spirituality of the audience, no matter how strong my personal beliefs.

- I will keep feedback in perspective, knowing that I'm never as good as the highest rating or as poor as the lowest; my self-esteem comes from within.

- My materials and publicity will accurately reflect who I am, and I will never take credit or make claims that are undeserved or unsupported.

- I will help other speakers, through sharing experiences, providing ideas, referring business, and mentoring, because as we all grow, so does the profession.

- I will make a contribution to my community and environment through pro bono work, financial contributions, and volunteer activities.

- I will have made a difference in that my presence will have been felt.

Maintaining Perspective

In the movie *Mr. Saturday Night,* Billy Crystal plays a comic who, in one memorable scene, has just knocked the socks off a crowd in a Catskills resort. As he leaves the stage while 500 people are on their feet applauding, his manager is shouting in the wings, "You were a smash! They want a long-term contract! We can write our own terms!"

But Crystal is only half listening and appears troubled. He's glancing back toward the crowd, which is still screaming.

"Didn't you hear me?" yells the manager. "What's wrong with you? You were the biggest hit they've ever had here!"

"Yeah," says Crystal, "but did you see that guy near the front at table 5? I couldn't get him to laugh all night."

That's the story of our profession. Unless every person is on their feet telling us how good we are, we're a failure. (My feeling has always been that a successful engagement means that no one has thrown anything and the check has cleared.)

I cannot make someone else learn. I can't even motivate someone else. I deal with adults. They are responsible for their own learning, and motivation is an intrinsic aspect of human behavior—it can only come from within.

So what good am I? What can I do? Well, I can establish an environment that is conducive to learning and motivation. I can provide content that is relevant, delivered in an interesting and entertaining manner. I can honestly answer questions to the best of my ability and relate the answers to the questioner's circumstances. I can provide personal examples to demonstrate my points. I can involve the audience, actually or rhetorically, to enable them to relate my points to their issues. I can prepare carefully for a particular group's needs and can adapt suddenly when the unexpected occurs. I can keep the audience's learning needs superior to my own ego needs.

You know what? That's a lot. I'm successful if I've managed to deliver on what I'm capable of doing. Then the audience probably will learn, will change, will take action, will be motivated. But I can't guarantee it. I can only guarantee my part.

The problem is that we can get the standing ovations, the superb ratings, and the outstanding comments without really having contributed a thing to the audience or the client except a temporary view of our dexterity on stage. I know how to get the audience to laugh. I know how to get them to applaud. If I wanted to, I even know how to make them cry. So what? The question is, can I get them to want to learn?

There is a great deal in our arsenal that rarely needs to be used. But too often, we haul out every weapon and fire it simply because it's there, creates a lot of sound and light, and never fails to get a reaction. I can get any audience off their feet. My measure, though, is can I get them off their duffs?

Earlier in the book, I mentioned Albert Bandura, one of the most renowned psychologists of our times, who has done extensive work on self-efficacy. He says that people with low self-esteem and low beliefs in their abilities tend to place great weight on external measures of their performance. They incessantly want to know how they performed in the eyes of others, and rely on instruments and evaluations that assess their performance.

Those, however, with high self-esteem and an intrinsic belief in their abilities and talents tend to use internal measures to gauge their success. Bandura's work suggests that these measures are usually clustered around learning and self-development. He calls this "self-mastery."

In our profession, we have the potential to grow more than any client, any audience, any sponsor. We have the capacity to learn from each engagement, from each diverse client, and from each new environment. Some of us do, and we are different speakers from the ones we were 2 years ago. Some of us don't, and we continue with the same hackneyed approaches and old stories that we were telling a decade ago. What's the difference?

If we're not growing, we're simply not increasing the value we bring to our clients and our audiences. We need to have the perspective—and courage—to move away from the external measures of our often temporary successes and move toward the internal measures that indicate self-mastery. Just as there is a runner's "wall" and a test pilot's "envelope," there is a transcendent place where speakers can move from hearing the applause and being concerned about the guy at table 5 to listening to themselves and being concerned about the degree to which they are fulfilling their own potential. That transcendence has arrived when you can walk out of a room reverberating with your applause knowing that the session wasn't as good as it could have been, and when you walk out of a room to a tepid reaction knowing that no one could have achieved more with that group under those circumstances.

We are neither triumphant, nor do we "bomb." Some groups, some days, some places are better than others, perhaps, but what we do is put forth our best effort each time. It is the quality of the effort, not the quantity of the hoorahs, that matters. Helping 10 people out of 30 acquire skills and techniques to improve their situation, in a cynical, resistant group, is a far better result than emphasizing to 100 motivated high-performers how good they already are. We'll all wind up doing both, but let's not become confused about relative worth.

I'll preach to the choir anytime, but burly sinners run the world. It's the latter who are tougher, but ultimately more important, to change.

Personal Rewards

The subtitle of this book is not inconsistent with this epilog. The fact is, if you don't help yourself, you can't effectively help others.

A sophomore at a high school youth conference asked me, in front of a hundred students and teachers, "What's the shortcut to success? You're here as an example of success, so save us the trouble. What's the quickest route?"

After the laughter died down, I responded without hesitation, "Find something you love to do and throw yourself into it, body and soul. Don't try to find something that pays a lot and learn to love it. If you do the former, you'll get rich, however you define it, and you'll have a great life. If you do the latter, you'll be miserable."

Our lifestyles and our aspirations reflect very personal belief systems. I would never hold mine up as the avatar to which all others should aspire. I've found that the extraordinary financial rewards available in this profession can provide the ability to help others through the luxury of pro bono work, contributions, volunteerism, and flexible terms with clients. I've also found that the better I'm able to take care of my family and personal responsibilities, the better I'm able to handle the inevitable stress and pressures of dealing with diverse clients in different settings on a routine basis.

As I've become more and more successful in the profession, I've been able to become more selective about my work. I've referred lower-paying and lower-learning assignments to others who can use them; I've stopped doing the full-day programs that I never enjoyed and found to be exhausting; I've reduced my travel from 85 percent at one point to under 25 percent today. I've been able to travel the world with my wife, send two kids to the finest private universities in the country, and pursue the hobbies and interests that help maintain my energy, *all out of cash flow.* Don't forget, I was one of the kids hovering over a sewer, holding on to Berger's ankles.

Speakers tend to overemphasize what they *do* and underemphasize what they *contribute.* Their focus is on the task (a training session) as opposed to the result (increased profits). Consequently, for all the ego and self-centeredness in this business, *most speakers consistently undervalue what they contribute and undercharge their clients.* Ironically, only by understanding the internal measures I've alluded to in this epilog, and only by moving away from the ephemeral external measures, can we achieve a real appreciation of our contribution and our results.

I've heard of speakers aligning their fees with the evaluation sheets. The higher the rating, the higher the fee. *That's the equivalent of a doctor being paid based upon bedside manner and not whether your health has been protected or improved.* I've heard speakers say, "I knocked 'em dead," in response to "How'd you do?" But I hear others say, "I made a difference. They just don't know how much, yet."

If you can't evaluate your own contributions, no audience's evaluation sheets do you any good at all. If you need to be loved, get a dog.

Mounting a lonely platform to speak the truth isn't a profession for the timid, irresolute, or uninspired. Nor is it the proper setting for someone needing adulation, validation, or congratulation.

We, each of us, are engaged in a most noble calling, one whose roots are millennia old and whose future is assured despite globalization, technological change, and political strife. We are professional speakers, capable of affecting the hearts and minds of millions, who can in turn influence millions of others. That is a unique and profound accountability. In so doing, we can enrich ourselves, thereby enhancing our ability to continue to enrich others.

We might as well get good at it.

Appendix

The following lists are far from exhaustive, and sources change daily, particularly on the Internet. However, these resources should provide a solid base of information and skills relative to savvy, steak, and sizzle. I'd appreciate comments and suggestions for future editions of this book. The annotated opinions are mine and those of my research team.

I. Speaking Skills Resources

A. Books

Detz, Joan, *How to Write & Give a Speech*, St. Martin's Griffin, New York: 1992. This is written by a speechwriter who backs up her points by deconstructing public speeches. She is pragmatic and covers issues such as special occasion speeches and international speaking. I liked her ideas about being assertive with the emcee or host and absolutely controlling your introduction. But she also advocates writing out the entire speech word-by-word and not taping your rehearsals, which is very poor advice. And then she goes into "planting" staff members to increase the applause. This one's a roller coaster from sage advice to questionable practices, not surprising for someone who's helped politicians with "spin control."

Drummond, Mary-Ellen, *Fearless and Flawless Public Speaking, with Power, Polish, and Pizazz,* Pfeiffer & Co., San Diego: 1993. Influenced by Toastmasters International, the author focuses on overcoming fears of speaking. There is, consequently, advice good for amateurs but not necessarily for professionals (dumb down your vocabulary). There are some minor but fascinating tips, however, such as if your lips stick together, use petroleum jelly on the front teeth. There is some good work on preparing outlines and a valuable section on extemporaneous speaking and question and answer sessions.

Fletcher, Leon, *How to Speak Like a Pro,* Ballantine Books, New York: 1996. An entry-level work, Fletcher is somewhat academic and bound to an outline format that is downright dull. He tackles comfort, getting to know the audience, and careful rehearsing and preparation. Some of his advice is absolutely bizarre, for example, a technique in which the speaker brings a heckler onto the stage. That's crazy for a pro and death for an amateur.

Hoff, Ron, *I Can See You Naked* (revised edition), Andrews and McMeel, Kansas City: 1992. Hoff focuses on good presenting skills. He emphasizes the need to build a relationship with the audience and provides scores of techniques to do so. Read with a grain of salt: Some ideas are excellent (e.g., dealing with resistant and disruptive audience members), and others are just wrong (e.g., that the audience needs help and the speaker needs approval). Situationally, there are some good tips, however.

Karasik, Paul, *How to Make It Big in the Seminar Business,* McGraw-Hill, New York, 1992: This is a rich work in source material and references for trainers and seminar leaders. The author provides helpful guidelines for setting fees, newspaper advertising, sample contracts, press releases, mailing lists, handouts, etc. Since most of the people making most of the money in speaking are actually trainers and workshop leaders, this is a valuable resource for most professional speakers. Karasik makes too many references to "winners" and "losers," but this is a good book to read and highlight for quick reference.

Klepper, Michael M., and Gunther, Robert, *I'd Rather Die Than Give A Speech,* Carol Publishing Group, New York: 1995. Oriented toward corporate speeches, the authors are strong advocates of solid content and careful preparation. They cite "grabbers" to gain audience attention and focus on interesting aspects such as "texture" (interactions) and "ear appeal" (clever phrasing). There's a comprehensive list for understanding the nature of the audience in advance, which is particularly helpful. (Their worst advice is to pursue all "lost lambs," even at the cost of slowing the group, which I believe is suicidal.) More for the corporate, in-house speaker than the professional speaker.

Peoples, David A., *Presentations Plus* (second edition), John Wiley & Sons, New York: 1992. Although a second and presumably updated edition, the book seems older and dated, with simplistic graphics and breezy language. It appears to be a primer for sales presentations and cites arbitrary and incorrect statistics (e.g., misrepresents the Mehrabian study and doesn't cite the source). Much too basic and not always accurate for the sales professionals it seems to be targeting.

Schloff, Laurie, and Yudkin, Marcia, *Smart Speaking: Sixty-Second Strategies for More Than 100 Speaking Problems and Fears,* Plume, New York: 1992. Not meant to be read cover-to-cover, these are common sense suggestions for keeping the throat healthy, using positive language, dealing with stress, etc. It isn't a light read and contains some silly advice, like excusing yourself to visit the rest room. May be handy as a reference for particular problems.

Slutsky, Jeff, and Aun, Michael, *The Toastmasters International Guide to Successful Speaking: Overcoming Your Fears, Winning Over Your Audience, Building Your Business & Career,* Dearborn Financial Publishing, Chicago: 1997. This is a good, basic resource for those entering the speaking profession. There are techniques for stimulating audience participation, specialized events (i.e., invocations, eulogies, etc.), use of visual aids, and marketing approaches. It's well-written and fun to read, authored by two successful platform veterans.

Walters, Dottie, and Walters, Lilly, *Speak and Grow Rich,* Prentice Hall, Upper Saddle River, NJ: 1989. The Walters, mother and daughter, have put together a virtual encyclopedia on the speaking business. They are bureau principals, so the book is overwhelmingly weighted toward the advantages of working with bureaus, with nary a disadvantage. The authors correctly emphasize the diligent work required to succeed in the business and provide copious specifics for marketing success. There is a multitude of lists and some excellent tips (don't use testimonials that are obsolete) and sample documents (contracts, invoices). Major drawback: The book is blazingly self-promotional, is enamored of "celebrity" speakers, and is not very innovative.

Walters, Lilly, *Secrets of Successful Speakers: How You Can Motivate, Captivate & Persuade,* McGraw-Hill, New York: 1993. This is a thinly veiled sales promotion of this bureau principal's favorite speakers. Like the other Walters' book, it is egregiously self-promotional. However, it is geared toward true professionals, and keynoters at that (a small percentage of the overall speaking profession). She gets her credits mixed up, frequently citing speakers she likes as the developers of approaches that, in fact, they appropriated from the original sources, which she either is ignorant of or ignores. There are some excellent examples (e.g., of a preprogram questionnaire), but this is not the book to fill that single remaining space on your shelf.

Weiss, Alan, *Million Dollar Consulting: The Professional's Guide to Growing a Practice* (revised edition), McGraw-Hill, New York: 1997. My work on consulting. Its approach to establishing objectives, establishing value, creating options for the buyer, and raising fees based upon value provided is as applicable for the speaker and seminar leader as for consultants. It's especially timely because the traditional buying point for speakers—the meeting planner—has to be abandoned in favor of line executives and business leaders. It includes annotated sources and references for the consulting profession.

Yudkin, Marcia, *6 Steps to Free Publicity, and Dozens of Other Ways to Win Free Media Attention for You or Your Business,* Plume, New York: 1994. A well-constructed, conversational book by a woman who is an expert in generating publicity from scratch. She advises the reader to use only the techniques that are personally comfortable and provides wonderful detail on press kits, tip sheets, surveys, sponsors, etc. Her "ten keys to punchy publicity copy" may be worth the price of the book alone. *6 Steps* is like a one-on-one consulting session.

B. Newsletters, Periodicals, Reference

Burt Dubin's Market Letter, Personal Achievement Institute, 1 Speaking Success Road, Kingman, AZ 86402. Burt Dubin is a speaking coach and author of the Speaking Success System™. His newsletter is filled with specific techniques ranging from how to motivate an audience to how to pack when traveling. (Quarterly, $97)

Business Phone Book USA™, Omnigraphics, Inc., Penobscot Building, Detroit, MI 48226. Contains the address, phone, fax, etc. for virtually any company doing business in the United States. Invaluable.

The Consultant's Craft, Summit Consulting Group, Inc., Box 1009, East Greenwich, RI 02818. This is our publication focusing on how to establish fees, gain entry to the economic buyer, provide value options, use proposals to summarize conceptual agreement, etc. Includes tips, trends, and letters. (Bimonthly, $98)

Consultants News, Kennedy Publications, Fitzwilliam, NH 03447. Focuses on consulting, but still valuable for speakers because it highlights trends in business that also reflect the speaking and training topics that are relevant and in demand. Some of the consulting is, actually, training. (Monthly, $229)

National Trade and Professional Associations of the United States, Columbia Books, Inc., 1212 New York Ave. N.W., Suite 330, Washington, DC 20005. Every trade association in the United States, complete with annual budget, convention themes and dates, membership demographics, contacts, etc. Invaluable.

The Yearbook of Experts, Authorities & Spokespersons®, Broadcast Interview Source, 2233 Wisconsin Ave. N.W., Washington, DC 20007. An excellent place to be listed, since it is circulated to producers, assignment editors, reporters, etc. nationwide. A listing also appears on their Internet site.

C. Tapes

The Consultant's Treasury, Summit Consulting Group, Inc., Box 1009, East Greenwich, RI 02818. Four cassettes and two workbooks on marketing, sales, and publicity. Cassettes were recorded live at speaker and consultant trade association meetings and include question and answer sessions. Workbooks include sample proposals, questions to ask to establish value, techniques to achieve conceptual agreement and closes, etc.

D. Bureaus

Here are some bureaus located around the country that I've found to be top quality in their ethics and investment in speakers. If you've never worked with bureaus, here's the drill: Don't call them. Send them a professional package and follow up 2 weeks later. The package should include a professional set of text materials, testimonials, audio and/or video, fee schedule, references, and your areas of expertise. If you don't have these available, then you're not ready to contact them.

Convention Connection, 18133 Coastline Dr., Malibu, CA 90265

Gold Star Speakers, Box 37106, Tucson, AZ 85740

Great Speakers, 626 Santa Monica Blvd., Santa Monica, CA 90401

International Speakers, 5740 Prospect Ave., Suite 1160, Dallas, TX 75206

Leading Authorities, 1720 Rhode Island Ave. N.W., Suite 1100, Washington, DC 20036

The Speakers Bureau, 800 N. Washington Ave., Suite M104, Minneapolis, MN 55401

Speakers Corner, 15332 Antioch St., #209, Pacific Palisades, CA 90272

E. Internet

The Internet changes so rapidly that any listing here would be obsolete within 30 days. However, use the major search engines (Yahoo, AltaVista, etc.) to find a wide variety of speaking topics, from bureaus and coaches to books and tape cassettes. There are many speaker sites where, for an annual fee, the administrator will list you with descriptive material, fees, topics, photos, etc. Some even feature audio clips of your speeches for potential buyers to hear. (If you want to sample one, visit my home page at http://www.summitconsulting.com.)

The Internet is also valuable for speaker "chat" rooms and support groups. You'll find regularly scheduled as well as spontaneous discussions ranging from marketing techniques to lead referrals. A particularly interesting source, which ranges from maximizing fees to avoiding dehydration on airplanes, is SpeakerNet, run by Rebecca Morgan and

Ken Braly. There are certain rules for subscribing. Contact her at RLMorgan@aol.com.

Finally, see the Levinson and Keeler books listed later under II: Small-Business Resources.

F. Seminars, Workshops, Coaching

Beware! As colleague Jeff Slutsky (see his book listed earlier) points out, "Speaking coaches have ruined more good speakers than any other source." Nonetheless, if you're interested, you can find them on the Internet or in the listings of the National Speakers Association. Here are a few whom I know and can vouch for:

Ron Arden, Speech Dynamics, 3728 Dixon Pl., San Diego, CA 92107. (Focus: Platform skills, use of dramatic techniques; for the advanced speaker.)

Max Dixon, Max Dixon Communication, 1268 N.E. 69th St., Seattle, WA 98115. (Focus: Performance skills, voice control, movement.)

Roger Herman, Herman Assoc., 3400 Willow Grove Ct., Greensboro, NC 27410. (Focus: Practice management, growth strategies, marketing.)

Vickie Sullivan, Sullivan Speaker Services, 2708 N. 68th St., #2-470, Scottsdale, AZ 85257. (Focus: Promotion, increasing bookings, publicity.)

Juanell Teague, People Plus, Inc., Box 742047, Dallas, TX 75374-2047. (Focus: Market positioning.)

G. Associations

Note: Beware of speaking and/or consulting groups that provide a set of initials to place after your name or guarantee a certain number of leads, all for the cost of your membership dues. The general public and most buyers don't recognize specialized credentials to begin with, and those that are awarded should be based upon some test of competence and/or history of achievement. Join an organization for the learning, networking, and support potential, not for imaginary status.

American Association for Training and Development, 1640 King St., Alexandria, VA 22313. If you're primarily a trainer, you can't afford not to belong to the ASTD. It holds an annual convention, and local chapters are active to various degrees. Although it's too often "consultants and trainers speaking to each other," there is a core membership of practitioners who can be key recommenders for your services.

Networking is valuable, and they publish the monthly *Training &
Development* covering trends and methodologies. Ironically, the head-
quarters provides probably the worst service and slowest responsiveness
of any association I've yet encountered. (Annual dues $150).

American Management Association, 135 W. 50th St., New York, NY 10020.
An important organization for serious businesspeople. It publishes the
excellent *Management Review* monthly and hosts seminars and break-
fasts around the country. Research library and specialized reports are
available. This is a fine organization both to keep in touch with business
trends and to network among key decision makers. (Annual membership, depending on status, from $150–$300).

International Platform Association, Box 250, Winnetka, IL 60093. About
5000 members. Professionals on stage: speakers, musicians, actors, etc.
Promotes public awareness and professionalism. Wide variety of newslet-
ters and magazines, such as *Secrets of Successful Public Speaking: The
Public Speakers Handbook*. Includes bureaus and booking agents.
(Annual dues $45).

National Speakers Association, 1500 S. Priest Dr., Tempe, AZ 85281.
About 3700 members, of whom perhaps 20–30 percent support themselves full-time as professional speakers. Annual convention and two
major workshops (plus smaller "labs") cover topic development, marketing, platform skills, etc. Very effective at the chapter level for networking, mentoring, and support. Monthly audiotape and magazine,
Professional Speaker. Provides "Certified Speaking Professional" designation for those meeting qualifications (about 10 percent of membership). Annual dues $275 plus local chapter (optional). Note: Many of its
local chapters will allow a year's membership at local level only (typically
about $90) to test the water. This is a very good value.

Professional Speakers Network, 8502 E. Chapman Ave., Orange, CA
92669. About 500 members. Trains and promotes professional speakers. Library, resource center, educational programs, referral services, in-
house bureau, annual convention. Probably more like an organization
for self-promotion of limited membership than a true trade association.
(Dues $75)

II. Small-Business Resources

A. Organizations

National Association for the Self-Employed, 800/232-6273.

National Association of Women Business Owners, 301/608-2590.

National Federation for Independent Business, 800/634-2669.

National Small Business United, 800/345-6728.

Small Business Administration Answer Desk, 800/827-5722.

U.S. Chamber of Commerce, 202/463-5600.

B. Periodicals

Entrepreneur, 2392 Morse Ave., Irvine, CA 92714.

Home Office Computing, 411 Lafayette St., New York, NY 10003.

Inc. Magazine, 38 Commercial Wharf, Boston, MA 02110.

Success, 230 Park Ave., New York, NY 10169.

C. Books

Berner, Jeff, *The Joy of Working from Home,* Berrett-Koehler.

Carruthers, William, *999 Successful Little Known Businesses,* J.J. Publications.

Edwards, Paul, and Edwards, Sarah, *Working from Home,* Putnam Berkley Group.

Goldstick, Gary, *Romancing the Business Loan,* Lexington Books.

Kennedy, Dan, *Getting into Business* (four-part series), Self-Counsel Press.

Martin, Charles L., *Your New Business,* Crisp Publications.

Merrill, Ronald E., *The New Venture Handbook,* Amacom.

Suchocki, Dennis, *Banking Smarter,* BCS & Associates.

Weiss, Alan, *How to Maximize Fees in Professional Service Firms,* Las Brisas Research Press.

D. Internet Marketing

Keeler, Len, *CyberMarketing,* Amacom.

Levinson, Jay C., *Guerrilla Marketing Online,* Houghton-Mifflin.

III. Preparation and Quality Resource Tools

A. Targeting the Audience

What is the message you are to convey, the objective to be met?

Describe the audience:

- Who are they?
- How many will attend?
- How much time is available?

- What is their level of knowledge of the topic?
- What is the relevance of your message to them?
- What potential problems might arise in understanding?
- How will you prevent and/or overcome those problems?
- What are the key stories, examples, and visuals to employ?

B. Opening Options

What is the primary intent or objective?

Choose effective techniques to gain early interest:

- True story (We once sold products in Alaska . . .)
- Humor (I am probably the oldest living product manager . . .)
- Relevant statistics or facts (There are more baby boomers than . . .)
- Audience involvement (Does anyone have experience with . . .)
- Examples (Gillette tried to give away the razors because . . .)
- Demonstration (Here's how you pack this briefcase . . .)
- Visual aids (This slide shows your competition . . .)
- Personal experience (The worst sale I ever made . . .)
- Challenge or question (Can this profession survive . . .)
- Unusual point of view (Coaching can be disastrous . . .)

C. Building Interest

1. Eye Contact
   - hold for 3–5 seconds
   - begin with "friendlies"
   - don't threaten
   - reach everyone you can

2. Voice
   - alternate volume
   - use dramatic pauses
   - alternate inflection
   - keep a moderate pace overall
   - speed up or slow down for emphasis
   - accept silences and don't fill with chatter or sounds

3. Nonverbal Behavior
   - move around
   - use your hands for emphasis
   - don't hold notes
   - avoid nervous habits and repetitive gestures
   - use positive facial expressions—smile

4. Other Factors
   - get proper rest
   - eat reasonably prior to presenting
   - get some exercise
   - wear comfortable clothing which you've rehearsed in
   - be conversant but not choreographed

D. Influential Phrasing

Uncertain Phrases	*Influential Phrases*
I think we should	We will
What I would like to propose	I propose
We might be able to if	We can do this if
Is it possible to hear your ideas	Let's hear your ideas
Can we discuss	Let's discuss
I would really like to try to	I want to
It might be a good idea to	It's a good idea to
I'll try to explain how	Here's how
I would like to try to answer questions	What questions do you have
You may want to consider	You should consider
We really should try to improve	We must improve
Is there anyone who knows	Who knows
I would like to try to summarize now	In summary
Is it possible to get your attention	Let me have your attention please
I will try to answer that	Here's the answer

E. Handling Errors

Three Steps

1. Acknowledge immediately.

   Avoid continuing as if nothing happened.
   Avoid failing to correct the error.
   Avoid interpreting laughter as a personal comment on you.
   Use humor if appropriate and comfortable.
2. Check the accuracy.

   Test for understanding after correcting.
   Ask if there are any questions.

3. Continue.

 Don't linger over the error.

 Don't apologize excessively.

 Regain the continuity of your presentation.

F. Selecting Visual Aids					
Requirement	Easel	Overhead	Slides	Video	Computer
dim lights			✓	✓	✓
stop at key points	✓	✓	✓		✓
utilize remotely			✓	✓	✓
easy backup for malfunction	✓	✓			
spontaneous	✓	✓			
response to questions	✓	✓			
immediately correct errors	✓	✓			
focus on speaker	✓	✓			
large groups			✓	✓	✓
sophisticated graphics			✓	✓	✓
expense level	low	low	moderate	high	moderate

 Examples assume multiple screens or projection for video and laptop computer-generated graphics.

Index

About the Author

Alan Weiss, Ph.D., is an internationally known speaker, author, and consultant. He is the founder and president of Summit Consulting Group, Inc., an organization and management development firm that has clients that include Merck and Hewlett-Packard. He has spoken professionally for General Electric, GTE, Mercedes-Benz, the Institute for Management Studies, and hundreds of other firms and groups. He is the author of seven books, including *Managing for Peak Performance*, *Million Dollar Consulting*, and *What Happened to Excellence?*